STAGES OF TERROR

STAGES OF TERROR

TERRORISM, IDEOLOGY, AND COERCION
AS THEATRE HISTORY

Anthony Kubiak

INDIANA UNIVERSITY PRESS   BLOOMINGTON AND INDIANAPOLIS

The paper used in this publication meets the minimum requirements of American National Standard for Information Sciences—Permanence of Paper for Printed Library Materials, ANSI Z39.48-1984.

∞™

Manufactured in the United States of America

Library of Congress Cataloging-in-Publication Data

Kubiak, Anthony, date.
    Stages of terror : terrorism, ideology, and coercion as theatre history / by Anthony Kubiak.
      p. cm.
    Includes bibliographical references and index.
    ISBN 0-253-33146-3 (alk. paper). — ISBN 0-253-20663-4 (pbk. : alk. paper)
    1. Drama—History and criticism. 2. Terrorism in literature.
3. Violence in literature. 4. Theater—Political aspects.
I. Title.
PN1650.T47K8   1991
809.2'916—dc20   90-25521

1 2 3 4 5   95 94 93 92 91

To Herbert Blau,
   who first named the terror that haunted me,

and to my mother and my friend Emmett
   who met it, and faced it down.

BLACK CAT

Still, a ghost is like a place
your eye glances upon, sounding.
But here, within this black pelt
your most powerful gaze finally disappears:

Like a raging madman,
who howls and pounds in the dark,
then stops at the padded
cell wall and dissolves.

She seems to conceal within
every look that has ever met her,
and examines them all, somber and menacing
before she lies down to sleep with them.
Then suddenly, seemingly awake,
she turns her face to yours
and in the glassy amber of her eye
you see yourself seeing,
trapped in the golden circle
like a primordial fly

> —Rainer Maria Rilke
> (Translation by the author)

CONTENTS

ACKNOWLEDGMENTS

The thank yous are always easy. What is more difficult is expressing the profound debt owed to those who have cheerfully suffered through this project with me. First, to Susan Anderson, who accepted the peaks and valleys with far more equanimity than I could have expected; to Herbert Blau, whose encouragement and many suggestions convinced me that this book was worth publishing; to Alan Ackerman, whose relaxed diligence, imagination, and good humor moved the project through its most intense and anxious period; to my earliest readers, Kathleen Woodward, Bernard Gendron, Ihab Hassan, Patrice Petro, and Jamie Owen Daniel; to Harvard University, and the Hyder E. Rollins fund, which saw the project to completion; and to Daniel Anderson Kubiak, who put it all in perspective.

Portions of this book have appeared in *Theatre Journal,* 39.1 (1987): 78–88 and are reprinted by permission of The Johns Hopkins University Press. Other portions have appeared in *Comparative Drama,* 23.1 (1989): 3–30, and *Journal of Dramatic Theory and Criticism,* 4.1 (1989): 3–30.

STAGES OF TERROR

1 INTRODUCTION

A PANEGYRIC ON ARISTOTLE'S *POETICS*

1. A history of tragedy—Mimesis and the terrorist epic

In 1984, news anchorman Ted Koppel, who with Ronald Reagan rose to national fame during the terrorism of the Iran hostage incident, expressed a now familiar (and largely unexplored) sentiment in a *Harper's* magazine interview.[1] "The media, particularly television, and terrorists need one another," he said. "They have what is fundamentally a symbiotic relationship."[2] Now this is a rather curious statement, for in symbiosis each element functions as a complementary other; thus terrorists would not only create an economy of the media event, but the media event would *create* terrorists in a kind of mutual mimesis. And not merely in the sense of providing would-be revolutionaries with a medium within which to function: the news media, by providing us with what *is* new and seemingly original, represents and informs terrorism for the first time. Terrorism first appears *in culture* as a media event. The terrorist, consequently, does not exist before the media image, and only exists subsequently *as* a media image in culture.

This bio-economic association was developed along a slightly different axis later in the same article when journalist Charles Krauthammer called terrorism since 1968 (apropos 1968), "media terrorism;" an essentially new, international form of violence that "needs" and manipulates media as the raison d'être for its existence: "Since the outlaws cannot buy television time, they have to earn it through terrorist acts. Like the sponsors of early television who produced shows as vehicles for their commercials, media terrorists [sic] now provide drama—murder and kidnapping, live—in return for advertising time."[3]

The title of this special, provocative issue of *Harper's* is "Lost in the Terrorist Theatre." The issue in fact begins with a series of direct associations between terrorism and performance: terrorism's "bloody theatrics" follow closely the "script" of the "terrorist productions." Sprinkled throughout the interviews and essays are numerous quotes from various sources explicating terrorism's theatrical theory and production practice. Taken together, the assumption seems to be that the theatricalization of political violence did not really occur until the great age of video began during the height of the Vietnam action, but nowhere do we see the explication of the other aspect of the symbiosis, the aspect that sees the appearance of terrorism as a natural extension of performative terror, a terror that precedes the mediadrome and gives it birth.

I would then suggest an inversion: I would suggest that while the symbiosis between terrorism and media is an authentic one, the emphasis ought to be reversed—the media do not merely need and support terrorism, they construct it mimetically as a phenomenon. And the phenomenon is so constructed because American culture as a whole needs it, desires it, is fascinated by it, and utilizes it as a central impulse in its foreign and domestic policy.[4] I would further suggest that while terrorism is not theatre, terrorism's affiliation with political coercion as performance is a history whose first impulse is a terror that is theatre's moment, a terror that is so basic to human life that it remains largely invisible *except* as theatre. The history of theatre's filiation with psychic and political terror is the perfect twin of terror's own history as politics. That history—the operation and objectification of terror as a first principle of performance, from thought, to *mise en scène,* to terrorist act—is the subject of this book.[5]

The performative history of terror was first rehearsed in thought as *myth*. Hesiod, writing on the far side of the great classical age of theatre, describes the birth of this terror from a curious union: the marriage of Kytheria and Ares, eros and war. The conjunction bears a malignant fruit, the twins Panic[6] [Phobos] and Terror [Deimos], the stage stars of the theatre of war, the remembrance of myth, and the enactment of dream. This marriage suggests the extremes of sex and violence erupting from the riddle of performance and embodying the relation between terror, terrorism, and their showings.

Two hundred years later, these sibling Terrors dream another kind of showing, the "goatsong" tragedy, and the classical stage articulates itself specifically *as* theatre within the omnipresence of catastrophe. But catastrophe is also supressed in this theatre in an injunction to silence and secreted acts of violence. Even as Euripides' Medea nominally submits to silence, the hidden and violent crime that obsesses her threatens to rupture the tragic circumscription of the law, but draws back in the face of what is literally unspeakable and so unthinkable.

In Seneca's *Medea,* appearing some five hundred years later, the breach again threatens in the interpenetration of theatre and terror crystallized in the later Imperial Roman spectacles of the Circus Maximus. These spectacles displaced the theatre of the Republic and demanded a state terrorism grounded in real death, blood, and pain, extracted from the bodies of its slave-performers. Seneca prophesies through his Medea a political counter-terror erupting through the theatricalized violence in the political spectacle of law: "Whatever stood within this royal house has fallen. . . . Is there no limit to catastrophe?"[7] The warning might have been directed to theatre itself, silenced as it later was by the ethical preoccupations of an emerging Christianity, and by the suspicions of an encroaching barbarism.

On the other side of the great medieval theatrical silence, the tradition of terror reemerges (or so we have been told) with the appearance of the *Quem Quaeritis* trope in the tenth century: "Whom do you seek," asks the angel at the tomb. "Jesus of Nazareth," the women reply, "who was crucified." Theatrical scholarship in the west thus locates its origins in the reappearance of a disappeared victim of state terror, an identification that defines hope as the repressed terror of torture and death repositioned in the Church's censorship of the drama.

The laminations and permutations of mythic and theatrical terror continue in the English Renaissance tragedies.[8] In the works of Kyd, Shakespeare, Marlowe, and Webster, terror's image takes center stage in plays such as *Edward II* or *The Spanish Tragedy.* Ultimately, in the productions of the Jacobean period, terror emerges in the split between what seems and what is, and spills quite literally into the pit, bleeding, finally, into yet another abysmal fissure, the repression of the Interregnum. Terror's deployments reappear on the Restoration stage, but are now carefully regulated and applied with surgical precision in the maintenance of social appearances in the cruel and witty "comedies" of Congreve, Etherege, Wycherley, and others. These plays mold the later attitudes and beliefs of middle-class, bourgeois culture in a way that Puritanism could not.

Into the nineteenth century, theatrical terror seemingly exhausts the physical and is redirected inward, where it redefines and gives literary substance to the forces of the psyche in the terror-stricken dramatic works of the Romantic poets. Plays such as Byron's *Manfred,* Shelley's *The Cenci* and *Prometheus Unbound,* and Coleridge's *Remorse,* eventually inform the space of a modern psyche, and give place to a psychology and social engineering whose darker side emerges in the practices of psychosurgery, electroconvulsive therapy, and mental incarceration; "another reign of terror" as Michel Foucault puts it.[9]

In the modern period, the inheritance of the Enlightenment seen.s to collapse inexorably, under the impact of techno-industrialization, world wars, and holocausts. From Ibsen on, humanism begins to dissolve into the very information systems that gave it birth, and the shards and fragments appear in the drama in the images of yet another, solipsistic, terror that is ironically terrified of its own disappearance. Beckett's bums, aliens in a blasted landscape, cannot seem to leave terror's site, and cannot bear to stay.

Thus in theatre's recent history—as Genet marks out the terrorizing topography and psychosexual gamings of love's suspicious history, and Beckett exposes the self-destructive violence of culture and consciousness in performances that often rely on the actual implementation of the bondage, physical pain, and psychic torture that he abhors—the problematic is compounded by the appearance of real violence in the body art of Bruce Naumann, Vito Acconci, Chris Burden, Gina Pain, and others. Meanwhile, in the womb of the mediadrome, the Red Brigades kidnap and execute Aldo Moro in a terrorist "morality play" while the Baader-Meinhof Gang is silenced, both literally and theatrically, "off-stage" in the dark and hidden cells of Stammheim prison.

More recently, as bombs explode in the Frankfurt airport and terrorists hijack luxury cruise ships and throw the handicapped into the Adriatic, the "terrorist" MOVE community in Philadelphia is snuffed out in a self-fulfilling, prophetic scenario of gratuitous and mediated "anti-terrorist" violence almost unsurpassed in the performance documentations of broadcast news.

Eventually, as "real" terrorism develops its own audiences and theatricalizes its presentations, and the "real" theatre begins staging plays *about* terrorism in an attempt to "understand" the phenomenon that has seemingly appropriated the name and form of theatre, form and concept begin to blur. Terrorism is now called "theatre" while we try to convince ourselves that what happens on stage can have anything to do with the real terrorisms of ruptured bodies and wounded minds. Finally, as the actual practice of terrorism is dissolved into the numbing repetitions of terror's mediated images, violence and terror *seem* to be everywhere, and theatre and terrorism become, ironically, *emptied* of terror. Both theatre and terrorism become evenly distributed in the agonizing search for substance beneath the "mere appearance of mere appearance" of culture and its hidden violence. And yet real terrorisms remain, seemingly autonomous, working their way from the outside in. From the threat of global holocaust or "natural" disaster, to the viral inflections of failed immune response, the terror is still with us, shadowing our thought.

This appearance of terror in theatre's history is certainly not a new observation, nor is there anything particularly novel in the recognition that theatre has always been the vehicle for social ideology and control. But these observations are not the point of this study: for I am proposing that theatre is not merely a means by which social behavior is engineered, it is the *site* of violence, the locus of terror's emergence as myth, law, religion, economy, gender, class, or race, either *in* the theatre, or in culture *as* a theatricality that paradoxically precedes culture.

Thus while numerous theorists have recently written about power *in* the theatre, as well as the very theatricality *of* power,[10] I am claiming a certain priority for a theatre which precedes power—a theatre that is the precondition of socio-political power, a sociopolitical power that is impossible without some implied and already recognized structure of performance. Not only is power "deeply theatrical," in Jonathan Dollimore's words, theatre is the very locus in which the "self-division" that is "intrinsic to . . . subordination" is produced.[11] So what may seem at times an essentializing of theatre—the presentation of theatre as a unified and transhistorical phenomenon—is actually an argument for theatre as difference, as the site where cultural and historical diversity is seemingly unified through a sometimes overt, concealed threat of violence. In other words, theatre is the site in which cultural consciousness and identity come into being through fear; it is the proleptic locus of terror's transformation from thought into culture and its terrorisms, staging the very birth of that which seemingly gives it birth—namely Tragedy.

2. The six provisional elements or aspects of tragedy

Plot and character—myth, structure, and ego-consciousness

I am suggesting that theatre constructs, and is constructed by, thought-consciousness—"consciousness released into structure," in Herbert Blau's words—the source of performative questions of subject/object, watcher and watched, actor and spectator, reality and "mere appearance."[12] This moment of thought's structure materializes before the institutional/political theatre both synchronically and diachronically; not only does the *mise en scène* of thought and perception precede the theatrical *production* in all cases—a point I will discuss at length later on—but also the terror of theatre's thought precedes classical performance itself in the literature of myth and epic.

To begin with the classical theatre, and what came *before* the classical theatre, might seem to be an appeal to the very problematic of origins that deconstruction has warned us against—the notion that something like a "purer" or "truer" theatre happened "back then." But that is not my strategy. I am suggesting that in the work of Greek classicism there exists a premonition or sign, a metaphoric prolepsis, that names theatre's terror before theatre names itself as an institution. Thus the formulation of the Terrors in Hesiod, for example, is carried out in a highly theatricalized manner, and this formulation stands in historical relation to the eventual emergence of the classical Greek theatre in much the same way that the *mise en scène* that is thought leads, ultimately, to the "actual" theatrical production. In the metaphor of the Hesiodic Terrors, we can see a theatre emerging from the alienated violence of thought, but thought that is, *in its alienation,* constructed as theatre.

Consequently, if we look at myth and see in its contours the appearance of theatre before the fact, we are not merely engaging in a critical sleight of hand. The very relation and metaphor of thought-terror-theatre that we see in Hesiod is indeed theatre *before* the theatre—the theatre as the condition of perception, shimmering ghostlike in the image of its realized double. The "theatre" of Hesiod articulates, as we will see, a dialectic[13] that displaces the terror of chaos with form or *structure* (plot), while simultaneously indicating the possibilities of that lurking chaos as coercive threat. The Hesiodic theatre, then, articulates and *historicizes* a politics of tragedy, which develops over the next two hundred years into the proto-terrorist structure of the *Oresteia.*

Hesiod's work—in showing us a theatre before the theatre, a tragedy before Tragedy—historically contextualizes the idea of the tragic that appears in the later classical period. The Artistotelian formula then appears as a historically bound *description* of *classical* tragedy, and not a prescriptive formula for reconstituting or identifying the elements of "the tragic." Consequently, the various features of tragedy in the *Poetics* are subject to the rather radical reinterpretations of theatre in history. Indeed, one might attempt a redefinition of the tragic as a form exemplifying the painful ideological displacements that in part explain the appearance of Aristotle's philosophy, or indeed *any* philosophy, in the first place—displacements that construct (either through Marxist "dialectic" or Deleuzean "nomadism") history itself. These displacements are already richly articulated in the Hesiodic vision through the fissures of thought-perception released into mytho-political structure.

Unlike the theories that seek the origins of Greek theatre (and theatre in general) in Dionysian festivals or other "carnivalized" or para-theatrical rituals of culture, in those cultural and religious performances that in some sense celebrate the cohesion of a society already born into the law, Hesiod's vision elucidates through its anti-mythic mythos a theory of terror's theatre that is grounded in the chiaroscuro of perception itself. The Hesiodic description of terror's appearance illuminates the later development of theatre and performance in ways that have been largely ignored by other historical or anthropological approaches to theatre's history; indeed, the Hesiodic illumination places the beginnings of theatre and its terror in thought, and in the long series of displacements that develop, eventually, toward an emergent humanism.

Hesiod, we are told, is "the first Greek who names himself," a mythographer who looks with both bitter skepticism and nostalgia on the dogma he records. His mythic narratives, "vast and heavy, dark and shadow veiled," mark the "cross over into history and reality" from the radiant and brutal world of Homeric retribution. Hesiod was, to anachronize metaphors a bit, an anti-*scop,* his work antiscopic.[14] Indeed, the genesis of the sibling Terrors in Hesiod's work reveals the concerns of a proletarian and tragic man who nursed a hatred of violence, an intense distrust of judicious appearances, and a deep dread of social harmony's secret affiliation with terror and war.[15] Phobos first appears in Hesiod's *Theogony*[16] in a familial context:

> Now Kytheria
> to Ares, stabber of shields, bore Panic [Phobos]
>   and Terror [Deimos], dreaded
> gods, who batter the dense battalions
>   of men embattled
> in horrible war, they with Ares,
>   sacker of cities. She also
> bore him Harmonia. (934–938)

The Hesiodic Phobos appears again, figuratively and literally, in *The Shield of Herakles,* adorning that hero's circular shield:

> And there were folds
>   of cobalt driven upon it
> In the middle was a face of Panic,
>   not to be spoken of,
> glaring on the beholder
>   with eyes full of fire glinting
> and the mouth of it was full of teeth,
>   terrible, repugnant
> and glittering white. (143–147)

This passage describes Herakles' shield in images of grotesque and nightmarish violence, images that evoke the blood-maddened mind of Herakles himself. The face of Phobos occupies the central space of the shield, at the graven nightmare's navel, where the articulation of meanings is both lost and circumscribed by terror's repugnant and speechless mouth. The figured silence of the screaming image echoes back to the concealed and unnamed Deimos, that other terror "not to be spoken of."

In the figuration on the "gold-glowing" mirror-like shield, Phobos appears as the reflection of his brother, as the mask of Deimos that, like a mask, proclaims in its form and conceals in its function the essential dialectical nature of thought itself: the split between materialism and idealism, reality and appearance, inside and outside, disappearance and return, repression and exclusion, thought[17] and representation. Deimos disappears behind the image of Phobos, while Phobos generates the "seeming substance" of terror in mere appearance.[18] At the same time, the dreamlike circumscriptions on the Heraklean shield represent the inevitable displacement[19] of dream/performance by artifact or *narrative*. This displacement is indicated by the appearance of a dream text on the inscribed shield—thus thought, dreamed-desire, is usurped by representation and production, but a production that is, in this case, still closely linked to its ontologic bloodlines, to "Terror, the dream-diviner of/ this house."[20]

In Hesiod the terrible brothers appear in a theatre of war, indicating their filiation with the violence of the father, Ares. Although Hesiod does not specifically mention any interaction between Phobos and Deimos and their mother Aphrodite (Kytheria), terror appears as the child of Desire and Violence frequently enough in the later history of drama, often as an indication of an epiphanic chaos that subverts the seeming harmony of law and order. "If I be Venus, thou must needs be Mars" says Bel-Imperia while seducing her lover Horatio in Kyd's *The Spanish Tragedy*, "and where Mars reigneth, there must needs be wars."[21] A few lines later Horatio is horribly and gratuitously murdered in an act of passion and political intrigue that sets into motion a series of assassinations and retaliations that strike at the foundation of the political order, revealing *avant la lettre* the phobias of a somewhat later Jacobean age—terrors that are conceived and violently exteriorized through Horatio/Mars' seduction by Bel-Imperia/ Venus.

In Kyd as in Hesiod, then, Phobos masks a showing. In Lacanian terms, he represents within the text the abolished presence or *forclusion* (the denial of experience's access to the Symbolic, experience's a priori expulsion back into the Real)[22] of Deimos projected outward into the scene of violence—a theatre of pure cruelty. This is a manifestation of a terror that is both specular and performative. The apparitions and concealments that describe the relationship between Phobos and Deimos mark both the dislocations and the disappearances that are central to theatre and performance—the essential unlocatability of the vanishing Deimos, for example, or the secretions of meaning in the appearance of Phobos, who plays out war and performs acts of violence that are later inscribed on the "magic writing pad" of the Heraklean shield, much as a modern performance artist might document his work.[23]

Phobos reveals himself in these performative spaces—the theatres of war, the circular shield of remembrance, the *mise en scène* of thought/desire and representation. He paradoxically embodies in carefully inscribed images of disarray, chaos, and dislocation the violent resistances that define the difference between thought and its representations: Phobos, as the image of Deimos, locates displacement and repression in his very appearance. Deimos, on the other hand, describes a critical absence or lack, a "hole" in the fabric of consciousness that indicates a pathology of deficiency:

> a *béance* of some sort, resulting from the way in which the original tissue [of consciousness] itself was woven; *forclusion* would be sort of an *"original hole,"* never capable of finding its own substance again since it had never been anything other than *"hole-substance."*[24]

This pathology is also congenital in theatre, a pathology in which we can trace either the repression or the *forclusion* of terror by theatrical representation. And this distinction is critical, for when political terror is *repressed* through theatre—or more precisely, when the *relation* between terror and its implementation in the images of terror*ism* is repressed—when it is dislocated into the image systems of spectacle, it often displaces cultural terror and terror's pain into the strategies of information until terror and its isms become formalized, objectified, and gradually neutralized into concealed ideologies, "hegemonies," or mere habits of thought.

When terror is displaced by *forclusion* in the theatre, however, and then re-presented, it appears not as representation (because it cannot *be* represented), but as hallucination, as some unnameable thing that returns in the Real like a Jacobean apparition.[25] This *forclusion* often seems more potentially subversive in its relation to actual terror because it seeks not to conceal terror (although it must to some degree), but to reject the repressive signifying order itself—the order of law—in its entirety. Artaud perceived this when he wrote:

> The theatre will never find itself again—i.e. constitute a means of true illusion—except by furnishing the spectator with the truthful precipitates of dreams, in which his taste for crime, his erotic obsessions, his savagery, his chimeras, his utopian sense of life and matter, even his cannibalism, pour out, on a level not counterfeit and illusory, but internal.[26]

"True illusion"—in other words, the hallucinatory return of what has been excluded in the Real—rediscovers its connection to terror in the immediacy of thought, in the perception of the terror that *is* thought.

We can see this distinction between repression and *forclusion* by comparing the response to terror of Euripides' Medea—in which the relation between terror and its implementation in terrorism is repressed in the law of language, in the very inscription of the word "silence" itself[27]—to the final act of Marlowe's *Edward II,* in which the assassin Lightborne comes to the jailers who are holding Edward in the cloacal dungeon "to which the channels of the castle run." Lightborne carries a letter:

> *Enter* LIGHTBORNE
> *Light.* My lord Protector greets you. [Gives letter.]
> *Gur.* What's here? I know not how to conster it.
> *Mat.* Gurney, it was left unpointed for the nonce; *'Edwardum occidere nolite timere,'* That's his meaning.
> *Light.* Know you this token? I must have the king.[28]

'Edwardum occidere nolite timere bonum est' is from Holinshed's *Chronicles of England* in which the story of Edward's grisly death is recounted:

> Withall the Bishop of Hereforde under a sophisticall forme of wordes signified to them by his letters, that they shoulde dispatch him out of the way, as thus: Edwardum occidere nolite timere bonum est: To kill Edwarde will not to fear

it is good. Whiche riddle or doubtfull kinde of speech . . . might bee taken in two contrarie senses, onely by placing the poynt in Ortographie called *comma,* they interpreted it in the worse sense.[29]

The two senses of the phrase, "Fear not to kill the king 'tis good he die," or "Kill not the king, 'tis good to fear the worst." (5.4.9–12), depend upon the placement of a comma, but the phrase within Marlowe's text is left unpunctuated. Edward's fate is determined by the "missing poynte" that leads to his disappearance.[30] The unpunctuated text, or rather the point that is missing from the text, marks a hole or rent in the textual tissue, corresponding to a *béance* in the tissue of consciousness. Furthermore, the *forclusion* comes again in a horrifying form; the missing comma returns in the Real as the hollow horn pushed into Edward's anus to guide the red-hot poker that kills him: "They kept him downe, and withall put into his fundament an horne."[31] The guiding horn appears as a "punctuation without a text," and thus the "castrated" or disembodied phallus/comma comes from without as a real object of violence in the hand of the Luciferian Lightborne, who embodies the disappeared lover Gaveston:

> K. *Edw.* Who's there? what light is that? wherefore comes thou?
> *Light.* To comfort you, and bring you joyful news. (5.5.41–43)

In the performative site of *Edward II,* Lightborne/Phobos functions as gestus, glyph or cipher; Gaveston/Deimos as the exclusion of that inscription. The affiliation and interval between them is a space of theatrical possibility in which relations of power become thought at thought's extremity. Thus while it is obvious that Marlowe's play—or any play, for that matter—must always repress terror as performance or text, this repression operates *within* Marlowe's play as an exclusion, as a rejection of the signifying order, which reverberates beyond the play and calls into question the very hierarchies of power that depend upon that signifying order for entrenchment and stability.

These last comments on *Edward II* will suggest several questions: although all performance is to some extent repressive, to what degree does any given performance reveal its repressive mechanisms? To what degree does a performance, in its rejection of the signifying order through *forclusion,* show its own relation to violence and terror? To what degree does any performance re-present hallucinatory expulsions from the "political unconscious"? Although there can certainly be no play that is purely a repression or a *forclusion,* determining the degree to which a given performance is operating in one or the other mode can reveal the critical movements of terror and terrorism in history.

The Phobos/Deimos relation represents, in this context, several different types and levels of meaning in performance: the relation between neurosis and schizophrenia; the breach between thought and its "theft" by language; the difference between theatre and its double; the reference between the Symbolic/Imaginary (representation—Phobos) and the Real (what cannot be represented—Deimos); the collusion between terror (which cannot enter systems of information or representation) and the terrorism that ends, in the ceaseless cycles of mediations, as the information system of the absent terror; the opposition between self and Other. In each case Phobos (the unpunctuated text) displaces Deimos (punctuation without a text), and Deimos is either repressed or cast into the Real through the discharges of performance.

By the same token, these performative ideas in Hesiod, while quite evocative and perhaps in some ways perfunctorily theatrical, must at the same time be differentiated from performance itself. When we speak of theatre or performance, we are speaking of a place where what *is* is what is shown "out there" in real bodies living and dying in real time. What we see in the tragic theatre (differentiated from "tragedy" as a literary type or genre) is the appearance of what had been unarticulated. This showing is in fact the primary business of the theatre; language, words, letters, signs must be embodied, voiced, shown, made present. What we see in Hesiod is theatre *as forclusion,* performativity as disavowal exemplified in the terror that is both revealed and repudiated in a single line: "In the middle was a / face of Panic, / not to be spoken of."

Here we are faced with a paradox, however, because in performance what cannot be articulated must be shown, and when it is shown, it ceases to be what it was. Thus when terror enters the information systems of performance, it ceases, in a sense, to be terror—which is unspeakable, and unrepresentable—and becomes a mask of itself. Terror is transformed into the imaging system of terrorism.

There is a chasm here between what we might term the ontologic theatre, the theatre that *is* thought, and the "ontic" theatre, the theatre that *represents* the theatre that is thought.[32] This is further complicated by the difference I have already suggested between theatres that repress terror by displacing it into the reforming sign system of terrorism, and theatres that direct thought back to the unrepresentability of terror—the difference between theatre, once again, and its double.[33] The issue, finally, is not merely to determine a given theatrical performance's relation to signification, but also to determine the ways in which that relation mystifies the linkages between signification, theatre, and political violence. These linkages are the traces, as it were, of the mind's terror upon itself, exemplified, once again, in the image of the shield as that which marks the boundary between life and death, between body and Other/Enemy, between thought and the unthinkable.

The breach between the genotypes of terror (Phobos and Deimos), then, is born of the cleft in solipsistic consciousness that constitutes primary identity—what Jacques Lacan calls the mirror stage, in which the child perceives the (w)holeness of body/self only in the image of an other. This perception is at once a perception of integration and a recognition that integration (identity) can only be had in an other.

The mirror stage is thus simultaneously the apprehension of an essential wholeness, and a self-alienation in which the self can only be composed and apprehended apart from and outside of the self. The other in this case becomes a specular principle of discord/harmony through which the individual is realized. This is what Anthony Wilden identifies as the *"Imaginary Other,"* a kind of proto-Symbolic Other who represents the locus of a law that is *necessarily* violent because it is based not on difference and correspondence (communication), but on opposition and identity (conflict).[34]

This rhetorical silence—what comes to be called in the postmodern period "theoretical terrorism"—is represented in the theatre by the relation between those figures who function as an absence, as an empty screen for the phobic projections of terrorists, and the terrorists who carry out the bloody deeds. I have already mentioned the relationship between these two figurations in the characters Gaveston and Lightborne, but we also see it in the recessive, seated figure in Beckett's *Catastrophe* who is manipulated by the ideologue director, for example, or in the projection of terror onto the image of the female/Other in the drama—the Other who serves as the empty space through which desire and its terror(ism) formulate themselves. I am thinking here of Desdemona and Othello, or the Duchess of Malfi and her brother, or any number of plays in which characters formulate their own terror against an Other-as-absence.

This relationship between a terror that is (or seems to be) a withholding or recessiveness, and a terrorism that is an acting out,[35] is yet one more relation between the Deimic and the Phobic, a relation that enters the theatre in these kinds of plays as a self-reflexive discourse in which the Imaginary relation between Phobos and the unrepresentable but now-shown Deimos is represented in an Imaginary Other.

The appearance of the imaginary Other is, according to Lacan, a necessary stage in the realization of the Symbolic Other, a realization crucial to the final development of the individual in society. Thus while the Symbolic Other comes, finally, to represent the locus of language and law, this law is not *necessarily* exploitative or violent, according to Wilden.[36]

Theatre is not really of the Symbolic order, however. It is specular and as such is the site of seduction and "capture" by the Imaginary Other. In its guise as a political-cultural institution theatre is the specularity/spectacle of the Imaginary and of the violent law that is "always already" part of the symbolic order. This is different from the *drama,* from the theatre that exists as text/criticism and not as spectacle. The drama exists more specifically as a part of the Symbolic order—the order of difference and correspondence—and not, as does performance, in the Imaginary order of opposition and identity.

This affinity between theatre and the Imaginary order explains, in part, why *forclusion* becomes the means by which the connection between violence and law is most clearly revealed in performance. Even though it is obvious that theatre must exist to some degree within the Symbolic, the seeming immediacy of theatrical perception wants, in every instance, to exclude or repress the Symbolic in favor of the Imaginary. Consequently the only means by which the repression of the Imaginary is revealed is the complete rejection of the Symbolic *and* Imaginary orders through *forclusion,* through the recuperation of symbol and imagination as hallucination.

In any case, whether we identify the theatre's Other as Imaginary or Symbolic, the alienation of the self in the locus of the Other eventually causes what Lacan calls *aphanisis,* or disappearance, as "I" am displaced outside the locus of "my" self, and seem to vanish into the Other. This is the essential performative circumstance of theatre and generated the particular agony of Artaud, that patron saint of the modern theatre, who felt himself continuously bereft of a language adequate to his agony.[37] Artaud's tormented disavowal of *aphanisis* eventually led to his descent into a hell of pain, terror, madness, and finally death. There are a few better examples than Artaud's madness of *aphanisis in extremis.* This is the terrorizing and lethal aspect of the Other as it becomes what Herbert Blau calls the Enemy, "all that survives of the Beloved—what makes your hair stand on end."[38] The threat of disappearance in/by the presence of the Other generates this kind of terror out of the differentiating space, the rupture in consciousness that displaces the self into the power of an other. This is the same terror that either defines or conceals the ruptures or disunities that characterize culture itself.

Diction—the Symbolic, language and law

The simultaneous perception and denial that this rupture exists initiates the obsessive and blinded insight that develops into one of the major theoretical principles of tragedy in Sophocles' *Oedipus Rex* and beyond, leading us by increments to the seemingly endless, self-silencing ratiocinations of Kyd's proto-Hamlet, Hieronimo, into the exhaustion of thought in Beckett, and ending with the flat recitatives and silences of postmodern performance.

As I suggested at the outset, the burgeoning intuition in Greek culture of the essentially infracted nature of consciousness emblematic in *Oedipus Rex,* to name but the most obvious example, emerges concurrently with the growth of a complex and exteriorized legal and economic system.[39] This helps to explain why Greek tragedy's preoccupation with crime seems, paradoxically, to anticipate legal systems after the historical fact. Crime in tragedy appears both as an individual lack, and as a fault line or stress fracture[40] in the social structure in which the individual (the hero) lives. Crime is ultimately the origin both of the hero, and of civilization and culture. In the *Oresteia,* for example, the concealed Orestes (who describes himself, according to Richmond Lattimore's translation, as a "Daulian stranger out of Phocis") is eventually resolved and defined through the remembrance of a murder generating murder, recounted mythically and mimetically over and again back through time, ending (beginning?) with the tribunal of Athena that judges and abolishes the threat of an infinite, recursive vengeance, and establishes order and identity as the result of the remembered crime.

Nietzsche sees a similar situation in *Oedipus Rex* when he identifies the Oedipal myth not as the cause and explanation of individual and collective neuroses, but rather as the result of some more primal, unspeakable crime which is eventually adjudicated through the displacement of the "divine" king by the law, and then by the collective will of the demos.[41] This recalls the displacement that occurs in (Lacanian) psychoanalysis, when the specular power of the king, the "Imaginary Father," is (at least partially) deposed by the subject through the symbolic exchanges (laws) of language and analysis.[42] The crime that resolves the individual and creates society is brought to justice (language) in an act of Symbolic exchange in which the primal infraction— the desire for incest or the incest that is desire—is adjudged and punished by the very system of signs it generates: the heroic silence of the classical stage is, in other words, the appearance of the Lacanian unconscious, the space or *stage* of articulation in the Other, thus the lineation of a theatre that emerges as thought, and a thought that emerges *as theatre*.

Thought

This cross-penetration between thought and theatre is pivotal in Freudian theories of individual memory and consciousness, and, I would suggest, in the social memory and consciousness that is myth and history. But while many writers have recognized a theatrical context in Freud's dramatization of the primal moments of psychosexual development ("the primal scene," "the seduction scene," "screen memories," the spatial and theatrically bound idea of the re-presented), these moments are often assumed to have taken on theatricality *after the fact* so to speak; Freud merely uses the theatre as a preexisting metaphor for certain psychic mechanisms, or he assumes that both psyche and theatre emerge from some common perceptual apparatus that inflects each with the peculiar sense of spatiality, separation, and rememoration that somehow characterizes basic psychic operations as theatrical production.

But if we look at any of these Freudian "performance metaphors" from the standpoint of theatre *or* trauma theory, we come to realize that there is nothing, that there can be nothing, preceding these Freudian mechanisms but theatre itself (or what Derrida would call "writing"). I have already pointed out that the pained moment of perception by which the character of the self emerges in consciousness through the "mirror stage" is the moment of theatre's perception, and it is the psyche itself, emerging as *structure*—as dream, memory, plot, ego—that occurs after the theatrical fact. It is fruitless, then, to argue for this theatricality simply as a ground for the figuration upon which perception appears, just as it would be absurd to call a play like Beckett's *Breath* "pure" theatre because of the absence of actors.

We cannot, therefore, think of thought, of dream, or of mythic-memory and their associated traumas as phenomena that occur "within" a performative context. Rather the performative itself is the necessity through which something like the myth-as-seduction scene and its ensuing trauma comes into being. Freud seems, at some subliminal level at least, to presuppose this; although he never uses theatre as a *paradigm,* he develops his theory of sexuality and trauma along theatrical lines when he "metaphorically" places such phenomena as memory or dream within a preexisting and essentially performative context—a "scene" or *theatre* that is "always already" there to receive it.

Similarly, when Walter Benjamin, in *The Origin of German Tragic Drama,* reframed what is perhaps the most critical perception in Nietzsche's *The Birth of Tragedy* (that the Greek tragic theatre, and perhaps theatre generically, is the product of the psycho-cultural passage from myth/religion into law), he was articulating the sociopolitical axis of the Freudian theatre metaphor. That is, the appearance of the "actual" theatre in the West represents the forensic, representational space of the passage from myth to law, from the wreckage of war to veneration and reconstruction, from a divisive and *spectacular* thought to a codified forensic practice, from the dismembering structure of thought itself to its remembrance as *theatre.*[43]

Accordingly, what Nietzsche describes problematically as the "mere appearance of mere appearance" in the theatre articulates the entrance of an earlier, "sacred" terror onto a new stage. This would be a theatre of jurisdiction, a reactive violence against terror that in turn reappropriates terror's Chaotic power as law: "The bright image projections of the Sophoclean hero—in short, the Apollonian aspect of the mask—are necessary effects of a glance into the inside and terrors of nature; as it were, luminous spots to cure eyes damaged by gruesome night."[44] The induction of this "gruesome night" into the theatre, where it might be *tragically* "cured," was and is asymptotic with the emergence of a "luminescent," recuperative law, a law perceived earlier in the terror-strewn work of Hesiod.

The simultaneous emergence of tragedy and law suggests a more fundamental relationship than a mere tactical support by theatre in the establishment of legal codes. It represents a necessary conjunction of law and theatre in history. Although this relationship is often described (as it is in Benjamin's work) in terms of the formation of a culture/law that *allows* theatre to appear—that theatre in some sense always "looks back" to its origins in the law—what is usually forgotten is the sense in which theatre enunciates the very instant of perception that exists before culture and its laws can appear. Theatre is, in other words, in a dialectical tension with culture—or seen in another way, there is a dialectical tension between theatre and the seeming life that emerges from it.

This instant, as Nietzsche tells us, is deeply ambivalent: in the expanding field of thought and perception that is culture, thought itself seemingly holds the violence of chaos at bay. Yet this instant is also the moment of an other terror—the moment of the many against the one, but also, and perhaps more profoundly, the instant of alienation, fragmentation, and death that is the dark and violent aspect of perception itself. This is the terror that what is perceived is always Other, always suspect, always a lie: "Men should be what they seem," says Iago, even as he teaches us that perception itself is "always already" infected by desire, a desire that Freud tells us is, at mind's end, the desire for the "true illusion' of death.

Perception is absolutely infused by terror—a confrontation with the imminence of a non-being that defines life. Pain and death and madness are "feelingly perceived" in the terrorizing play of human thought itself, the play that is theatre, the *"initiatory breach* which remembers the primal violence" in the meeting between "life and death, art and life, the thing itself and its double." [45]

In the institutionalized theatre (the inevitable end of all performance), within the reverberations of theatre's relation to the law in tragedy, the terror of non-being is ultimately crystallized as the threat of terrorism—an objectification of terror in the ideology of the violent image. [46] This objectification of terror is used as a disciplining force applied to the body and mind. Moreover, this force is historically determined, and takes different forms in different theatrical periods. The forms of terror and its isms are historically unique to each age of the theatre. The history of performance becomes, in this sense, a history of the ways in which terror is objectified as ideology/law and deployed as a means of sociopolitical conditioning. These forms of conditioning can be traced along several axes: the creation and use of gender, race, or class as a means of terrorizing control, for example, or the ideological coercion couched in the representational systems (Cartesianism, Hegelianism, etc.) that theatre generates in any given age. [47] These ideological coercions, moreover, suggest real practices on real, albeit concealed, bodies in the political order of the law, an order that in turn deploys its own terrorisms theatrically in the spectacle.

Spectacle and musicality

The *tragic* institution of law, grounded in the expiatory concept of *lex talionis* ("an eye for an eye"—the economization of violence in systems of exchange) defines culture and the individual, as Hegel suggests, in negative terms through the painful breaks, dislocations, disappearances, and *forclusion* that appear in the individual and collective psyche. The individual and culture come to being, in other words, through infractions, real or imagined, judged and disposed in the locus of the Other. The recurrence of absence, *forclusion, aphanisis*—the returning, painful expulsions that mark the irruption of culture and identity—are the substance of theatre's crime, and are theatre history.

René Girard discusses this performance of expulsion at the cultural-political level in terms of *mimesis*. In *Violence and the Sacred*,[48] for instance, he delineates the ways in which *desire* is produced through competition with an other for the possession of some object that comes, in the desiring struggle, to emblematize desire itself.[49] Here Girard seems to be describing something like an Imaginary Other, an *imago* that haunts the Symbolic order and reduces difference and correspondence to opposition and identity. This reduction is the essential operation of repression that I described earlier, and is the seeming image of power and force that Girard sees as the generator of culture, the seeming image that I would call theatre.

As the other becomes Double becomes Other becomes Enemy through the struggle of opposition and identity in Girard's thought, s/he is spectacularly and ritualistically expelled, through either exile or sacrificial execution in the guise of the Double. This expulsion of the Other is not, however, an expulsion of the law, *per se,* but an expulsion of the *relation* between law and violence that is repressed in the image of the Double. As this relation seemingly disappears beyond the frontiers of culture and thought, the community experiences its *apparent* cohesion through the exercise of its *unanimous violence*. This, according to Girard, is the meaning of tragic theatre in general, and the meaning of *Oedipus Rex* in particular. Consequently, the appearance of a unified impulse in theatre practice—the idea that theatre represents the interests of the dominant culture—is indeterminate. Theatre's terror in fact represents the radical uncertainty of theatre's violence. What is crucial in this process of identification and expulsion is, as Girard tells us, that the link between the unanimous law and violence remain hidden. It is of utmost importance that the connection between *mimetic desire,* or desire in general, and the reality of cultural violence (even "subcultural" or oppositional violence) remain concealed (unconscious) as well.

Mimetic desire finds its means of concealment in the theatrical spectacle itself, and the systems of sign and spectacle that are chosen are therefore historically "selected" to conceal specific relations between law and desiring-violence, between tragedy and its generative terror. Thus tragic mimesis, or the particular form and language that tragedy takes on in order to imitate and so possess desire, conceals within its lineaments the particular mode of repression that identifies the connections between the tragic form and the cultural powers it upholds.

We might seek, then, a kind of Brechtian antitoxin, the traces of a para-tragic theatre within the tragic tradition that disarticulates its mimetic mechanisms beneath its own terrorized gaze, that discovers the Imaginary Other and sees in that delusion, and in the hallucinations of terror's violent *forclu-*

sion, something like Artaud's "truthful precipitates of dreams" in the dream of the political unconscious.

3. Tragedy, terror, and katharsis

Aristotle, writing this dream on the far side of the passage from mythic society to law, named the various mechanisms of violent *forclusion* and dislocation—the "laws of expiation" grown from the substrate of purification rite and religious dictum—*katharsis.*[50] The dislocative phenomenon of *katharsis* was, according to Aristotle, effected mimetically through the now famous invocation of pity and terror[51], and has since been relocated as the central, pivotal term in Aristotle's theory.

Although no other theory of performance has had the impact or generated the volume of discussion that Aristotle's theory has, the disturbing and problematical nature of the meaning of *katharsis* that resides at the heart of Aristotle's theory remains. What seems at first to be a rather simple homology of effects in the Aristotelian formula—manic music expelling mania, mimetic terror expelling actual terror—becomes more problematic as we search for a clearer understanding of the term as it is employed. The precise meaning of *katharsis* becomes fraught with questions and difficulties: what, precisely, is being expelled? some morbid terror lying hidden in the mind of the subject? and who or what is that subject—the audience, the actor, the "character"? and of what is this terror terrified? what object? what situation? Indeed, a fundamental problem in understanding *katharsis* is related to its pivotal role in Aristotle's theory—pity, fear, and *katharsis* are more experiential than categorical. But the problem still remains, what is this *katharsis* that is induced by the experience of pity and terror?

Although I can make no pretence to classical scholarship, and so cannot support or refute the specifics of the various philological analyses of the terms, I would suggest that the "problem" of the meaning of *katharsis* delineates a condition of dislocation that is the precise reflex of *katharsis* (and phobos, its attendant term) itself.[52]

The fundamental sense of the word *katharsis* seems to be grounded in the history of medicine, or even earlier, in rites of purification and proto-legal expiation where the word indicated not a condition or state of mind, but a kind of expurgation, a casting away or removal of some impurity, sickness, or crime through "ceremonies that wash clean and cast out the Furies."[53] *Katharsis* indicated not the final circumstance of purification, but the process of disgorgement itself.

As a philosophical term, *katharsis* retained this sense of dis-location. At one point in the *Rhetoric,* for example, terror (phobos), the precondition of *katharsis,* is defined as "pain or disturbance due to imagining some destructive or painful evil *in the future.*"[54] Terror, then, and in a different sense, *katharsis,* are neither objective nor subjective phenomena, but are instead the manifestation of a fundamental and violent expulsion or disappearance of the subject and his pain into another locus—either the repressive Other or the Real. The intensity of this disappearance produces a loss of identity: the collapse of the subject/object into a third term, an Unnameable.

Katharsis then, is an expulsion inaugurated within the field of terror. Generated by the terror born of fragmented consciousness, *katharsis* is what it produces—a perpetual unlocatability, a continuous *aphanisis,* an infinite series of displacements, disgorgements, emeses that serve in the end to eradicate all sense of a vulnerable, locatable self (what we might call theatrical "characterization"). The presumed "healing" effect of *katharsis* comes about because these expurgations and dislocations eventually seem to engender terror's Imaginary opposite in the returning sense of a sublime following the expulsion of non-being. In terms of terrorism, this sublime is perceived as a sense of harmony and stasis in a world "restored" by the violence of unanimous law,[55] or as the end of repressive history engendered by the individual violent act. In either case, the difficulty in finally locating meaning behind *katharsis* is the root meaning of *katharsis*—and phobos—itself: a word that conceals a lack of significance within its inscription.

The conflation of the medical and political senses of *katharsis* is clear in the Greek drama: "We must use medicine, / or burn, or amputate, with kind intention," says Agamemnon in the *Oresteia,* "take / all means at hand that might beat down corruption's pain."[56] *Katharsis* and its tragedy, then, might be understood as the historical displacement of one ideology by another through the seeming dismembering processes of terror. *Katharsis,* terror, and *pity (eleos)* intersect in a desire to eradicate a literal or metaphorical ("false consciousness") dis-ease from the *polis* through the amputation with "kind intention" of the gangrenous member.

Conversely, the modern dismissal of pity as a noble virtue ("the *worthlessness* of pity," writes Nietzsche, that "pernicious, modern effeminacy") stems in part from its dissociation from the blooded brutality of *katharsis* and terror. When Artaud dismisses pity in favor of a cruelty by which the body and psyche is scourged and purified—the plague—he is invoking the older sense of pity that sees its violent, *reforming* aspect. But this reformation can move in two different directions. While Artaud saw in cruelty/pity the possibility of a complete reconstruction of consciousness, Nietzsche, and Foucault following him, saw in the union of cruelty and pity the means by which pain and punishment have been objectified, reified, and economized as crucial elements in the irruption of a "merciful" and just law.[57] In these views pity is the other side of terror, its perversion, the "bright projection of the Sophoclean hero" that covers over the dark violence concealed in a "gruesome night."

Although pity normally evokes the seemingly benign aspect of desire— pity is empathic, contiguous, the corrective to *demand* in the sentiment that pretends to proclaim "I want what is good for you"—there is much that is suspect in pity as it appears in theatre, especially in tragedy, where the warpings of desire become so complete that it is often impossible to ascertain an *object* of desire at all. Indeed, one of the most powerful ideas to surface again and again in the drama is the recognition that desire does not desire any object, but desires only itself. Theatre is what Gilles Deleuze and Felix Guattari would call a desiring machine.

Desire is the engine that subverts pity and regenerates the terror within it, a painful recognition that the union implied by pity might be a lie spoken by the Other to cover up an emphatic and absolute alienation or absence of being in desire. The desire for what the Other desires (the objectified desire of the Other) that is implied by pity is transformed into terror when desire cannot capture the Other, or the Other's desire, as object. When desire is frustrated in this way, the threat of non-being appears, and either an object is substituted for the desire of the Other, or the Other is absolutely denied. When a replacement object is substituted for the Enemy-Other, desire becomes phobic. When the Other is categorically denied or expelled, a "hole" or lack opens in consciousness, and desire/terror is displaced into the Real.

Freud characterized a phobia as a fixation on an object of dread that functions as a mask concealing the space of an other, repressed, desire. He gives the example of a young man who wishes to murder his father, but cannot admit his desire to himself because it is too fearful. It is so fearful in fact that he cannot even admit its existence as an object of fear, and so he substitutes another fearful desire in its place, and fears that; he becomes phobic and will not go out in public because he is afraid he will murder people indiscriminately. This is a particularly provocative example because both phobia and the particular example of phobia given are instances of dislocation.[58]

The object of a phobia in Freud is not the true terror, but a terror dislocated. The Phobic object—the graven shield, the mask, the image of terror—both represents and hides the feared and desired Deimos. We might seek, then, a repudiated desire in the tragic experience of terror, the concealed wish that draws us to the theatre in the first place: perhaps a hunger for obliteration and death in the Other suggested in different ways by both Freud and Lacan, or the craving for some primal bloodlust already noted by Nietzsche and Foucault. Or perhaps we are drawn by the longing for a totality in which all correspondence and difference is obliterated by a desire "firmly wedded to the law in the pure detachment and elevation of the death instinct"—a desire for death in an object that will replace the dispersive tedium of history, the boredom of hearing the "hypocritical doctors explain what it all means."[59]

At the level of state terrorism, the public performance of the desire for death in objectification transforms it into a socio-political ideology. This is the structure and function of tragedy raised to an extreme virulence: the violent displacement of one ideology by another through the enactment of a tyranny that absolutely denies its dispersion into history and language (and theatre). Tyranny's resistance to dispersion is enforced by terror's embodiment in the words and images of state violence and terrorism. In order for tyranny to operate, in other words, its terror must be deployed as a sign within the systems of exchange. It must, in fact, become the sign system of its own terrorism. Yet paradoxically, the terror that is the result of this terrorism—the real pain inflicted on the body—can never become a sign, can never enter a system of information and exchange. It remains unsignifiable, unrepresentable. This distinction between terror and terrorism, the difference between real pain and the techniques of its production, represents the reification and commodification of terror into terrorism.

Terrorism, in other words, is an extreme, theatricalized violence that operates in what Roland Barthes would have termed "the regime of the signifier." But when terror's roots and causes are repressed in the formation of performance, media, and theatre events, and the connections between the socializing, disciplining power of terroristic violence are cut off from the ontologic terror that generates them—when terror loses itself in the Imaginary—we lose sight of terrorism's mechanisms and are denied the possibilities of resistance. Violence then seems to return in the Real, individually and collectively, in new and abominable hallucinatory forms. This is the terror of socio-political madness—that the reality we think we know may only be the hallucinated remains of a denied enormity, cast back into the world, returned in another monstrous form in the Real. Thus at the level of the "political unconscious" the repressed (for most of us) connections between the mediated state terrorism of the Vietnam "theatre," and the psychotic terror of national non-being that supported it, eventually caused that war to erupt again in American movie theatres in the figure of various sorts of reflagged Rambos. Meanwhile, the psychotic footsoldiers of the *mediated* campaign— the *spectacle* of the war—suddenly began to carry Vietnam-era automatic weapons into fast-food restaurants, shopping malls, and playgrounds, falsely proclaiming themselves battle-crazed vets before opening fire. All of this while performance artists and experimental theatres initiated their own explorations into the ethos of violence and self-mutilation in ways that sometimes did more to confuse the issues of violence and theatre than to clarify their relations.

This confusion arises because whenever acts of terrorism of any sort are mediated, causing us to lose sight of the critical, terrorizing impulses that gave them birth, violence reemerges as a mystifying, disconnected system of signs whose causes and reasons become permanently lost to us; they become, in Guy Debord's word, *spectacle,* a fragmentary or schizophrenic "ideology par excellence" ruled by "the despotism of the fragment . . . completed in the immobilized spectacle of non-history."[60]

The ultimate danger for us in this is that the fear of national non-being that led us into the theatre of Vietnam, aggravated by the sense of theatricalized irrationality surrounding domestic and foreign anti-state terrorist acts, becomes transformed into a kind of proto-fascism, a terror of formlessness and fragmentation which is eventually displaced by the law as a formal object of fear, fascination, and desire. The law becomes spectacular, it becomes a phobic object which hides this terror of non-being, the terror of the chaos beneath the harmony of law, the deep and resolute void beyond the imagery of violence. This finally echoes Lacan's understanding of phobia, which is quite distinct from Freud's:

> Not the fear of an object, but the confrontation of the subject with an absence of object, with a lack of being in which he is stuck or caught, in which he loses himself and to which anything is preferable, even the forging of that most strange and alien of objects: a phobia.[61]

The Lacanian concept of phobia suggests a repudiation, not a displacement, the traces of schizo-psychosis and not a "mere" neurotic repression. Thus tyranny's phobia "covers itself over" with Debord's *béance,* the spectacle, an object *contra* situation that is perhaps best exposed or "deconstructed" in performance *as* performance, and through performance in culture itself. Forms of theatre that conceal the filiation between terrorism and ontologic terror by substituting a phobic object to cover a "lack of being"—performance modes that are essentially or largely spectacular—must be discovered and properly situated so that we can gain an understanding of their ideological alignment and the effects of that alignment on memory, on history.

4. Terror and history

History, as Nietzsche points out in the *Genealogy,* is linked spectacularly to the creation of a memory in man. This memory is created by inflicting pain on the individual, and history becomes the residual pain of the collective scar tissue.[62] The creation and recreation of this collective memory of pain was, moreover, a critical point in humankind's passage from "protohistoric" myth-religion into history and law.

Clearly, the collective repetition of the trauma, of that "which never ceases to hurt," suggests the necessity of a "being-witness" to hurt—the necessity of an audience in a *theatre* of pain. History is thus made to appear *as* theatre—an endless reenactment of the perception of pain, and the pain of perception. The present work, then, suggests a history of pain displayed as theatre before the subject of culture, a pain generated out of the split within/without the self that is the moment of perception—the oscillation between terror and its shield that is something like the movement of history itself.

In the astigmatic eye of perception, then, in the context of the "becoming" and disappearance that *is also* the (Deimic) theatre, the history of terror in theater would not be an attempt to see things "as they really might have been." Nor would such a history appear as an effort to reconstruct the political and economic forces of past periods. Rather, we might look at terror's history in a provisional way as the truth of some present, historical distress traced by that history on the contemporary body and mind. These traces might be recognized by their particular sensitivity to pain, a sensitivity that is related in various ways to its methods of production, but a pain-terror that is, finally, locatable only in the *aphanisis* of perception disarticulating itself "in the locus of the Other." This is the preoccupation with the terror of *aphanisis* that has been formulated and reformulated throughout theatre's history *as* history, culminating in its foregrounding in contemporary performance and theatre.

And thus the painful irony: while it may be true that the original impulses to liberation or knowledge that underlie the contemporary "terrorist act" or violent performance—the impulses that provide the critical connection between terror and its terrorism—are in certain cases courageous and deeply committed, those deeply committed impulses are ultimately transformed into a denial of the reality of pain. Pain, in other words, loses its impact when, through history, it becomes foregrounded—or "repressively desublimated"—in contemporary performance. This "repressive desublimation" of pain suppresses the real pain of history within the development of an increasingly historicist (linear, positivist) postmodernism. This suppression is then *dis*played in the theatre in "real" acts of violence as performance, but the terroristic nuances of these *signs* of violence finally obscure the coercive, historical necessity of actual violence and terror as they are produced within politico-economic systems in the Real, the Real that Fredric Jameson says *is* history.[63]

In contemporary performance, this level of mystification assigns the work of artists like Chris Burden or Vito Acconci to the tradition of tragic theatre; literal violence in performance eventually upholds, as does tragedy, the spectacle of the law in the endless permutations of terror's images, images that ultimately, I would argue, always represent the same thing—an *ontological confrontation with the non-being* that generates theatre, the terror of nothing, Deimos, the missing presence in the shield of Herakles. Any particular historical tracing of terror's threat in the theatre would perhaps do no better than to observe the places where each play folds itself into this disappearance, this "original hole," the empty mouth of Phobos.[64]

Such a tracing, then, is not merely qualitative. It does not try to legitimize "correct" plays, or condemn others as examples of some sort of "false consciousness." On the other hand, it also refuses to invest itself in new historicist studies of the "empirical" conditions of theatrical practice, for those "conditions" describe the very scandal against which the anti-empiricism of theatricality defines itself—as we will see later on in the handkerchief as incontrovertible "ocular proof" in *Othello,* or in the presumed corporeal presence of an absent body that grounds the Western theatre tradition in the *Quem Quaeritis* trope. Such a study would instead describe in each case the degree to which the connections between terror and its isms are discernible *only* through the meticulously "perjur'd eye" of theatre itself. The study would see how, in each case, terror's threat appears both as an ontologic condition of perception, a condition of theatre, and also as the mechanism by which social reformation and discipline is concealed and enforced as theatre's double.

Thus this study could never be a primarily empirical or positivist undertaking—it could never be a historicism or a historiography. Indeed, the model for such a project might be the very transformative and perjured vision of Iago, or the warping eye of Genet through which theatre's lie becomes the limiting condition of knowledge, thought, and perception.

This would be a history of disappearances, a history synchronous and coterminous with a history of terror's effects *in* the theatre, but also a history of terror's fading image in the performative traces of its practice.[65] In such a history we could note the specific changes in the historical movements of terrorism as it becomes organized, economized, and deployed within and through various modes of performance—from the display of the state-sanctioned terrorisms of the Roman spectacles to the political-aesthetic terrorism of Surrealism[66]—but we would also insist on terror's existence prior to articulation, a terror that is, in its reality as disappearance, "passed over in silence," to use Wittgenstein's words, only to be appropriated later by the various theatres of signs.

Yet even within these various theatres of signs, no easy distinction can be drawn between a terrorism that is deployed referentially in the theatre, and one that is deployed in culture *as* theatricality. As the examples show, the two bleed almost imperceptibly into one another: were the Roman spectacles, after all, more theatre or more a "spectacle of the scaffold"? Was Breton suggesting a politicization of art, or is he aestheticizing politics? No easy answer can be given, but what is clear is that there is a necessary, a priori appeal to a Nietzschean theatre in each case, an appeal that manifests itself in a terrorism that sometimes appears first *in* the theatre, that at other times formulates itself *as* theatricality in culture, and sometimes indeterminately as both.

Finally, in such a historical approach, I would caution against privileging pain merely for its spectacular effects. Such an alienation of violence would run precisely counter to the ethos of the present work. Rather, I would suggest a theatre history that foregrounds pain because theatre itself seems to do so, and because, as Derrida has written in his essay on Freud, "Life is already threatened by the origin of the memory which constitutes it"—a memory of pain, if we are to believe Nietzsche—"and by the breaching which it resists."[67]

The critical issue, then, would not be pain itself, but the often hidden

systems of pain production in theatre's history. The assumptions and concealed terrors of these systems might help us better articulate some of the
issues raised throughout the present work: what are the sources of our individual and collective traumas, our "crimes," the enormities that have been
torn from the tissue of remembrance in thought and culture? when those
memories have been repressed or expelled, how have they reappeared as
mechanisms of social engineering and ideological disciplining? how can we
come to learn, especially at the political level, what has been dislocated, or
excluded? is it possible in *any* proposed investigation to stand somehow outside one's own cultural-historical warp and reveal these mechanisms of
repression and exclusion with any kind of clear vision, or does the perversion
of seeing that *is* theatre make any such project impossible? should we instead
resign ourselves to our historical reality as a play of madness, illusion, hallucination, theatre? This is, after all, the show that has been playing in the
Grand Guignol of State since the beginning, and the beginning was, after all,
merely theatre.

2 TRIAL AND TERROR

MEDEA PRIMA FACIE

In the third act of Seneca's *Medea,* Jason, in a spasm of guilt occasioned by his decision to divorce Medea and marry Creon's daughter, cries out to his spurned wife, "What could I do?" "For me?" she responds, "a crime." But Jason, both fearful of the law and hungry for the power that it will confer on him, is paralyzed by such a challenge: "But how, with kings on either side?"[1]

Jason is indeed encompassed by the law in different and corresponding ways. He is constrained as the *mythic/historical* Jason to obey the demands of myth and history and replay his already consummated fate in "the bliss of memory." He is likewise obligated as the *citizen* Jason to submit to the laws of propriety and common statute laid down by Creon ("There's . . . harshness in a ruler's wrath" 495). Finally, he is compelled as the *character* Jason to perform whatever the *text* demands of him *in the theatre:* "Jason, lift up your swollen eyes to me . . . do you now know your wife?" (1020–21). The interplay of these strata of law and propriety and the compliance they demand denote, as I have suggested in the previous chapter, a performative correspondence. The constraints of legal statute, the historico-mythic traditions that authorize them, and the limits of theatre are all revealed in a folded, forensic space; the site of the legal hearing and the theatrical performance appear superposed. Theatre and law betray in this a critical affiliation that is delimited by representation and exhibited as performance.

In both the Euripidean and the Senecan *Medeas,* for example, the bound-
aries of the stage mark the limits within which essential questions of law are
investigated. Thus in Seneca's play, Jason speaks:

> JASON: Cite one specific charge against me now.
> MEDEA: Whatever crime I did.
> JASON: This is too much.
>   To be held guilty of your crimes as well.
> MEDEA: They are your crimes, they're yours! You gained by them
>   so you committed them. (495–501)

Staging legal debates such as this produces conceptions of justice and law
that necessarily coincide, either openly or covertly, with the conventions of
the form—theatre, in this case—that articulate them. The enunciation of evidence through syllogism, the stichomythic Q and A of the arraignment, the
taking of depositions, the manipulation of carefully staged conflict as a means
to truth, in short, the quantification of evidence through performativity—
surveillance, interrogation, indictment, correction—all demonstrate the profound cross-penetration of theatrical structure and legal technique in the
maintenance of limits on the acting body.[2] In his book *Attitudes Toward History,* Kenneth Burke speaks to this specific aspect of Greek law/theatre:

> The greater complexity of relationships that went with the development of
> trade and urban living led to a proliferation of the *forensic,* as exemplified in
> the law courts and in parliamentary procedure. Out of legal sophistication there
> grew the vast *metaphysical* structures, that eventually imposed *scientific* concepts
> of causality upon the earlier patterns of magic and religion. The new attitude
> reaches its culmination *explicitly* in Aristotle, but we find it *implicitly* in the
> great writers of tragedy that preceded him. Their plays, we might say, are
> complex trials by jury, with plaintiff, defendant, attorneys, judges, and jury
> all rolled into one—or otherwise stated, we get in one piece the offence, the
> sentence, the expiation. . . . The events of tragedy are made to grow out of
> one another in keeping with the logic of scientific cogency, the Q.E.D. of
> Euclid and the political oration. (39)

Burke's larger point is that although the obsession with the tragic terror of
failed insight—a failure demanded by the keepers of the divine order who
had to retain all powers of insight and omniscience to themselves—may seem
to stand in an exact counterequivalence with the proclivities in Greek thought
towards the rational and the empirical, both tendencies (the rational and the
phobic) have their origin in the consolidation of an economic power base.
The legal system functions, then, not only as a corrective to the vicissitudes
of divine mania and mythic chaos, but also as a bulwark against the exploitation of myth and religion for political purposes by the priestly classes, and
it begins the disarticulation of the expensive (both at the societal and the
psychic level) cult of the hero.

Hartvig Frisch also discusses the passage from divine right to tyranny and finally to democracy, but with a somewhat different set of observations from Burke's. According to Frisch, the rise of tyranny was a double-edged proposition. While the tyrants ended the rule of incompetent and extravagant kings, and eventually opened up the possibilities of "democratic rule," they also imposed cruel and excessive punishments as adjuncts to the institution of their legal prescriptions. The interesting point to be made here, though, is the distinct correlation drawn by both Burke and Frisch between theatre (specifically tragic theatre) and the systems of economics, legislation and philosophy.[3]

In particular, it is worth noting that the correspondence Burke sees between theatre and law is a *forensic* correspondence, one born of specularity and performance. Even though tragedy emerges from a concern with edict and rules of evidence, law itself is born of the ontological split, translated, as Nietzsche shows, to the domains of exchange. This is the ontological split that designates the theatrical—what is seen in the *mise en scène,* bodies of evidence, the body *as* evidence, corpus delicti.

The laws of theatre and the theatre of law determine their limits on the acting body by rehearsing, through the repetition of testimonies, the *appearance* of transgression which is consequently reformed in the staged *appearance* of correction legitimated by convention—the judicial sentence, the tragic "fall" and resolution.

Yet while legal codes define criminality through statute, judicial proceeding, precedent, and rule of evidence describing every degree and nuance of the transgressive, theatre sets its own precedent and *determines* the evidence in the staging of representative, mimetic *images* of life. Consequently theatre's perverse claim to truth is that it is not "real" but is a *true perjury* that is determined and upheld by the conventions of the stage.

But theatre must suppress this claim to truth as it pursues its illusions in the double bind—it can only find its truth in an illusion, and thus what is "real" ontologically is false empirically. Moreover, as theatre establishes its "ocular" evidence in the bare *appearance* of illusion and embraces the truth of that suspect specularity, it conversely supports the legal code's claim to veracity in a wholly negative, double repression. The truth of the legal hearing is, after all, subject to the same specular distortions that theatre is, but the legal hearing proclaims "ocular evidence" as airtight proof in the "eyewitness account." The theatre finally encompasses the law and completes the double repression by falsely maintaining the opposition between law (truth) and theatre (lie) in its continuous *representation* of the trial as the *means* to truth—the trial that is the center and substance of the tragic form.

In addition, Greek drama provided the legal institutions with an additional affirmation by portraying the gods and mythic/heroic culture as criminal and violent, promiscuous and dangerous. The classical Greek tragedy, with its "complex trials by jury," repressed divine excess by decree as the law usurped power from the seeming precocities of divine or heroic rule through the ontology and representational structures of performance. By representing the criminality of the gods on stage, performance exhibited a simultaneous movement of transgression and normalization—an *ideological* movement, in other words.

The affiliation between theatre and law, then, exceeds any mere surface similarities of form—the stage in the courtroom, the courtroom on stage. Nietzsche, writing a century before Burke, already saw that the complicities of theatre with politics are deeply inscribed in each: "Dionysus had already been scared from the tragic stage by a demonic power speaking through Euripides." But "even Euripides was, in a sense, only a mask: the deity that spoke through him was neither Dionysus nor Apollo, but an altogether new-born demon, called *Socrates*."[4] Socrates casts out Dionysus. The truth of science and the intercourse of reason displace the revelations of ecstasy, as written criminal codes had earlier displaced "customary" or religious law.

In the written law, the gods become less than human. The tragic hero's realization of the gods' inferiority in the face of legal codes *terrorizes* him into silence: "In tragedy pagan man realizes that he is better than his gods," writes Walter Benjamin, "but this realization strikes him dumb, and it remains un-articulated."[5] Yet it is through the realization that the mythic order *is* inferior to the law that myth, the myth that *grounds* the law, is seemingly repudiated. This is a profound irony, for in showing us the superiority of legal institutions over the mercurial divine order, and in repudiating that order, tragedy also shows us the consummately fragile footing upon which both the law and tragedy surreptitiously rests—the representational order that is *exempli-fied* by myth. Accordingly, in order for the legal codes to operate, they must mystify their violent *connection* to myth/religion.

If the silence of the tragic hero is the result of terror engendered through the recognition of debased gods, it is likewise the result of a terrifying *recognition* that the law that religious myth covertly supports is founded upon the same squalor, strife, and emptiness that are the substances of the disparaged mythic/religious order—a recognition that is subjugated by silence. This is "the realization that strikes . . . dumb," a dumbness that articulates in its repressive function a double terror. In the first instance, tragic silence indicates a terror of crime or infraction, which is engendered by the threatened violence of the impermeable order of signification—the state and the state's theatre that will at all costs maintain the appearance of propriety. In the second instance, what eludes articulation is a terror generated through (c)overt opposition to the orders of signification, a terror that breathes in the fractures that it opens between myth and law, appearance and reality, self and Other; fractures that appear as countless theatres sustained in the exclusion of the signifying order and the *disruption* of appearances. As these terrors move into their signifying systems, they define the difference between tyranny (the terror of legalized and concealed violence), and anti-state terrorism (the terror of theatricalized violence).

In the theatre, both the terror of infraction and infracted terror are *states of disease* marked in each case by a movement into different forms of the inarticulate. We spoke earlier of the theatre as the enunciating space of history's effects. The hero's "silent" utterance, his in-articulation, transpires in the theatre, where it must be heard in its silence. The theatre, we said, must "presence" the absent word—the echo in the mind, the hum in the brain, the broken gestus, the exhausted breath—by giving voice. When faced with what cannot be said, the theatre must say it anyway. It must, in other words, fail at the moment of enunciating its most intense necessity, its most important truth—that the law that gives form to language, culture, and the state, nourishing and sustaining them as myth sustains law, that generates its own reproduction in systems of exchange,—this law *is* theatre born in the fragmentation of thought. This law is a metapsychosis, a kind of "framing madness" concealed in the semblance of reason and revealed in the impasse of silence. The different methods employed by Seneca and Euripides to enunciate this impasse and articulate the silence, at one level at least, define the difference between the infracted terror of exclusion, and the repressive terror of infraction.

In Euripidean drama, centralized terror and the horror of its effects—a terror*ism* proper to legal prescription and signification—seek to preserve their power undiminished through the exercise of political repression. Indeed, even though Euripides sees this through his Medea, in this play at least he seems unable to approach the problem at its base in the repressive power of representation.[6]

Seneca, on the other hand, shows us a power that is clearly positioned against the state, a terror generated through an attack on signification, code, theatre, and representation itself. In his *Medea,* we are assaulted by language and image, which immerse us in disarticulate delusions that shake the foundations of reason and power. The irony here is that Seneca was apparently a believer in "law and order." His plays were reputedly written to demonstrate the evil effects of lawlessness, and yet they demonstrate more clearly than Euripides' drama a terror generated *beyond* the scope of law and propriety.

Gilles Deleuze and Felix Guattari write that "The law does not begin by being what it will become or seek to become later: a guarantee against despotism." Rather, the "Imperial" law, the law of the "barbarian," possesses two features that are opposed to this "guarantee": there is first of all a *metonymic* aspect concerned with establishing a series of paradoxical "discrete contiguities" and measurements in order to forbid communication between parts, and thus organize and eventually deflect power into the structure of the state. This aspect of law, the "paranoid-schizo" aspect, ends up by establishing a "formal but *empty* Unity," a structure that seems logical and necessary, but whose "necessity" rests only on its *organizational* claims to power. This is the law of the tyrants, the law that Euripides understood, the law of Phobos: the grand structures of legalized state terror whose sole titles to legitimacy are based on representative series—the appearance of order, or legality, or violence, or "civilization." *In extremis*, this is the jurisprudence of state terrorism, the logic of the state taken to the limit; it is, as Herbert Blau states, "the mind's revenge on itself."[7]

In contradistinction to this, there is a second, *metaphoric* aspect of the law, an even darker, psychotic semblance:

> The maniacal depressive trait. . . . according to which the law reveals nothing and has no knowable object, the verdict having no existence prior the penalty, and the statement of the law having no existence prior to the verdict. . . . As in the machine of "The Penal Colony," it is the penalty that writes both the verdict and the rule that has been broken. . . . the body . . . now becomes the stone and the paper, the tablet and the currency on which the new writing is able to mark its figures, its phoneticism, and its alphabet.[8]

This is the Senecan vision of law, the hidden power of terror as *non-being*, a terror whose psychopathic presence-as-absence is *masked* by the spectacular structures of a paranoid—or Phobic—*secretion* of law: the secretions that congeal into Nietzsche's "Euripidean mask" through which we hear the voice of Socrates. And yet Euripides, speaking in the voice of Socrates, writes at the far end of the Greek drama, and approaches the dark limn of Deimic terror perhaps more closely than any other Greek playwright, but he stops short at the transgressive extreme, as he must.

In Seneca, though, Jason's inclusion within the legal system counterbalances Medea's transgressive rejection by it. His willingness to embrace and be embraced by Creon's power functions in apposition to Medea's *forclusion* by it ("You erase . . . me, erase everything I've done? / Have I died inside your memory? / Am I cut out?" 560–63), and her ensuing disavowal of it ("What source can I tap for vengeance now? . . . There must be some crime that cities Greek or savage, do not know, something your hands have never tried before" 125–27).

Jason's circumscription within legality and Medea's obsession with what lies beyond it denotes a phenomenon that is distinctly Senecan and essentially theatrical—the suggestion of a transgression and a violence lying *outside* the purview of legality entirely, beyond the inscribed limits; an outrage that supersedes "mere" crime, a violation that not only defies the law but rejects its claims entirely. This is the theatrical violence that precedes the law, the violence of the terror of thought, a terror that strikes at the very basis of both law and the theatre of state by threatening representation itself. This terror is, paradoxically, the *embodiment* of non-being.[9]

The terror of non-being, the terror of thought, are more powerfully expressed in the classical Roman plays than in the Greek works that antedate them, although the bias against Roman drama in theatre histories might obscure this fact.[10] The terror that appears in the Roman theatre exceeds and amplifies the terror that remains implicit and self-contained within representation in Greek drama. Euripides' earlier version of *Medea,* for instance, clearly demonstrates the subjection of tragedy and the tragic hero to a terrorizing law, but it is a concept and subjection that is, as I have already suggested, socially prescribed, proprietary, and appalled at excess; it is the result of a long and arduous passage from myth and ecstatic religion to science and state statute.

The Roman theatre appears at the decadent end of this passage. The esteem with which the legal system was held in the writings of some of the early Greek Stoics has clearly eroded in the Senecan period of Roman culture. Although Seneca the philosopher may have defended the necessity of the legal codes, Seneca the playwright displays a harsh cynicism at the tyrannical power of the state and the dissolution of personal ethics, a cynicism that translates into an appalling violence which threatens to cancel the law at each level of its manifestation—not only as legal statute, as in Greek drama, but also as theatrical constraint, as language and representation, as the Imaginary/Symbolic itself. For clarification let me first attempt a somewhat more exhaustive analysis of the Euripidean text.

Euripides' *Medea* opens with a mythic retelling of Medea's story by the Nurse (a preservation of the tradition of myth), followed by several references to Medea's laments: "I heard the voice, I heard the cry of Colchis' wretched daughter."[11] Medea's initial lament is a cry that is, at least as indicated in the text, unheard. It is a *reported* cry, a *represented* moan.

The enunciation of the narrated complaint passes from the Nurse to the Tutor, and is translated to the Chorus. The Chorus, the apparent emblem of public forum in Greek drama, gives further testimony to the pain and suffering of the oppressed Medea, who repeatedly proscribes for herself a self imposed silence as the remedy for her rage.

This self-injunction to silence, demarcated by the numerous references to silence in the text, is undercut by speeches that immediately intrude upon any *performed* silence. For example, when Medea says to Creon that his "greater power subdues me to silence," she immediately engages him in a long debate followed by a lengthy speech. Although in production Medea might in fact observe silence, there is no indication in the text that she falls silent when she says she must. Furthermore, a silence at this point, followed by a long speech, seems awkward in performative terms, where such a lapse would seem incongrous and illogical. We see a similar injunction to silence in Seneca's play, but there Medea is instructed *by others* to keep silence, which she refuses to do—because to do so, even tacitly as in Euripides' play, would be a submission to the laws of discourse.

In contradistinction to the proscribed silence concealing her rage, the injustices done to Medea are announced in a public arena, within the inter-course of Corinthian society depicted on an Athenian stage—demonstrating once again the *doubling* of two forums, the political and the theatrical, in a *hearing* determined by the exigencies of the Greek legal system *represented* by the Chorus. In this context, the hero's silence represents the tension between the old heroic society—of which mythic Medea is part and which has in reality existed perhaps only as a point of difference, a touchstone of political possibilities—and the new nationalist society within which Euripides lives, the Greek democracy, reputedly founded upon the principles of rationality, regulation, and description.[12] This *idea* of the Greek *society* is what fixes the Euripidean social concern.

Euripidean drama is illumined by this concern and is unique in Greek tragedy in its repeated condemnation of the failure of the rational society, and in its simultaneous suspicion of the hyporational—religion and the uni-verse of the gods.[13] The old world of gods and heroes is, on the one hand, deeply questioned: "I cannot tell / Whether you think the gods whose names you swore by then / Have ceased to rule and that new standards are set up, / Since you must know you have broken your word to me," (492–95); and the "new" society of public legality is condemned as corrupt and ineffectual: "Even though I have been wronged, / I will not raise my voice, but submit to my betters" (314–15). Medea's criminality is contained within these bounds. Although her actions are psychopathic, abhorrent, violent, "divine" in Ben-jamin's sense, the force of their criminality lies within law itself. The distance (between legality and illegality) is defined politically and socially. The Chorus speaks best of this context when it condemns Medea's vengeful machina-tions: "Since you have shared the knowledge of your plan with us, / I both wish to help you and support the normal / Ways of mankind, and tell you not to do this thing" (811–13).

Medea's murderous act, although excessive and criminal, indeed *insane* (a legal term), is an act designed to project into clearer refraction another, *legal* injustice, Jason's divorce and remarriage:

MEDEA:
    He has taken a wife to his house, supplanting me.
AEGEUS:
    Surely he would not dare to do a thing like that?
MEDEA:
    Be sure he has. Once dear, I now am now slighted by him.
AEGEUS:
    Did he fall in love? Or is he tired of your love?
MEDEA:
    He was greatly in love, this traitor to his friends.
AEGEUS:
    Then let him go, if, as you say, he is so bad.
MEDEA:

A passionate love—for an alliance with the king.
AEGEUS:
And who gave him his wife? Tell me the rest of it.
MEDEA:
It was Creon, he who rules this land of Corinth. (694–702)

Medea acts out of a sense of injustice as injustice is created within the purview of what is legal. We are operating in a world of criminality, to be sure, but it is paradoxically a world almost totally circumscribed by the *myth* of law: "God and God's daughter, justice! and light of Helius! / Now, friends, has come the time of my triumph over / My enemies" (764–66).

Yet in spite of this circumscription, there is no desire in Medea to actually strike down the law. Although assaulted, the law is left intact. In fact, Medea does not specifically plot to kill Creon, although Creon is himself the law (269–70). This is perhaps partly due to her precarious position within Corinthian society as a woman and as a minority, but it is also a clear reflection of her real desire—vengeance against injustice that is *disguised* as legality. This seems to justify Medea's desire to do what is illegal, but just—to extract revenge. In fact, there seems to be no way for Medea to act *but* illegally. She is bound to break the codes, has *already* broken them (the codes of propriety, at least) by remaining in Corinth as an embarrassment to Creon and Jason. We can begin to see Medea's crimes—infanticide and murder—as *tragic* acts in Benjamin's sense, the price demanded by history in the establishment of culture: the dispersal of violence into law, but a law that is "always already" deficient. Thus we might reformulate this dispersal of violence according to our earlier definition of tragedy—the force of Medea's crime represents the demand for an ideological displacement, by which an unjust law is *kathartically* displaced by another, presumably "saner" (but also deficient) law.

But "mythical violence is lawmaking," writes Benjamin, and "divine violence is law-destroying."[14] This mythical violence is the paradox of Euripidean drama. However much revulsion Euripides might have had for the older, barbaric mythologies of the Greeks, however much he may have supplanted a Dionysian demonism with "an altogether newborn demon, called *Socrates*," the Euripidean demonism is saturated through and through with the Athenian New Mythology of law. This is perhaps Nietzsche's point in his characterization of the Socratic demon that casts out Dionysus: "Wherever Socratism turns its searching eyes it sees lack of insight and the power of illusion; and from this lack it infers the essential perversity and reprehensibility of what exists."[15]

The seeming corrective to this reprehensible illusion, the tonic for the "mere appearance of mere appearance" is the law; but this system of economics that parses out pleasure in systems of pain is itself born of illusion, engendered by *theatre,* indeed woven from the same illusions of excess it seeks to eliminate—in casting away disease, irrationality, and crime, the law reflects the *kathartic* desire of tragedy. Tragedy thus represents both the crime and its seeming corrective; tragedy becomes, in other words, the inclusive term—it contains both the crime and the law. Tragedy thus defines the law after the crime and gives law its space, its *darstellung,* its *stage.* Thus in the end, the law is seen to *uphold* the "perversity . . . of what exists." We can see in the body of Euripides' drama his approach to this essential perversity, but it remains (as it must), throughout his work, only an approach.

The context of struggle in Euripides—struggles between legality and justice, power and rights, insight and illusion—is the hearing. From the beginning, the argument of Euripides' *Medea* is *framed* by the hearing:

> O God and Earth and Heaven!
> Did you hear what a cry was that
> Which the sad wife sings?
> . . . .
> Do you hear what she says, and how she cries?
> . . . .
> I heard a shriek that is laden with sorrow
> Shrilling out her hard grief she cries out
> Upon him who betrayed both her bed and her marriage.
> Wronged, she calls on the gods. (148, 170, 207)

Although we have what seems to be an appeal to the Symbolic order here, a privileging of hearing and testimony over spectacle, this is illusory because the evidence finally submitted in the hearing, the reasons proffered for Medea's exile, are based on an "ocular proof," a *seeing* that interestingly, is itself ocular:

> I've seen her already blazing her eyes at them
> as though she meant some mischief.
> . . . .
> Will she come into our presence?
> Will she listen when we are speaking
> To the words we say?
> . . . .
> You, with that angry look . . .
> I order you to leave . . . (92, 174–75, 271)

Conversely, Medea's own complaint, reinforced at times by the chorus, is characterized by her perception of the insufficiency of ocularity:

> A just judgement is not evident in the eyes
> When a man at first sight hates another . . .
> . . . .
> Why is there no mark engraved upon men's bodies
> By which we could know the true ones from the false
> ones? (220, 518–19)

Here, the act of seeing is itself the ocular evidence submitted to the hearing. This synesthesia is powerfully enunciated when the Chorus incredulously and fatalistically exhibits Medea's most hideous crime—a crime we have not seen but have only *heard* committed—in the evidential corpses of her children: "Open the gates and there you will see them murdered" (1313).

The result is judgment, first on Jason ("Heaven, it seems, on this day has fastened many / Evils on Jason" 1231–32), and then on Medea ("I will lament and cry upon heaven / Calling the gods to bear me witness / How you have killed my boys" 1409–11). The place of judgment is the theatre (the seeing place); the agency of judgment, the audience (they who hear). This is the case not only in the performance of Euripidean tragedy, but in the text as well. The Tutor's report, for example, based on his eavesdropping, frames the audience/player relationship in tension between the seeing and the hearing: "I *heard a person saying*, while I myself *seemed / Not to be paying attention* . . . / That Creon, ruler of the land, intends to drive / These children and their mother in exile from Corinth" ([emphasis mine] 67–71).

The audience's sense of justice is appealed to as the corrective to what the law *is* in opposition to what the law should be. As a result, the audience is imagined in the chorus not as an example of an *ideal* theatrical audience, but as an Imaginary Other. Thus there is an apparent contradiction in the chorus's reactions. Earlier there had seemed to be an identification between the "citizen chorus" and Medea in her crime:

> MEDEA:
> This much then is the service I would beg from you:
> If I can find the means or devise any scheme
> To pay my husband back for what he has done to me—
> Him and his father-in-law and the girl who married him—
> Just to keep silent. . . .
> CHORUS:
> This I will promise. You are in the right, Medea,
> In paying your husband back. (259–67)

As the murders proceed, however, the Chorus finally stands transfixed in opposition: "Shall I enter the house? Oh, surely I should / Defend the children from murder" (1275–76). We can also see this paralysis in Nietzschean terms as an expression of a Hamletic nausea produced by knowledge (the evidence of guilt) inhibiting action. The Chorus, engaged in the representative function of theatre, pierces its illusions *as* illusion, and, as "action requires the veils of illusion," the chorus is left immobilized and bereft.[16]

Yet even at this point in the play, representation *as* representation remains intact: the Chorus responds to its paralysis by recounting the story of Ino's infanticide. Once again, mythic narrative is surreptitiously employed as the means of maintaining the semblance of law and order over and against chaos and madness—and yet all *is* mere semblance, because during the time that the Chorus recounts the "harmonizing" myth, Medea murders her children (1279–92). Here, myth literally "covers up" the unthinkable.

In suggesting that the Chorus is only an *Imaginary* coherence, I am of course implying that the Chorus, and indeed the entire structure of democratic systems, are destined to fail because there is in reality no consensus, no *demos,* no *real* or even Symbolic Chorus. And yet paradoxically, the entire play, and most notably the opening segments, depend heavily on the structures of exchange and communication, which would seem to *imply* a consensus. The repeated appeals to hearing and seeing seem to articulate an affirmation that is not *primarily* suspicious of representation or it would not so glibly invoke the seeing and the hearing. Although there are some notable exceptions (Jason's repeated invocation of the gods as witnesses to his honorable intentions, Medea's dissembling compliance with Creon's proclamation), the seeing and the hearing are usually not presented as a problematic— what is seen is generally to be trusted, what is heard is normally to be believed. The seeing and the hearing are invoked as testimony, as judgmental proof of injustice done and legality obtained.

But although there is no quibble over the basic, empirical fact of representation, there is a clear failure of the *orders* of representation. Systems of signification and legal codes, techniques of violence as means to understanding, are questioned and found wanting. The failure of justice is seen as a failure of culture and political systems, but it is not seen as a failure of the concept of law itself, which is grounded in representation and generates the representative function of language as well.

For this reason, Euripidean drama through its reservations about the law in the end affirms the law, or at least the Symbolic idea of law, as the means by which injustice, violence, and criminality might be measured and addressed in the forensic silence of the hero—the paralytic loquaciousness of the Chorus marks a performative counterpoint to the silence-in-action of the tragic hero.

In *The Origin of German Tragic Drama,* Benjamin writes: "Tragic silence, far more than tragic pathos, became the storehouse of an experience of the sublimity of linguistic expression."[17] The collation of "the sublimity of linguistic expression" and silence exists as a conceptual musicality in Euripides' *Medea.* Musical, because the moments of professed silence occur as intervals in the carefully scored orchestration of vengeance plotted against injustice. Conceptual, because the silence does not occur as act, but as idea. The silences that are invoked in the play exist as injunctions—Medea secures the silence of the Chorus, Medea exclaims "I will keep silence" before Creon's injustice to her, Creon himself commands her silence as he sends her away— but no real silences are enacted, no silences are actually *heard* as they are, for instance, in a Chekhov play or in Beckett's work. Silence is, like sight, like hearing, mediated through language, through the law. See, Hear, Judge, Fall Silent.[18]

The silence of the Euripidean hero is not, then, a *literal* silence but a literary one, a representation in the word itself of the inadequacy of speech in the face of injustice. This silence calls out, on the one hand, for a structure of mediation (language) through which injustice can be remedied without recourse to *criminal* violence. On the other hand, true mediation is ultimately inadequate, even inimical, to Euripidean drama, because the very possibility is repressed in the silence that marks the theatre's concealed relation to law and violence.

Silence, then, the silence of the isolated hero, describes a terror that is tightly circumscribed within Medea's consciousness. It is a solipsistic terror that eventually explodes and wounds those beyond the family cell, and when it does, it ceases to be solipsistic and becomes collective.[19]

Seen in this perspective, the play begins in Medea's mind in Jason's house. The shock waves of violence radiate beyond the family and disrupt (but do not destroy) the social order. The social effects are a secondary effect of the violence that radiates outward from some epicenter in the hero's consciousness through the enucleated family into the community, where it serves as example and as lesson in civic responsibility and restraint. This is, consequently, a terror that must enter systems of language and exchange in order to become a functioning sign of terror within the society—a terror that then ceases to be terror and becomes terrorism.

"There's no quarreling with the Terror from a position outside the Terror—and within the Terror there can be no quarrel at all," writes Herbert Blau.[20] Similarly, there can be no representation of terror outside terror, and inside terror there is no representation at all. When terror and pain assume signification, they assume meaning; when they cease to be meaningless, they are no longer terror and pain. When terror moves into signifying systems it is consequently transformed into terrorism. It becomes the annihilating force of the Other-as-Enemy, the Other who is the locus of the tyrannic law.

The Greek tragedy was staged, as I have suggested, *in situ* between heroic myth and law. Thus as tragedy supports tyranny,[21] and theatricality itself abets the state and its specular power,[22] so myth supports law (language, structure) while law ensconces myth within literary and aesthetic canons. This is inevitable, for, as the a priori condition of law, myth contextualizes the law, just as the law secularizes and regulates myth, eventually causing it to disappear *as* myth, and returns it as pure structure by transforming it into mythology.

In Seneca's play, Medea attempts to reverse this process. She grounds the power of her incantations in a disarticulation of the mythologies and thereby shows her understanding of the ontologic relation of myth to law:

> Silent hordes and gods of death, I call upon you
>   all in prayer:
> Chaos—unseeing and unseen abyss—dark home of
>   ghostly Dis,

caverns of decomposing Death, dungeoned by
   Tartarus' steep slopes,
tormented souls, take respite, run and see this
   novel wedding night.
The limb-wrenching wheel must stop, and Ixion must
   touch the ground;
Tantalus must slake his thirst at Corinth, fearing no
   deceit;
one exception: Sisyphus, forbear of Jason's new
   in-laws—
increase his torment, let the slipping stone roll
   him across the crags.
You Danaids whose leaking urns mock your attempts to
   fill them up,
come, be fulfilled together. This day needs your
   husband-killing hands. (739–49)

Medea evokes in her cursed disavowal the true terror of "Chaos—unseeing and unseen," the upheaval that follows from the destructuring of legal codes *through* the disarticulation of myth.

The d/enunciation of mythologies on stage was perhaps natural in a Roman society in which real violence, staged in events like the *naumachia*, eventually became the preferred mode of performance. This was a society in which the theatre itself became so obsessed with reality that actual murders and catastrophes were staged to satisfy the demand for less (or more?) theatre.[23]

Accordingly, the context of legality and justice in the theatre and in society would change as the nature of their representative functions came into question. The presuppositions of the possibility of justice, law, speech would be supplanted by a deeper belief in violence, vengeance, and terrorism as the mode of power in the world. This seems a natural response to a world in which representation itself—and representative structures—had come to be regarded with cynicism or Stoic resignation. Thus we have the appearance of the Roman "anti-representational theatre" which sought to replace representational plays with actual violence, and in the doublebind of theatrical truth/illusion ironically turned violence itself back into mere representation, back into theatre.

Although Seneca the philosopher argued against the excess depicted in these spectacles, one can see how the terror in Seneca's own plays was engendered by the presence within the Roman social warp of that very "divine violence," that "law-destroying violence" that we might today equate with terrorism:

>   . . . Don't think
>   of anything as crime. . . .
>   You must attack
> along a path no one can think could be
> a path from which to fear attack. Be bold!

Undertake whatever lies within
Medea's power, whatever lies beyond. (564–66)

Yet the terrorism in Seneca's play is not actually realized until the last moments of the play when the incipient, unimaged and *unimaginable* terror of
the earlier scenes—the Deimic terror of thought—finally enters the signifying
systems of language and sign as the infanticide is carried out in full view.
The spectacle of that violence finally alienates us from its causes in the dead-
ening horror of its image: "Wade through the deep expanses of boundless /
shining sky," says Jason to Medea, "Wherever you may go, / you will be
proof that gods do not exist" (1025–27). Medea, in the final image of the
play, is assumed by the gods into the realm where, following the "proof,"
no gods exist. She is translated into the locus of the Other, into the realm of
signification, the realm of law, where the relationship between myth and
law, violence and theatre, remains concealed.

In Euripides' theatre signification falters as the Phobic shield of tyranny
because it can no longer sustain the law. But in Senecan drama, language
fails utterly in the face of terror "set on limitless revenge." Words no longer
refer to realities, but exist only as the mark of their own failure. Language
literally *sustains nothing,* but exists as the sublime articulation of a desire for
death in excess. "Oh the bliss of memory," cries Medea in "an ecstasy of
madness," "My infant brother slain, his limbs torn." As long as the desire
for death remains unfulfilled by demand, it exists as terror, the indescribable
face of Deimos. When terror desires itself and demands the fruition of its
own desire in the iconography of excess violence, it becomes terrorism. When
it gives itself up to the state by delivering itself to signifying systems (the
media, for example), terror becomes what it resists, and it fails.

Terrorism, then, represents an absolute necessity to reveal the incommunicable *as* incommunicable, what Jean-Francois Lyotard has described as
"representing the unpresentable." [24] Terrorism uses the seemingly incommunicable as a discourse of power over the brutalized body. This self-dispar-
ity conceals violence within its inscription like a tattoo on the body, and
legislates terrorism's ideology and political technique effectuated as statute.

Nietzsche (and Foucault following him) have pointed out that the law has
its *origin* in terror inscribed on the body, projecting the body and its pain as
currency into an economy of punishment and correction whose primary pay-
off is the pleasure of being witness, of *seeing* the violence. There is, of course,
a dialectical relation here, inasmuch as the pleasure of seeing violence emerges
from its very economization. The fact that it can be apprehended as violence,
in other words, imbues it with pleasure—there is nothing intrinsically plea-
surable in the violent spectacle. Its pleasure is an effect of its economization.
The appearance of legal code is, at any rate, radically dependent on the seeing.
When the seeing is categorically objectified, the *spectacle* of the law as terrorism emerges. This describes the manifestation of a spec(tac)ular law in the

appearance of Creon the king in Euripides: "But look! I see our King Creon / Approaching. He will tell us of some new plan" (269–70).

In Seneca's play the Euripidean desire for the mediated spectacle of sanctioned violence is displaced by a desire for the violence of spectacle—the direct and relentless presentation of the thing in its unrepresentable immediacy.[25] Moreover, in Seneca there is no adjudication *but* the adjudication of spectacle, the appearance of appearance as the supreme expression of the ethical/aesthetic in the face of the nonrational—the terror of the unrepresentable represented by Medea's alchemical powers.

Here even language seems to operate more spectacularly than rationally. The silence that signified the tragic condition in Euripides opens out into sheer verbiage in Seneca, a kind of glossolalic or eulalic refusal of silence that finally expels silence in its function as indicator of the inarticulate:

> MEDEA: Your pain has little bite if it retains the power to conceal itself. Great sufferings do not lurk in disguise . . . .
> NURSE: Stillness of body and tongue scarcely protects . . . (155–57)

The power of Seneca's *Medea* has traditionally been ascribed to its rhetorical excesses—a play meant to be intoned and not acted. But the play's force exceeds mere rhetorical effluence—Euripidean silence exists as *forclusion* in Seneca, and the rent in the fabric of language is "patched over" by a torrent of speech that finally outstrips the dramatic function of silence in Greek tragedy. In an expression that defines the very notion of Lacanian *forclusion,* Medea cries out to Jason, "Am I cut out? Have I died inside your memory?" But she will not keep her silence in the exclusion: "I'm sowing seeds of verbiage," she says, and proceeds with her endless, horrific curses and death spells. This "verbiage" cannot, however, express the terror of its own deficiency, especially in the face of terror.

The excesses of Senecan speech cover over the *béance,* the radical lack within language that cannot enter the Symbolic, and so is cast out into the Real, where it returns as the hallucinatory spectacle of violent, jabbering, psychotic speech—a speech that *begins* to signify the terror of its deficiencies because it begins to lose its referentiality to reality. In Seneca's *Oedipus,* Jocasta, tearing out her uterus, speaks in a black, hemorrhagic language that pulses like her excised, "teeming womb," a speech gargling in the blood of an aborted universe:

> Come then, have you a hand to help your mother? If you could kill your father . . . this remains For you to do. . . . Then let me take his sword, The sword that killed my husband—no, not husband, Father-in-law. . . . Where shall I strike? My breast? Where plant the weapon—in my naked throat? . . . You know where you must strike—no need to choose—Strike here, my hand, strike at this teeming womb Which gave me sons and husbands! . . .[26]

Finally "the sword falls out / Expelled by the strong rush of blood" and she dies.

The difference between the Euripidean mythical violence, and that divine violence that desires the abolition of law as an ontological category, is what separates the Greek *Medea* from the Roman *Medea*. Reporting the discovery of the murder of Jason's bride, the Euripidean messenger exclaims, "You who have done such a dreadful thing, / So outrageous, run for your life, take what you can" (1121–22). The legal system has been assaulted, and in fact Creon is killed, apparently by accident, trying to save his daughter. The Senecan messenger, however, speaks in profoundly more pessimistic, onto-logically catastrophic, terms: "Death is everywhere. Whatever stood / within this royal house has fallen now. . . . Is there no limit to catastrophe?" (879–86). The assault on law has struck at the very base of power and order and being. The cosmos, stretched to the dark threshold of divine psychosis, be-gins its gravitational collapse back into a terminal chaos: "Laws of astrology break down . . . I have bent the laws that govern time" (755–59).

While the origin of violence in Euripides is hidden, inaccessible, *discrete,* like Medea herself in the opening scene—she is not seen or heard for some few hundred lines, after the Nurse and the Tutor recount her story—Seneca's play opens with the present figure of Medea chanting violent curses as *she* recounts the injustices that have been dealt her, and the revenge she will exact:

> I will tear wedding torches
> out of their hands, I'll tear the very light
> out of the sky . . . butcher
> the beasts on consecrated altar stones . . .
> seek out an opening . . . ruthlessly
> slicing through their guts as if through wax.
> You must banish from yourself all fears
> a woman has. Take on your native mind,
> your Cossack mind, that hates all foreigners.
> Whatever acts the Crimea,
> Rioni River, and Black Sea have seen
> the Isthmus will soon see. Evil actions
> of brutality unknown—enough
> to send shivers through heaven and earth alike. (28–48)

Immediately following this, the Chorus begins its wedding chant for Jason and his bride. Here the rhetoric is open, airy, filled with bright images of celebratory grace and light:

> Bacchus' child, white-robed Hymen who carries the
>   thyrsus!
> Time to inflame the piny torch's myriad fibers!

Whip up that solemn fire with fingers no matter how
   listless!
Let us speak out our jest in style ribald and
   Italian.
Leave the crowd free for farce.

In contrast, the wedding party's "curse" of Medea is expressed as a *forclusion* of the Medean spectre, a spectre who will indeed return "from the outside" as a hallucinatory abomination by play's end:

> We consign to silence
>   and darkness
> Any Woman who runs from home, wedding veiled for
>   an alien husband. (109–14)

The contrast in imagery between these two long opening speeches is obvious. There is an immediate opposition delineated between who and what Medea is and what the society is like in which she lives. This opposition is represented in the contrasts of the writing itself. The violence of Medea's crime does not erupt out of a figurative, discrete, and idealized silence, but rather in *pure, repressive opposition,* the opposition between classes, languages, psyches, *forces.* It does not, as it does in Euripides, emerge from a center within Medea, hidden and originary, but from her stark antithesis from those others in the society she inhabits.

While *conflict* is certainly one of the key elements in the history of drama, conflict is not the same as opposition. Conflict indicates a difference in desire between characters that ultimately leads to confrontation and (sometimes violent) resolution. By opposition, I mean a broader and also more particular structure of forces opposing each other. Conflict suggests an often poorly delineated antagonism between characters. Opposition implies other *Imaginary* possibilities: class contentions; metaphysical, material, and ideological struggles; the resistance of sanity and madness; either/or; life/death.

Because of this broader oppositional structure of Seneca's play, the political texture is more dynamic than in Euripidean drama. Strife is attributed not to Fates or Furies, but to violent struggle and resistance. The dialectic of antagonism propels this *Medea* into a deeper ontopolitical violence than the Euripidean version: a disturbing vision of the tension between absolute power—Creon's force—and absolute violence—Medea's force. The tension between violence and power is similar in many respects to the ideological impasse behind the modern terrorist dilemma.

The relationship between power and violence is delimited by extremity—the character of each is defined by its manifestation *in extremis:* "Power and violence are opposites," writes Hannah Arendt, "where the one rules absolutely, the other is absent. . . . The extreme form of power is All against One, the extreme form of violence is One against All." Arendt invokes here the unanimous violence of Girard's "sacred culture," a violence that also de-scribes the opposition between Creon's tyranny (terrorism "from above") and Medea's anti-state terrorism (terrorism "from below").[27]

The binary opposition between the extremes of violence and power col-lapses at a point just beyond the extreme. This collapse is fundamentally a collapse of meaning—when power and violence are held in an equilibrium, when each supports and feeds off the other *as* Other, their opposition is maintained and "meaning" is preserved in the binary opposition itself. But when the equilibrium is upset, the polarities collapse into a sameness that is electrifying: "it would be difficult to say in which way the order given by a policeman is different from that given by a gunman," writes Arendt, and thus identifies the threat of collapse in terms of a radical uncertainty in per-ception: what am I seeing: how can I *know* what I am seeing, what I am hearing? is the Enemy here? This is yet another way of understanding thea-tre's terror which is born in the fractures of perception and concealed in the doublebind. The outcome of such a collapse is unforeseeable because it is a collapse of signification itself.

Arendt goes on to say that "terror [tyranny] is not the same as violence," it is instead "the form of government that comes into being when violence, having destroyed all power, does not abdicate but, on the contrary, remains in full control." This was the condition of Creon's Corinth and Botha's South Africa, but it is also the potentiality of tyranny's opposition in anti-state ter-rorism, a potential that gives that terrorism its form and substance.[28]

Anti-state terrorism, realizing its perpetual alienation from power, can also never abdicate violence, even when the particular goals of a particular terrorist act have been met: "Violence can always destroy power; out of the barrel of a gun grows the most effective command," but "what never grows out of it is power." In this equation the equilibrium becomes a crucial and delicate thing. Real terror—terror that cannot be signified, the terror that is thought—seeks to upset that equilibrium. Terrorism, on the other hand, in its unavoidable complicities with power, in its desire and need for structures erected in the shadow of what it opposes, must seek to maintain its opposi-tional equilibrium with power, because it is that opposition that gives terror-ism its visibility and thus its force.[29]

As the force of thought's terror in Seneca's play, Medea upsets the bal-ance, and threatens to throw the entire society into chaos. But in the final movements when she becomes a terrorist "in exile," resistance fails and power is, we presume, restored to the state.

The entire mechanism of opposition, along with the assault on represen-tation as the *basis* of law, mark Seneca's play as more modern in flavor and sensibility and as profoundly disturbing in its implications. In the "modern" world of Seneca, lawlessness is not mere criminality (even though Medea herself uses the word "crime" over and over again to describe her plots); it is terror generated by an enormity that cannot be thought by law:

Like the sea her madness swells. When will
its moaning breaker crash upon itself?
What she turns over in her mind will be
no ordinary deed; she will surpass
her median of crime; she will conquer
herself. The moment I saw them, I knew
the ancient hallmarks of her angry rage.
Some enormity looms over us,
some bestial act of inhumanity. (392–96)

As the Enemy in Euripides (Medea? Jason? Creon?) stands within the structures of ordinance and its violation, so in Seneca the Enemy is precisely that which cannot be known in relation to any law, like one of the mysterious and deadly creatures that Medea invokes in her incantation. Thus while Jason is not able (or says he is not able) to exceed the legal codes, Medea exceeds them. Moreover manic obliteration of the law—in the shape of Creon, the king—becomes extremely important to her: "Creon's to blame. . . . It's solely his responsibility, / and he alone should pay due penalty. / Go after him! I will bury his home / in ash and cinders" (142–46).

The law for Medea, then, is not something by which she measures Jason's injustice to her; it is a limit, a historical and metaphysical boundary whose annihilation will engender abject terror in the culture that has propagated that law. Medea's desire is not a desire for justice through revenge as it is in Euripides, it is a Luciferian desire for the sublime generated by the sheer enormity of the transgression she contemplates: "My solitary chance / of calm comes when I see the elements / shattered with me as I fall. I want / the world to die with me. When you pass on, / there's joy in taking everything with you" (426–28). Thus whereas in Euripides infanticide is tragic, in Seneca it is obscene:

If the slaughtering
of only one could satisfy my hand,
I would have killed no one at all. And two
are trivial repayment for my pain,
If, even now, there is, unknown to me,
some fetus spawned by you inside my
    womb,
I'll use this sword and tear it out with steel.
(1009–11)

The transgression of the law in Medea is transgression of a much higher potential than the mere breaking of customs, proprieties, civil statutes. Medea seeks the destruction of these powers that have oppressed her—identity and opposition, correspondence and difference, the bases of knowledge and perception, of law and sanity. She becomes the location of the cross-penetration of the Dionysian and Apollonian, a place where the forces of unity and opposition collapse into the Same, the locus of *that* unarticulated terror.

Seneca's Medea—who sees beneath veils, whose eyes pierce illusion, who knows that law, even the law of theatre, must be, *is,* in essence, the bare appearance of itself, its trappings, delineations, shapes, illusions—this Medea knows that violence must burst open the ground beneath the law if justice is to be redefined. Violence must destroy the appearance of law, and make it seem what it is: monstrous and psychotic. This is the vision of terror that, when effectuated in the demand for a pure and sublime violence translated into image and sign, is finally transmuted into the vision of terrorism.

Although I have thus far framed the infractions in *Medea* in terms of the law, and although it is important to recall that the law is, in this play, the only means by which a more fundamental injustice is adjudicated, this very injustice is itself generated in the psycho-political economy of Greek and Roman culture as represented *by* socioeconomic law.

At this socioeconomic level, we might begin to see the ways in which Medea's complete devaluation by a colonizing power has completely translated her original *use-value* into an exchange value that is then emptied of worth through the action of male legal decree. In both versions of the play, Medea recounts over and over again the immense value she held for Jason on his voyages, both in terms of what she was able to do for him, and in terms of the value that accrued to her because of her position within Colchian society as princess, daughter to the king. Now back in Corinth, that usefulness, based upon an alien and alienated power that has (until the beginning of the play) been usurped and neutralized by Jason's imperialist seduction, is emptied of significance—emptied, that is, until it rediscovers its power in vengeance upon Jason and the royal family. Medea's original *value* has been transmuted into *violence* or *pure expenditure* as a result of the socioeconomic exploitation by a powerful political gender/state.

It is important to understand, then, that the focus of concern in both plays is on Medea's place in the *polis*/state. The major concern of both playwrights centers on the potential impact of her violence and threatened chaos on that community. In these terms, Medea indeed seems a kind of demigod, a sheer force that can find no niche, no definition in the community. She is a quasi-marginalized source of both fascination and fear, a latent phobic/fetish object, an object that finds its definition always withheld and concealed in an other.

What we see developing in the theatre in subsequent periods is the isolation and definition of this body-as-object as a digital unit within the *polis*. Theatre concerns itself more and more with the ways in which that unit is interpreted and organized in the efficiency of the social project. In Greek and Roman theatre this concern is defined largely in terms of *citizenship,* and thus questions of law and propriety emerge as the preeminent locations for the formation of the body's discipline in the community. At the end of the Roman period of theatre, however, citizenship and its concerns undergo a radical reevaluation as Christianity and its concern with the *moral/sexual* body gradually emerge as the new ethos. Fear and fascination thus become even more critical as the means by which the body is defined, especially the body of woman.

The *béance* in the history of the drama following the decline of the theatre of Rome, and the subsequent reemergence of that theatre within the very Church that suppressed it, might be seen in this regard as a latency, an inertia, during which the techniques of regulation that later emerge in theatre and culture are already incubating in the Medean womb of medieval Church dogma.

3 TROPE TO TRAGEDY

RUBBING OUT THEATRE'S CORPUS

In the history of theatre's disappearances, in theatre's history *as* disappearance, the medieval theatrical silence suggests a particularly intriguing historical moment during which the body is seemingly positioned at theatre's focal/vanishing point. Indeed, the disappearance of theatre in the early Middle Ages and its reappearance within the medieval church—first in the ritualized drama of the Mass, and later as the theatricalized trope known as the *Quem Quaeritis*—were realized through the performative image of an "absent/present" body. Moreover, the period in English drama from the late Middle Ages up to the appearance of *Gorbuduc,* the "first English tragedy," represents a crucial, formative stage during which the image of the effaced body becomes a metaphor for an operational principle of terror essential to drama, the terror of disappearance and disaster represented by the body "under erasure."[1] This image of disappearance first irrupts in Western drama in the execution of the medieval Mass—the single most important performance event in the Middle Ages—and is a representation that is carried through theatre's history and reverberates even today in the consciousness of the postmodern.[2]

It seems almost too simplistic to suggest that an essentially theatrical desire within a nascent Christian culture might have been absorbed at an early date by the performance of the Mass of the catacombs, and later by the pageantry of medieval ecclesiastical politics. Still, we cannot help but wonder if the assumed disappearance of theatre during the Middle Ages, in which there was no *officially sanctioned* theatre,[3] might not in fact represent a "remythologizing" of the classical drama through its expulsion and subsequent return "from the outside" in the politico-ecclesiastic spectacle of the Eucharist.

From its initial appearance as a subversive political and spiritual philosophy, to its transformation into pure spectacle during the later Middle Ages, the Mass was at each phase of its development the institutionalization of a performative, specular, and murderous desire inherited from Roman culture and passed on to the ambience of the Middle Ages, a period in which "torture and executions [were] enjoyed by the spectators like an entertainment at the fair."[4]

And yet these violent pastimes of the medieval period revealed much more than a mere continuance of the Roman predilection for violence as entertainment; they also demonstrated the survival of a fundamental and all-pervasive theatrical ontology. It was a *theatre* of punishment, after all, that provided those spectators with the pleasure of the gaze directed upon the spectacle of pain, just as it was *theatre* that supplied the Church with its powers of divine sanction and canonical authority through the excesses of liturgical spectacle— the administration of the sacraments which represented the "outward show" of Christ's presence and power. And it was, finally, *theatre* that provided an entire metaphysics of appearances to support the central authority of civil/ Church law displayed in the daily spectacle of the Mass.

Yet while the Mass was perhaps the central performance event in medieval life, and while it was grounded in a theatrical ontology, it, like other spectacular medieval entertainments, was not precisely theatre but a dramatic inversion of it. The Mass did not openly declare the illusory nature of truth, but was perceived instead through the eyes of faith as a *real* event, an actual historical return (albeit "bloodless") of the events of Christ's passion—the torture and murder of an obscure political subversive executed under the sign of the Messianic king, a Derridean *pharmakos* disappeared beneath the sentence of death.[5]

One can appreciate the complicated texture of this mimetic inversion in the central sacramental image of the Mass, the Transubstantiation, in which the problematic of appearances central to theatre is turned inside out: whereas in the ontological perception of theatre, illusion is embraced as truth, in the Mass empirical reality is presented as an illusion that conceals truth (as, for example, when the actual bodily presence of Christ is revealed under the *appearances* of bread and wine). It was the Church's profound intuitive grasp of this oppositional identity between faith and illusion that forced it to repulse the drama. Theatre's truth could simply never be thought in the logic of faith. Yet ironically the Church's attempt to expel theatre did not eliminate it, but only forced its concealment and its eventual return *in the Mass,* in the disruptive sonorities of the Easter tropes chanted "after the third lesson": "Whom do you seek? Why are you here?"—the questions addressed to the faithful assembled in the theatre of faith—questions that might also have been directed to the theatre itself.

This is not to say that the earliest form of theatre to emerge following the decline of the classical stage was a religious, or ritual, theatre. Indeed, I am suggesting the converse—the Mass was not merely an instance of theatre remembering (again) the spectacle of some elemental bloodletting. It was both a ritual and a performance event, supported by a concealed but fully operative theatrical ontology of "specular desire." The Mass was in this sense the celebration of specular violence secreted by theatre.

The interval between theatre and its violence is always a virtual space, unlocatable before the fact and only realized in performance. This lacuna— both minuscule and gaping, the very place where theatre masks violence and violence effects the theatrical—is the location of *terror,* a terror inaccessible to language. As René Girard says in his commentary on Sophocles' *Oedipus the King:*

> *Violence is the father and king of everything!* Jocasta affirms this truth in declaring that *Oedipus belongs to whomever speaks to him of "phobou"*—*of unhappiness, terror, disasters, nefarious violence of any sort.* . . . The *logos phobou* is ultimately the wordless language by which mimetic desire and violence communicate with one another.[6]

Thus the *logos phobou* of the Mass allowed the fierce, anti-mimetic, statutory ideology of the medieval Church to be concealed in a kind of "repressive desublimation" of the Passover meal as a reenactment of the human sacrifice/ assassination of the crucifixion. But this sacramentalized dislocation of mimetic desire was, ironically, effected performatively, causing the apparent return in the Church of the very thing it sought to expel—theatre (which returned in the form of the medieval Easter tropes, as discussed below). This mimetic struggle was linked, in turn, to the power emanating from the location of the ecclesiastical/Imaginary Other—the confessor, the bishopric and Papal See, the locus of the concealed Christ.[7]

The Mass, then, mimicking theatre, finally supplied the same support for civil law that tragedy did in Greece and the spectacles of the Circus did in Rome. The Mass was another instance of the appearance of a "real institution . . . constructed on a purely illusory basis," an institution of illusion designed to maintain the law, and supported by the "laws" or delimiting elements of performance itself. Thus for all of the Church's supposed anti-mimetic bias, it was mimetic representation itself that allowed an unworded terror to enter the ecclesiastical systems of power, where its force could be utilized as a political weapon.[8]

This return of theatre as what is real—the delusive appearance of torture and murder as an emanation of divine desire, and the apotheosis of that desire in the canons of faith as the Mass—was the apparition of a sublime psychosis.

The final r/enunciation of this apotheosis, an event that initiated the secularization of the drama and repopulated the disembodied, disappeared medieval theatres, was reputedly the trope known as the *Quem Quaeritis*. This trope represents, among other things, the reformulation of the performance event (the Mass) specifically as theatre.

The *Quem Quaeritis* was a responsory chanted during the Mass in Eastertide that reenacted the visit of the three Marys to the tomb of the crucified Christ. In its simplest form, three acolytes, representing the three Marys, arrive at the gravesite, and are met by another acolyte, representing an angel of the Lord, holding a palm leaf and sitting in front of the empty tomb. The angel intones, "Quem quaeritis, in sepulchro, Christicolae?" ("Whom do you seek in the sepulchre, O followers of Christ?"). The three women reply, "Iesum Nazareum crucifixum, o caelicolae" (Jesus of Nazareth, who was crucified, O heavenly dwellers"). The angel then responds, "Non est hic, surrexit sicut praedixerat" ("He is not here, he has arisen as he had foretold"), and commands the women, "ite, nuntiate quia surrexit de sepulchro" ("go, announce that he has risen from the sepulchre"). The trope ends, rather provocatively, in a switch from the angel's third person reportage to a first person pronouncement, "Resurrexi" ("I have risen"): the "absent presence" of Christ, ghosted in the continuously displaced responsorial voice, is now established as the sign of the dislocated, disappeared body itself.[9]

This dislodged body, the "presence of absence" within the empty tomb, becomes, like Plato's missing, *pharmakos*,[10] the "sign"[11] or signifier of an expelled body of violence to which, as Girard puts it, "desire clings . . . like a shadow." The empty tomb itself, in turn, becomes a doubled sign of desire (for the absent divinity) and terror (of death, emptiness, the lack of divinity) subtending an absent object,[12] a Phobic object that points back to and covers over the Deimic terror of non-being. The inscription of violence (the sign of the empty tomb) that conceals the missing, crucified body becomes "the signifier of the cherished being, the signifier of divinity."[13]

This signifier performs a double action according to its double inscription. It seemingly consecrates the "violent regime of the signifier" and simultaneously, through a *self-expulsion,* withholds the signifier's claim to divine being. Consequently, the "divine" signifier of the empty tomb, mimicking signification itself, is forever hollow and absent to itself. It is a "cure by *logos,* exorcism, and catharsis," a "pharmaceutical operation" that "must . . . *exclude itself from itself.*"[14] The signifier of the missing body conceals within itself its lack of significance; it operates as a space of expulsion within the field of terror, as the action and sign of *katharsis* itself.

The importance of this negative image, the image of the absent body, or the body "under erasure," is suggested in the question that is sometimes raised regarding the appearance of this particular segment of the Easter story as the "starting point" or return of theatre: why was this particular text, with its central image of the absent body, chosen for a "first" performance? But the question is usually dismissed with a tautology: "The texts appointed to be read or sung during Passion week . . . inevitably lend themselves to histrionic presentations."[15] The question as to *why* this particular text from the liturgy of Passion week "lends itself to histrionic presentation" more than any other is rarely pursued. Certainly as the central event in the mythos of Christianity this scene has immense theological importance, but there is also perhaps no better image, no other sign, that could convey the double bind of a historical impasse which looked at once back to the medieval world of faith, and ahead to the burgeoning but as yet uncertain economic and political world of the Renaissance. The latter was a world that would, more and more, find the body and the desire it represented reconstituted and dispersed within the increasingly fluid dynamics of trade, the flows of currency, and the discourses of politics.

Johan Huizinga, in *The Waning of the Middle Ages,* writes that late medieval culture made "desire itself the central motif, and so create[d] a conception of love with a negative groundnote." This love, furthermore, had "to be elevated to the height of a rite" because "the overflowing violence of passion" demanded it: "Only by constructing a system of forms and rules for the vehement emotions can barbarity be escaped."[16] The desire in/of the body which had initially lain hidden within the silence of an ecclesiastical *ascesis* now erupted outward. This desire was gradually reformed and regulated through its conscription onto the body's surface, where it could be seen, corrected, and remodeled according to the political and economic needs of culture and the state.[17]

This formal rule-making process, this preliminary reformation of the passions was, as I have said, effected through the body, and was counterpoint to the Reformation itself, which intuited the "secularization of the divine" and the consequent dispersion of divine force into the body of the state as the means to achieving autonomous political power.[18] Ironically, in light of the later Reformation's ban on theatre during the Interregnum, the forensic space within which the reconstitution of the body was first and most effectively demonstrated was theatre.

And yet, in still another paradoxical twist, the periods of presumed exclusion in theatre history, the spaces during which there *seemed* to be an absence of theatre, or when theatre *seemed* to be "in decline," were often the periods during which the reformation of the body *seems* to have taken its most violent hold, as evidenced by the disruptive change in attitude toward the body and its control that emerges after each of these disappearances. Thus it is not in theatre as a static cultural institution or as an essential and unchanging monumental force that we see its socializing coercion, its violence, its political complicities; but in the flux of its disappearances and reappearances in history, as well as in the appearances and disappearances that constitute theatre itself. Consequently, what might seem at first glance a desire to "monumentalize" the theatrical in these pages should be understood in light of this definition of theatre *as* disappearance, disappearance always effected in the absolute uniqueness of a particular historical moment.[19]

We can see at this point that the question of whether the *Quem Quaeritis* trope is, in fact, evidence of the "reemergence" of the drama is both moot and irrelevant. Indeed, we might just as easily contend, recognizing the Church's collusion with theatre, that it was theatre that made the Church's political emergence, and eventual decline, possible. The *Quem Quaeritis* trope would then represent something beyond the emergence of theatre from the Church; it would enunciate theatre's repudiation of a politically dissolute Church law, a law that could no longer sustain itself in the face of changing economic and political reality. The *Quem Quaeritis*, then, would be the overdetermined *sign* of this subversion of ecclesiastic law, and the consequent reformulation of the body according to the tenets of a developing humanism.

It makes little difference, finally, whether the *Quem Quaeritis* actually represents an origin or a reemergence of theatre, or merely the biases of scholarship. In either case the choice of the trope, either by history or scholarship, belies a deep concern with the onto-politics of the inscribed body and the body's disappearance into the systems of exchange that define it.

Whether the medieval silence in theatre history—and the trope that punctuates it—are an actual rend in the terror-stricken memory of theatre, or the result of political repression, or simply an artifact of the biases of literary history,[20] several complex things happen in the space of this lapse, and in the "reemergence" of theatre that follows.[21] At the most obvious level, a simple religious zealot is apotheosized: "He is not here, but has risen . . ."[22] His murder, executed by the Roman state in its desire to quell possible "terrorist actions" against its authority in Palestine, is sanctified and consequently depoliticized: "It behoved Christ to suffer, and on the / third day / To rise again with glory." Torture, pain, and murder subsequently become sanctioned if undergone "for the faith" (e.g., adherence to ecclesiastical law) and, accordingly, pain in the body becomes idealized and reified while the body itself begins to experience its disappearance into the law that has sanctioned its pain: "Do not touch me, for I have not yet ascended to my father."[23] Subsequently, the reality of the body and its pain is no longer based upon evidence or simple ocular proof, but hinges instead on the perception of an "absence" or "lack"—the empty tomb ("See, He is not here").[24] Violence, then, is no longer "seen" but "read" in its absence, in its *signs* ("See my hands and my feet, signifying I am he").[25] This absence or lack echoes or *ghosts* the seeming absence of theatricality in history as that theatricality was disarticulated, inverted, and "derealized" by the do inr nt political institution, the Church, in its desire to control through repe .ion the "real" catastrophe, the "real" terror of the crucifixion as a means of political exploitation and subjugation.

The endless return of the catastrophic occurs as a "showing" or performance event that serves to demonstrate the divine power of the Church of faith, which simultaneously depends on this showing and repulses it: "Thomas, now examine closely the wounds / of my body. . . . Put your finger in the place of the wound. . . . Blessed are they that have not seen and have believed." Finally, at perhaps its most essential level, the locus of the absent Other (God, language, ecclesiastical law, heaven) is named as the true location of the body's substance: "There are many rooms in my Father's house. . . . I shall return to take you with me, so that where I am you may be too." Moreover, this *aphanisis,* or disappearance of the subject into the locus of the Other, is inscribed on the body itself. The wounds of scourging and crucifixion stands as the mark of a divine desire relocated in the imprint of state law.

Beyond these developments, the glorification of murder and political assassination in the Church's sanctification of the crucifixion also reverses the dramatic movement of the classical theatre and the movement of time and history which that drama had represented. Whereas Aristotle sees this movement linearly [26] in terms of *anagnoresis* (recognition), *peripeteia* (reversal), and *catastrophe* (which Girard equates with terror), the Church, in its sublimation of the theatrical to the historical in the enactment of the Mass, inverts the Aristotelian order, and posits the catastrophic event first (the Crucifixion), followed by the reversal (the Resurrection), ending with recognition (Christ's appearance to his followers). This inversion is clearly demonstrated not only in the Gospels and in the performance of the Mass, but also in the Book of Revelation—the historical vision of Christian culture in which the destruction of mankind in history is eventually followed by the salvation of the faithful through the reappearance of Christ. [27]

This inversion of terms not only represents a reversal of the movement of desire in classical drama away from the body "and its intensities" and toward a lack (the tomb); it also represents a movement—especially the a priori catastrophe and the growing disarticulation of the body into systems of exchange—that leads eventually and inevitably to a distinct view of history *as a theatre of terror,* a history that is, like theatre's body, continuously in danger of disappearing into itself, of vanishing as an object, a history whose substance seems to be locatable only *in* the painfully damaged and maimed body. Concomitantly, the emergence of a view of history as catastrophe or terror stimulates the theatre in history to shape itself more and more around terror as its central experience of desire. The history of theatre is thus the history of terror. [28]

The first site of this reversal in the traditional canon (apart from the *Quem Quaeritis*) is the mystery cycles that were popular during the late Middle Ages. Nominally propagandistic in the exposition of their ideology, these plays moved from the Easter story to other stories in the life of Christ and culminated, finally, in the great day-long *Corpus Christi* cycles that encapsulated the entire history of the universe from its creation, with *The Fall Man,* to its end, with *The Last Judgement*. Other kinds of mysteries were also played—the lives of the saints, for example, or apologies for certain tenets of the faith, or instructional plays on the evils of unbelief or sacrilege.

Just as the absence of theatre in history was reflected in the choice of the disembodied *Quem Quaeritis* texts—texts that served as the final punctuation of this medieval silence (a "punctuation without a text")—so the other performance manuscripts of this period reflected the reorganization of the body in the forms taken by the texts themselves and in the images they evoked; the cancelled, dismembered body as text, and the text as remembered corpus *under erasure* appear synchronously, each the documentation of the other. The eventual appropriation of the mystery cycles by the various and growing guilds that sponsored them is one of the earliest indications of the movement of this cancelled body from the ritual "theatre" of the Church into the secular and economic theatres of middle-class Europe.

The fact that the impetus for these plays apparently originated within the ecclesiastical sobriety of the Church did not prevent them from developing into entertainments of the most grotesque and bizarre form. *The Croxton Play of the Sacrament* is ostensibly about the conversion of a Jew, Jonathas, who attempts to disprove the real presence of Christ in the communion wafer. He and his associates plot to secure a Host in order to debunk the notion of divine presence in the bread: "might we get it onys within our pales, / I trow we shud sone after put it to the test." [29] He procures a Host from a Christian merchant who has stolen it from the sacristy. With his cronies, he proceeds to inflict all sorts of absurd and savage violence upon the wafer, finally sticking it with daggers until "It bledith as it woode, iwis!" (485) Frantic, Jonathas picks up the "ilke cake" and tries to throw it into a cauldron of boiling oil and so destroy it, but instead, the stage directions tell us, "the host . . . clings to his hand" (498). Jonathas begins running in "wood / nesse," or madness, until his compatriots catch him and nail the Host to a pillar in order to quiet him. But as they attempt to pull Jonathas from the host, his hand sticks to the bread/body, and he is dismembered: "Thay pluke the arme, and the hand shall hang still with the sacrament" (515). The bloody hand and arm of the heathen, hanging like Grendel's claw above the mead-hall door, is yet another sign of the destruction that must inevitably befall pagans, monsters, and Jews who deny the presence of Christ in the sacrament, and by extension, his authoritarian presence in the Church. Jonathas is later cured—literally re-membered—by sticking his hand into a cauldron containing the scalding blood of Christ.

This example denotes an implicit terrorism in the Church's ideological posture, a terrorism that becomes explicit during the great Inquisitions, those magnificent theatres of terror that ran concurrently with and after the mystery plays in Europe. But this terrorism, distinct from the classical plays, locates the operational site of violence explicitly on the body *in* the theatre. Jonathas is literally disarticulated on stage as he attempts to dismember the

Host in a parody of the theatricalized arraignment and sentencing of Christ described in the Gospels.

The message that is conveyed, that the power of Christ operating through the remembrance of Church dogma is more powerful than any who oppose it, is displayed on and in the body of the unbeliever, which, like the Host or *Corpus Christi,* then becomes the object of Phobic terror as it is reified and derealized through the torturous ideology of the Church. Simultaneously, this same body also becomes the object of a Deimic terror inasmuch as it is threatened with non-being by the imminent violence that the Host represents. This is an *aphanic* terror of disappearance into the empty tomb—the *kathartic* expulsion of the body's substance into the locus of the Other. The dismemberment of Jonathas represents a replaying of theatre's origins in the dismemberment of self in the creation of a phobic object, and the re-membrance of identity in the law (the blood of Christ, in this case) as an object of fascination—a fetish object.

The play also exhibits an additional lamination. Just as Hesiod foresaw the total reformation of Greek society in the Phobic/Deimic split reflected in the expulsion of religion by law, so the torture of Jonathas prefigures an even more complex reorganization of society around now primarily economic terms in the advancement of middle-class values. The wealthy Jew is torn up and redistributed according to the tenets of a "new" morality—his body functions as currency recouped in the submission of religious ideology to the terrorizing reality of economic power.[30] The developing signs of this transformation can be seen in the later morality plays, in which the value of the individual is transmuted into the currency of appearances that is imprinted on his body—the stage, itself compartmentalized into allegorical "areas" or domains of performance, is no longer inhabited exclusively by mythic or historical figures such as Adam or Jonathas, but is instead populated by emblematic "characters": Kindred, Goods, Discretion, Beauty, Knowledge. The appearance of the morality play marks the economy of myth/history dispersed into the field of allegory.

"In the field of allegorical intuition," writes Walter Benjamin, "the image [of the human torso] is a fragment, a rune."[31] The morality play represents a redistribution of those fragments, those runic images of the human and social body, into representations of middle-class values, values that inexorably support the power of the status quo that is tautologically defined by the morality play itself. Thus, for example, in the morality play *Everyman,* the companion that accompanies Everyman to the grave is not Knowledge, or Fellowship, but Good Deeds, which "consist not only of charitable acts but also of penitential scourgings."[32]

Even though *Everyman* is quite clearly a "Catholic" play, the orientation of its ideology and the means of effecting it—discipline and punishment—clearly show a desire to reform the body in order to bring it into accord with the power of the law, a law whose authorship was, at the time of *Everyman's* earliest performances, being hotly contested between the Roman Church and the Church of England (the Crown).

Certainly self-scourging and the importance of good works had been an essential part of the Catholic canon for centuries before this play was written. However, the translation of these ideological tenets into the discourse of performance, a discourse operating within "the field of allegorical intuition," was something quite new, and represented, I believe, a radically different modality in the process of reinscribing the law—a tactic that was employed by theatre to divorce the power of law from the Papal See.

"Allegories are, in the realm of thoughts, what ruins are in the realm of things":[33] the reorganization of terror onto the surface of the ruined/runed body, its inscription there the mark of pain, follows a tortured and fascinated path from the *Quem Quaeritis* through the mystery cycles and morality plays to the later "transitional period," during which a number of "pre-tragic" plays appear, works that have been largely dismissed as "bad theatre." Thomas Preston's *Cambyses, King of Persia,*[34] for example, for all its dramatic inconsistencies and excesses (or perhaps because of them), exudes some of the schizo-phobic terror that erupts centuries later in such early modernist plays as Alfred Jarry's *Ubu Roi* or the fevered fragments of Artaud's theatrical writings.

Appearing (as did Jarry's play) in a historical epoch that was in the process of losing its identity in the fragmentation of a past age, the text of *Cambyses,* like the characters within the play, bears in its peculiar construct the literal scars of the violence of its historical era. Although *Cambyses* was one of the most popular plays in medieval and Renaissance England, it seems at first glance little more than a hodgepodge of different styles and genres mixed in a seemingly random fashion to a produce a frenzied, and somewhat outrageous, theatrical effect. According to most scholars, elements of the history play, the morality play, folk theatre, and mummery are utilized primarily as gratuitous spectacle, and secondly to convey (albeit rather weakly) a moral point similar to the "Mirror of Magistrates" plays of a slightly later period in English drama—that it is necessary and good for the King (or Queen) to be wise and moderate in his/her rule.

But the actual effect of the play is quite the opposite; the whole notion of the "divine power" of kingship seems to be ridiculed and disparaged at every turn. The play is less an instruction than a hallucinatory inversion of the theatre of court; the ravings, flayings, infanticides, beatings and copulations are paraded through the text like deluded testimony in a schizo-paranoiac trial. The play bemoans again and again the seeming impossibility of justice in the realm of law:

> *Enter COMMON'S CRY running in, speak this verse,*
> *and go out again hastily*

Com. Cr. Alas, alas, how are the commons op-
   pressed
By that vile judge, Sisamnes by name.
I do not know how it should be redressed.
To amend his life no whit he doth frame.
We are undone and thrown out of door;
   His damnable dealing doth us so torment;
At his hand we can find no relief or succor.
God grant him grace for to repent.
                          Run away crying. (5.17–24)

Unfortunately, the wrongs of Sisamnes the judge *are* redressed—by the king,
a far crueller and more violent man than his proxy. Justice in the realm of
Cambyses is synonymous with the privileges of power, which must always
abuse and pervert it. There is consequently no way to reform power, no ideal
way for a magistrate to act. Power dictates its own code, its own ethics, and
its own models of behavior according to a single principle, the pleasure of
cruelty witnessed and the ecstasy of the gratuitously violent act. In scene five,
the king, in order to demonstrate his ability to hold his drink against the
criticism of one of his counselors, has the counselor's child brought in. He
stands the child up, and to prove his undiminished abilities, shoots the child
straight through the heart. The act is simple and senseless: "I have dispatched
him. Down he doth fall." The gratuitous cruelty is compounded by gratuitous enormity: "Nay, thou shalt see, Praxaspes, stranger news yet. / My
knight, with speed his heart cut out and give it / unto me" (5.214–17).

The images of violence and cruelty are interrupted only by the intrusion
of cynicism (in Ambidexter), and by stupidity (in the personages of Hob and
Lob, the country bumpkins, and the three ruffians, Huf, Ruf and Snuf, together the perfect image of the banality of evil). Venus and Cupid, who
make a brief appearance in scene nine, do so only at the lazy urging of divine
whim; the gods have no interest in these cruel goings on—divine interven-
tion for the cause of justice is unthinkable. Athena is out to lunch.

There is, in this world, no one to redress grievances to. The universe of
Cambyses is circumscribed by violence, tyranny, and chaos, relieved only by
a crude and demonic humor. The world of the play, for all of its "open-
ended" structure, is suffocating and abysmally fatalistic. This "Mirror for
Magistrates" becomes another Heraklean shield, reflecting only a grimace
and a cruel wink; the single, pathetic instance of justice is supplied by Chance
in a *deus ex machina* ending: the king, at play's finish, accidentally falls on his
sword and kills himself, a contrived and terrifying absurdity, as if the machine of cruel desire could only be stopped by a collision with another, equally
absurd, death-machine.

Cambyses stands as an absolute subversion of the morality play. Disarticulation and reinscription appear right at the play's surface, both in its vision
of the world and in its structure. Apart from the nonstop litany of atrocities,

the form of the text—with its disjunctures, its psychotic characterizations, its ridiculous (and frightening) excesses of violence—seems to represent a social body and cultural psyche undergoing total fragmentation, as if the tenuously remembered body of Jonathas had suddenly flown apart again in the exploding cauldron of spiritual doubt, difference, and subversion of authority. Moreover, *Cambyses* brings to the surface the previously semi-articulated theatrical desire to reform the body in the most violent way possible. In this, *Cambyses* represents—albeit unintentionally—a truly revolutionary play. Although there is no ideology proposed here (as there is in the slightly later play *Gorboduc*, the "first English tragedy," a play of intense and somewhat tedious moral instruction), we are given a portrait of power in question, disrupted by excess of cruelty, crying out in its jagged contours for some vision of true peace and unifying justice; a fragmented vision that will too often be submerged beneath the finer lineaments of the "better" English tragedies to come. But in *Cambyses* we see that the transference of power from the Church to the state effected through the body is merely a stage in the development of the theatre of terror.

Looking back at the movement of drama from its supposed irruption in the *Quem Quaeritis* to its final "pretragic" forms in such plays as *Cambyses*, we can begin to see how the continuing tradition of English tragedy was at some level an attempt to quantify, constrain, and reduce to currency the energy and pleasure of passion and desire represented by the body—which ultimately become "love" and "sexuality" through the domesticating course of Renaissance and later drama.[35] Indeed, throughout the magnificent explosion of drama in the Elizabethan period, the tension between the energy of desire and its attempted domestication through the representational processes of performance produces some of the finest plays ever written. But the exclusions and uncertain "transitional periods" in the movement of theatre history often reveal the most basic impulses of performance—the terror, for instance, of the body under erasure.

We can perceive, then, through the development of the theatre the gradual retranslation of body as text, as "discourse" or written law. Moreover, this translation at every step looks back to and reaffirms the violence applied to a "real" body in society—the subjective, terrorized theatre-body as "the site of the inscription of the law."

This identity between body and text, and the concealed binary opposition that articulates it, suggest a prescient and embryonic insight into the transition from a medieval worldview steeped in simile and correspondence, to a later, neoclassical worldview explicated through differential representation.[36] Thus the movement from the defaced body of Christ as palimpsest to the *text* as a displaced body of violence is clearly visible in the slow but deliberate growth of the theatricalized metaphor of text *as* body. We see this metaphor quite clearly in plays like *Cambyses, King of Persia* or *Edward II*, and even more self-consciously in Kyd's *The Spanish Tragedy*—a play in which letters

and texts are circulated with dizzying frequency, and at certain points literally
bleed into the physical and Eucharistic body of the Other.

The Spanish Tragedy looks back directly to the Senecan drama and its
Hesiodic terrors for the energy of its worldview, and so it is not surprising
that the play invokes, as I have already suggested, those twins born of Love
and War:

BEL-IMPERIA
    . . . Whereon dost thou chiefly meditate?
HORATIO
    On dangers past, and pleasures to ensue.
BALTHAZAR
    On pleasures past, and dangers to ensue.
BEL-IMPERIA
    What dangers and what pleasures dost thou mean?
HORATIO
    Dangers of war, and pleasures of our love.
LORENZO
    Dangers of death, but pleasures none at all.
BEL-IMPERIA
    Let dangers go; thy war shall be with me . . . [37]

In this passage the terror that is born of a "warring peace" between Horatio
and Bel-Imperia is spoken literally "between the lines" in the metacommen-
tary of Balthazar and Lorenzo. This is a terror that is, in the play, still terror,
the threat of non-being which is as yet unsignified and unsignifiable—a
frightening and apprehensive "riddling of the Sphinx." This terror is, however, almost immediately translated into a terrorism through the murder and
display of the hanged, pierced body of Horatio, which now reads as the
bloody sign of Balthazar's tyranny.

The hanged body as sign appears again in Act III, when Pedringano, Lorenzo's toady, murders Serberine at Lorenzo's order and is subsequently executed for it on the gallows. What is worth noting in this incident is the
ontologic correspondence between Pedringano's body and its violent fate,
and a promised letter of reprieve that the messenger boy is supposed to be
carrying to the scaffold in his wooden box. The box is in fact empty because
of Lorenzo's betrayal of Pedringano, who is sent purposely to the gallows
believing that he will be pardoned at the last moment.

The "presence of absence" within the messenger's casket re-echoes that
ontologic conundrum that defines Western theatre, a mystification of the relationship between law and violence by which the displayed body of the
"criminal" is gradually dislocated into text (or "discourse") through the ex-
pediency of an "empty tomb" or casket which now appears as an overdeter-
mination of the law's metaphoric relationship to the body: what "is good for

the body / is likewise good for the soul," says Pedringano on the gallows' steps, "and it may be in that box is balm for both" (3.6.76–78). But the box is indeed empty, and the law's salvific power is transmuted through that emptiness into the vengeance of the Many upon the One: "For blood with blood shall, while I sit as judge, / Be satisfied, and the law discharg'd" (3.6.35–36).

It is worth noting here that the "disappearing appearance" of the letter/ law is enacted forensically on the gallows stage. It *occurs as theatre,* in other words, and becomes a metaphor not only for the theatre itself, but for the acting body *in* the theatre, a body whose very substance appears in the theatre only as *dis*appearance: "the insubstantiality of the self," writes Herbert Blau, seen "through the insubstantiality of performance"—an attenuation seemingly refused in the objectification of the body as corpse/letter.[38]

Horatio's murdered body becomes the sign of its own unseen terror and becomes other than what it was; it is obliterated, in other words, in the practice of Balthazar and Lorenzo. Likewise, the hanged body of Pedringano gives up the secret of its terrorism in/as text in the letter, found in the condemned man's hand, that proclaims the treachery of Lorenzo and Balthazar in the murder of Horatio. Terror, which is initially repressed in the sign system of terrorism, is retranslated throughout the play, and is finally revealed *exclusively* through the agency of the *sign/letter* which appears and disappears with bewildering regularity in the play. In fact, we see no fewer than twelve instances in which letters, papers, or books are passed between characters in the play, and in each case the letter passed translates—as either warning, threat, or lie—some extraordinary violence that awaits somebody in the play.[39] At times, as in the "empty box" example noted above, these letters are both appearing and disappearing at the same moment.

There is, moreover, a *direct* correspondence in some cases between the letter and the violence it reports, and the body of the recipient. In one instance Hieronimo receives a letter of warning from Bel-Imperia, who is imprisoned by Balthazar, which for want of ink she has written in her own blood. Here body and text literally become one through the transubstantiating act of writing.

In another instance Hieronimo, who has received a bundle of contracts and legal depositions in his position as Marshall, tears them apart with his teeth while crying out, "that Prosperpine may grant / Revenge on them that murdered my son. / Then will I rent and tear them thus, and thus, / Shivering their limbs in pieces with my teeth" (3.13.120–23). Text/body is thus disarticulated as Hieronimo dismembers the text and spits it out as speech, as voice sounding the body's disappearance into performance:

What is the voice? All we know is that something comes up through the nervous system which is incommunicable and disjunct, bereft of flesh once out of the body, silencing the body as it goes—all the more as it goes into language,

which is the history from which it came. Even when not voiced, words incit-
ing breath, breath becoming words in *a remembrance of breathing,* voice, giving
voice, voicing.[40]

Eventually, the body empties itself of language—like Seneca's Medea—through
its excess and enters into silence. The letter itself reappears out of that emptiness, in the real, as the sentence of death, the sentence that *is* silence. In this
complete, mutual exclusion of language, language *in the body* finally falls silent as Hieronimo bites out his tongue in a plenitude of despair.

This empty, silenced body is eventually repositioned in the theatre along
a new axis of organization. Attention now begins to shift away from the seen
body as the signified of the performance, and *seeing itself* becomes what is
signified. This is, in part, Joel Fineman's take on Shakespeare's sonnets, which
elucidate, according to Fineman, the formation of a subjectivity in the breach
between the seeing and the speaking. As one might imagine, the problematic
of seeing/speaking is raised to a different level in the plays, where the seeing
and the speaking are activated in all of their impossibility.

In Shakespeare's *Othello,*[41] for example, seeing appears as a problematic
by which power/terror is deployed as *misprision.* Taking up costume and
prop, Iago begins at once to prepare the show:

> When devils will their blackest sins put on,
> They do suggest at first with heavenly shows,
> As I do now: For while this honest fool [Cassio]
> Plies Desdemona to repair his fortunes,
> And she for him pleads strongly to the Moor,
> I'll pour this pestilence into his ear.[42]

The synesthetic reverberations are dizzying. Not only does Iago transpose
word into image—a "pestilence" poured into the ear—but this blighted image, this word-as-*lie* (I am tempted to say "fiction," which is indeed Stephen
Greenblatt's view[43]) is, in turn, later re-presented in Othello's mind as the
image of Desdemona's falsely seen adultery. As it is in *Hamlet*—where the
players pour hebona in the player-King's ear—this "pestilence" is the lie of
the play playing back an uncertain terror, the terror of death.[44] In the case of
Othello, however, the relation between image and word is reversed; the silent, Hamletic *image* of the mime is transposed into a *spoken metaphor* by
which Iago, through the enunciation, "represents for the first time" the spectacle of infidelity. In *Hamlet,* the image of the King's poisoned ear is a repetition of what has presumably already occurred. To further complicate matters, the *image* that is played out in *Hamlet* appears in the play text as word
(stage direction), whereas in *Othello,* one only imagines (images) Iago whis-
pering to Othello, so that he appears in the imagination pouring a metaphorical "pestilence" into Othello's ear with his spoken word.

In any case, between the inadequacy of word passing into image (the word's need of "ocular proof" in *Othello,* or *Hamlet's* need to enact the word into image) and the image's invocation as word, the tension becomes unbearable and generates an inevitable violence that erupts *between* word and image.[45] "Villain," cries Othello at Iago's lurid suggestions:

> Be sure thou prove my love a whore,
> Be sure of it; give me the ocular proof,
> Or by the worth of man's eternal soul,
> Thou hadst been better have been born a dog
> Than answer my wak'd wrath. (3.3.404–408)

Exiled within Iago's treacherous terrain of word-as-image, Othello counters with "a show of words," sounding the depth of his barely contained rage/desire. Iago, in turn, continues to terrorize Othello with the most subtle shift of seeing refracted through an almost imperceptible misdirection of the eye—a misdirection effected through Iago's words. Thus while the violence of Othello's threat rests on the sheer force of the imagery of his *discourse,* Iago's terrorism, much more potent, operates through the *effect of discourse on seeing,* a seeing that, to complete the circle, engenders the perjury and its vengeance.

This vengeance finally explodes in the capital sentence, the enunciation of death: "By heaven," cries Othello standing above the doomed Desdemona, confronting her with the "ocular proof," "I saw my handkerchief in his hand: O perjur'd woman, thou dost stone thy heart, / And makest me call what I intend to do / A murder, which I thought a sacrifice" (5.2.63–67). Othello's desire absolutely infects what he sees, and that desire has, at every step, been informed through Iago's words. Words, in turn, are tortured into a terrorizing violence by the seeing (Othello begins to ridicule and humiliate Desdemona publicly). Finally they move into the sheer terrorism of Desdemona's murder.

"Terrorist discourse," writes Roland Barthes, "is . . . simply . . . the lucid adequation of the enunciation with the true violence of language."[46] If we take *Othello* as a somewhat typical example of language's placement in the theatre, we can begin to see how the language of theatre *within the theatre* is, in Barthes's sense, always eminently terrorist. We can also see how the violence of terrorism occurs not as a result of this language aspiring to violence, but as the failure of language to attain the "adequation of the enunciation with violence." When language fails in this, its violence is redeployed as action. This threshold of failure, the threshold that holds violence in check, is clearly understood by Iago. His apparent calm in the face of Othello's "violent enunciation" is understandable because he knows that true terror is generated not by Othello's/word, but by the failure of perjured seeing. In essence, Iago, like the author, like the ideal spectator, like theatre itself, attends to the knowledge that the ocularity in which Othello seeks his truth is as much a failure as the language that directs it. Ultimately in the theatre, the terrorism of Barthes's "wish to adequation" is multiplied exponentially by the violence of failed seeing—the desire to see, seeing desire, seeing what one has been told (not) to.

The provocative relationship between seeing and the violence of language was developed centuries later in Brecht, who "adequated" the specifics of historical discourse and political ideology with the gestus in an almost seamless iconographic interplay of the visual with the enunciative. This relationship is the most impossible of theatre's conundrums. For the violence that is speaking, multiplied by the "ocular proof" that is theatre, is only "positive" (in the Brechtian perspective) when the proof in the seeing is *true*. Yet not only is that an unknowable proposition (that what is seen is indeed true); the history of theatre also seems to tell us quite plainly that what is seen is *in essence* false because what is seen is *inessential*. The "ocular proof," then, is always a lie, because it is always infected by the *desire* to see, and to see what one desires. Thus what at first appears as a problematic, now becomes an axiom: theatre's truth resides in the knowledge that we can only know that what we see is a lie. What Barthes (but not I) would call a terrorist discourse, is fed back into a more aboriginal terror in the realization that ocularity, the basis for all empirical truth,[47] the "truth" that forms the substance of discourse itself, is a perjury. Indeed, what theatre (exemplified by Iago) and politics finally demonstrate more than anything else is that the indeterminacies inherent in the seeing can be manipulated as *systems* of terror. The terror of theatre moves somewhere between the propositions of the axiom—what seems true is a lie—while deception itself seems to be the truth of what is seen.

This axiom provides a grounding for the deployment of a specific aspect of terror as ism—the terror that the primary condition of perception is failure. This terror has profound implications in a culture history whose identity rests largely in the seen, the empirical; a culture whose history, science, and economic and political order is, in other words, empirically bound. This is a terror that might infect this very work: to what degree can I, for example, "historically support" my own inquiry when all the means of historical knowledge open to me are empirically based? To what degree can I develop the work outward, in new historicist fashion, when such materialist directions emerge, according to my own argument, from theatre, from false ocularity, and not the other way around? The relative lack in this study of "other," "supporting" historical data is bound up with the impossibility of this central problem. Political-historical culture is not coeval and coextensive with theatre; theatre is the very condition of the violence of politico-economic history: *theatre is the essential condition of that and of all knowledge.*[48]

We can see this "knowledge problem" framed in *Othello* in different ways. The historical knowledge axis, for example, is called into question when the synesthesia of language-as-image is employed *as* theatre in the battle scenes falsely mounted through the mere evocation of images ("A sail, a sail . . . .").

Other battle scenes are falsely mounted *in* the play as a ruse or false "pageant" deployed by the Turkish fleet to distract Othello's attention away from the real intention of the Turkish military action.

This doubled ruse is further complicated by the trial that is being enacted concurrently with the battle, in which testimony is delivered through the eyewitness account. This testimony accuses Othello of bewitching Desdemon,[49] an account that is "supported" by reference to an ocular proof of Desdemona's own ocular innocence:

> A maiden never bold of spirit;
> So still and quiet, that her motion
> Blush'd at her self; and she, in spite of nature,
> Of years, of country, credit, everything,
> To fall in love with what she feared to look on? (1.3.94–98)

But Desdemona's seeming innocence is subverted later in the same scene when Braziano cautions Othello after the latter's acquittal: "Look to her, Moor, if have a quick eye to see: / She has deceiv'd her father, may do thee" (1.3.292–93). This warning is picked up again by Iago, "she that so young, could give out such a seeming / to seel her father's eyes up close as oak" (3.3.238–39). Against the backdrop of the false, ocularly conceived battle, Desdemona's seemingly "innocent" dissembling is seen for what it is.

Or is it? While the axiom of see(m)ing falsity is presented as caveat ("This cannot be / By no assay of reason. Tis a pageant / To keep us in false gaze") and developed through seemingly endless permutations ("I have a pain upon my forehead here," complains Othello, "Faith, that's with the watching; twill away again," comforts Desdemona), Iago enters and weaves his particular coercive violence from the terror implicit in the lie of theatre. Iago begins, bit by forensic bit, to dis-ease the mind of Othello with the implanted and disastrous presumption that what Othello sees will prove Iago's suggestions correct. This is an often-made observation, but one that ignores terror's deeper implication in the seeing of the "show"—Iago, after all, shows us the lie of the show through the show itself. He consciously creates an ocular lie—a play, in fact—on the stage, and shows us the lie that theatre is, infected as it is by our own desire. The question immediately arises: in the impossibility of these warpings, what is the truth, finally, of theatre's lie? What are we to make of theatre's self-revelatory falsity when we can only see it *through* that very lie, through Iago, whose great pleasure is *showing* us that seeing is "always already" held captive by hidden desire?

Although we have seen this terror of seeing before—perhaps most notably in the images of violence in the *Quem Quaeritis,* but also in the surveillance of/by Medea—we note here a distinct change: the terror of seeing is no longer revealed simply in the object seen (the female body, the tortured body), but in the subject who looks and in the looking itself. The terror of the effects of law upon the absent/present body of Jesus/Jonathas that we pointed to earlier has been enfolded by the ontologic problematic of the gaze itself, a gaze that terrorizes seen *and* seer, and forces him (most notably a him) to transfer that terror upon the screen/body of an Other (most notably a female). Attendant upon this problematic is a double transference, on the one hand between Othello and Desdemon, and on the other, between the audience and *Othello*.

Othello's transference works itself out in a kind of psychosis of seeing. The relatively "empty" character of a Desdemona marks the *béance* through which a denied enormity gains entry back into the psyche as truth: what Othello sees as real is a hallucinatory desire that casts terror back into the Real, and covers over the space of that denied terror with an emptiness. The terror itself then returns in the Real in the delusional *image* of woman. Woman thus becomes a kind of Lacanian phobic object, an image of Panic that points back to the unseen terror of seeing itself. The image of Panic here then assumes the image of innocence reflected in the relative lack of female identity as it is repressed and formulated by the gaze.[50]

The transference between audience and play resides in the desire to see desire's reenactment as seeing. The watching of the play thus represents the repressed action of desire upon the empiricism of the I/eye, the *gaze* that becomes, in the double bind, the deployment of a specific mode of terrorism.

What is critical in the *development* of this terrorism is the breach that theatre now suggests between seeing and speaking. This breach, the breach between revelation and deception, emerges in two opposing and complementary directions. On the one hand, the deception of the Imaginary, the deception and capture by the image of the Other, is *seemingly* arrested by the action of the Symbolic, the action of communication that corrects and rectifies the misread image. But in *Othello,* which appears here as the pure distillation of theatre, language itself operates in the Imaginary. Thus the perjured word cannot fulfill the image (which seems to be plenitude) and so *compounds* the deception. On the other hand, the image's creation in the duplicitous "language" of the Imaginary distills the dazzling ambiguity of the image into simple binarisms—good-evil, black-white, virgin-whore—which must, as Iago shows us, also fail as proof or truth function. Thus seeing and speaking are both identified and opposed in the forensic desire that one prove the truth of the other, in a never-ending escalation of deception and seeming. Both seeing and speaking are caught in the agonizing trap of a falsely assumed empiricism, an empiricism whose only real claim to truth resides not in its ability to "prove" but in its ability to reproduce or *rehearse* "the Same," that impossibility. The universe of correspondence that had anchored the Renaissance world dissolves in the growing recognition that the seen and the spoken are both of the same order, the order of the lack and the lie, the order of *representation*.

At the far end of Renaissance drama, we see the universe of correspondences continue to fragment as the fault line that circumscribes representation begins to split open the ground beneath language and history, reducing them by degrees to discrete signs, particular ruins. The pieces and parts of the universe of correspondence begin to appear more and more often as part-objects, letters, pieces of the world, runes and ruins.

Webster's *The Duchess of Malfi* is just such a play of ruins. Apart from the overt decadence and violence that is its hallmark and its warning, *The Duchess* envisions a society brought to destruction through the exteriorization of the incestuous desire that is representational mimesis, and the necessary violence that emerges from that representative desire.

When news of the Duchess's death reaches him, for example, her brother Ferdinand—the accessory to her murder—observes: "She and I were twins; / And should I die this instant, I had liv'd / her time to a minute."[51] But the Duke's profession of perfect filial union is offset by Bosola's observation that the Duchess's murder seems to confirm "the ancient truth, / That kindred commonly do worse agree / Than remote strangers" (4.2.272). Indeed, Ferdinand's mind-shattering ambivalence—the desiring passion of the sororicide and his equally passionate remorse—seems to imply that the intimacy between these twins necessitates a violence generated by the desire of the one to *have* the desire of the other. Ferdinand murders out of jealousy because he cannot have his sister's sexual love; indeed he is not even allowed the recognition of that desire in himself.

The demand to have the other's concealed desire forces its materialization in an object, a thing of revulsion and fascination, the phobic/fetish object.[52] The appearance of this object continuously oscillates, like the theatrical scene itself, between phobia and fetish, revulsion and desire, disappearance and reappearance. The corpse into which the Duchess disappears as subject and reappears objectively as the passive receptacle of Ferdinand's desire is just such an object: "Fix your eye here," says Bosola. "Constantly," replies Ferdinand, and then after a moment, "Cover her face: mine eyes dazzle." Finally fascination and desire triumph over revulsion: "Let me see her face again" (4.2.262–63, 266, 274).

The desire to see—and to *have seen*—desire entombed in the body draws our attention, once again, to the dramatic corpus as corpse, to the text as bodily remains, to the history of theatre itself as the desire to stop the disappearance of the performing body through its "death" in the unchanging inscriptions of the text. Yet we know that such an entombment in a "permanent" and unchanging text is also an impossibility, as the text itself, in its "permanence" and its "presence," continuously eludes our attempts at closure. The dramatic text, like the tomb in Palestine, continuously denies objectification in any sort of performative "final solution." Like the image of the tomb, it returns again and again throughout the history of theatre, always in a new context, each time with new riddles, new uncertainties, new mystifications.

Thus more than five hundred years after the *Quem Quaeritis* trope was presumably first heard floating on Gothic air, hushed acolytes again step cautiously among imagined tombs, and again the central character of the play exists only as an absence, a hole in the fabric of the text. The acolytes are no longer costumed monks, they are (presumably) professional actors playing out a monklike devotion to absent power and desire in the person of the missing, secretly murdered Duchess. Antonio, the humble and naive husband and accountant to the Duchess, and his friend Delio walk through the graveyard on their way to "work / a friendly reconcilement" with the godless Cardinal. Delio speaks:

> DELIO. Yond's the cardinal's window. This fortification
> Grew from the ruins of an ancient abbey;
> And to yond side o'th'river lies a wall,
> Piece of a cloister, which in my opinion
> Gives the best echo that you ever heard;
> So hollow, and so dismal, and withal
> So plain in the distinction of our words,
> That many have suppos'd it is a spirit
> That answers. (5.3.1-9)

The tombs among which Antonio and Delio walk are situated "in this open court" in which the "questionless" and sequestered dead lie "naked to the injuries / Of stormy weather" (5.3.12–14). The dead do not inquire, but give testimony and judgement in the osseous fragments that appear beneath the inscribed tombs like exhibits in the hearing.

But to what, precisely, do these ruined and runic exhibits stand as testimony? Who or what is on trial here? And who presides? The "fortification"—the seat of political power built upon the remnants of a medieval Catholic culture, the "ruins of an ancient abbey"—buttresses the sides of this court. The walls of the church ("Piece of a cloister"), against which the voice of tragedy is echoed in a "hollow" and "dismal" but "plain" voice, support the back wall. The audience, strangers united by the morbid gaze, sustains the fourth wall, because it is theatre itself that is on trial here—theatre circumscribing the very court within which it stands indicted, arraigned for its attempts to preserve the power of murderous and despotic states by preserving the ruins of culture at the expense of ruined/runed bodies.

The Duchess of Malfi demonstrates what I called earlier a "para-tragic" vision: the self-disarticulating gaze that sees, at least in moments, its own complicity with cruelty, tyranny, and terror. The exhibition or reappearance of the disappeared dead "in this open court" stands as mute testimony to this complicity with terror and death, and the runed bones attest to the violence of economic redistribution wrought upon the body as a result of its initial movements into the networks of currency and exchange.

As if to provide a counterpoint to these resonances, Antonio answers Delio with what might be a typical theatregoer's description of the experience and substance of theatre: "I do love these ancient ruins: / We never tread upon them but we set / Our foot upon some reverend history" (5.3.9–11). History and art are reliquaries, graveyards, and ossuaries filled with shards and bones. Theatre, when it operates as a museum for these relics, is little more than a mausoleum, a place to reverence the dead, while outside the living, like the Duchess herself, are tortured and murdered, or are disappearing before our eyes ("Why seek you the living among the dead?").

Thus while the theatre operates as a diversion, deflecting the gaze from the terrible power of the state and theatre's complicity with it, theatre itself becomes, like the Duke, the accessory to murder and the location of its disappearance, even as it tries to re-cover the evidence.[53] Finally, when theatre can no longer sustain its illusions separately from the state, it, like the cities and churches that it authors, will *seem* to disappear back into them: ". . . all things have their end," says Antonio, "Churches and cities, which have diseases like to men, / Must have like death that we have" (5.3.17–18).

"Like death that we have": the angelic voice of the *Quem Quaeritis* returns as the Echo of death, the mere breath of Being. The angel's "Resurrexi," the triumph over death, is now only an illusion—we are possessed of death just as surely as desire possesses us. The echo that "catches" Antonio speaks not in triumph, but with a "Deadly accent," as a "thing of sorrow," repeating at each turn the terminal fragments of Antonio's responses to Delio. This is the disembodied voice that once again articulates a black absence at the heart of desire, echoing through the bleak ruins of history, marking with a never present voice the forever disappearing locus of the self.

The peculiar, naive agony of Antonio marks the intersection of two terrors we have seen before: the politico-economic terror of state tyranny, and the ontologic terror of death-as-life (two different manifestations, it would seem, of the same featureless terror). These modes of terror meet in Antonio's refusal or inability to confront the terror of Ferdinand's despotism, and in the horror of the systemic failure of representation that ensues—a failure that forces terror to reappear, once again, "outside" as the hallucinated and *real* voice of the Duchess: " 'Tis very like my wife's voice. / ECHO. *Aye, wife's voice*" (5.3.27–28). The Duchess's voice drifts across time and space to re-present to Antonio what he has refused to see. At the same time, the echo also represents the *true identity* of the Duchess in Webster's play—all of the strength and power of her originary voice is reduced, ultimately, to the mere echo of her husband's banalities.

The echo here is the reverbation of a continuously disappearing Return, a Return that is at once identical and utterly different from what had come before. At each point, the disembodied voice of the dead wife matches the fragmented phrase exactly, except in two critical instances: when Antonio says to Delio, "'Tis very like my wife's voice," and the echo replies, "Aye, wife's voice," the affirmation comes floating across the ruins of history with something missing,[54] something that distinguishes it from the voice of the living Antonio—the letter *m*. A few lines later, Antonio (speaking to whom?) says, "Necessity compels me: / Make scrutiny throughout the passages / Of your own life; you'll find it impossible / To fly your fate." The echo replies, *"Oh fly your fate"* (5.3.32–35). Once again, the voice that returns from the far side of history (Necessity) comes fragmented, damaged; it is itself a ruin: the message is missing the letter *t*. *M* and *t:* the empty tomb upon which history is founded. The lack returns, as it does in Marlowe's comma, as the very literal return of the damaged text itself, this time naming itself *as* an emptiness.

Conversely, depending upon where one determines the "origin" of the true voice, in the spoken word or its "plain and distinct" historical echo, the missing letters are not missing at all but stand instead as "supplements" to the insufficiency of the spoken word, as *"letter[s]* installing [themselves] in a living organism to rob it of its *nourishment* and to *distort* (like static = *"bruit parasite")* the pure audibility of a voice."[55] In either case, the truth of history, the truth of the absent Duchess's voice is enunciated *in its difference from* Antonio's voice, a difference that is "empty," like the image of woman in the play, or like the damaged imagination that *is* remembered history. Thus the Derridean supplement operates as the lost power of the Duchess's voice; she is "always already" reduced to mere echo, but Echo here resists Narcissus in the shear fracturing of the Logos. Yet finally, along each axis, the truth of history in the theatre announces itself as a desire for disappearance into this fragmentation, into nothingness and terror: *"I do love these ancient ruins . . ."*

From the opening scenes of repressed and inflamed incestuous desire, through the degenerations into madness, murder, and bestiality, *The Duchess of Malfi* is an apt recapitulation of the formation and disintegration of representation and correspondence from the medieval drama to Renaissance tragedy, a disintegration itself represented in the progressive decomposition of the letter and its voice exemplified in the phobic/fetish response to the female body.

The character of the Duchess herself, constructed through male desire as an absence, represents an objectified desire that generates, in the civilizing impulse of violence, the myth of the incest taboo and its attendant transgression.[56] This taboo and its a priori transgression, depicted in the character of Ferdinand, exemplify the collapse of a primitive exchange system of correspondence in which desire, exemplified in the body of the Duchess, is not able to break the constraints of solipsism in order to find itself in another object, either of desire or of Phobic dread. This frustration in Ferdinand engenders the craving for an incest that goes beyond mere desire for his sister, and seems to demand that desire possess itself in the total fusion of familial blood:

> Damn her! that body of hers,
> While that my blood ran pure in't, was more worth
> Than that which thou wouldst comfort, called a soul. (4.1.119–21)

The impossibility of this desire produces madness and a regression of culture into bestiality: a degenerative movement from the Phobic terrorism of representation and exchange "back" to the Deimic terror of chaos and death. There seems to be no escape here. Either we suffer the terrorism of our disappearance into the informational systems of theatre/civilization, or we undergo the terror of madness, bestiality, and death when civilization disappears. This is a return and re-enunciation of the dark sensibility we encountered in *Cambyses, King of Persia*, a sensibility grounded in the imagery of the *Quem Quaeritis,* in which the "social ignominy and the cadaverous degradation of the torture victim" are equated with "divine splendor."[57]

Yet as the play looks back to its seeming origins in the reappearance of the absent/present body, it also looks forward, in a kind of prophetic pronouncement of yet another stage in the commodification of the body through terror, namely the body's further reformulation within and without the theatrical silence of the coming Interregnum (the years from 1648 until 1660, during which the Puritans supposedly closed the theatres because of their immoral influence). But it is not until the drama "reemerges" (yet another questionable "reemergence" of a theatre that apparently never really disappeared) after 1660,[58] in the full force of its representational reformation, that we can assess the effects of *this béance,* and the subtle yet profound changes that occur as a result of its particular violences. The voice of the Duchess, calling through time, prophesies that terror.

4

GESTURING THROUGH THE FLAMES

COMMODIFICATION, FETISH, AND VIOLENCE IN RESTORATION DRAMA

The many divorces and reconciliations in the "unnatural marriage of Freud and Marx"[1] during the past half century attest to the difficulty of creating a theoretics that adequately accounts for the two most powerful economic forces of theatre's history: the class economics of the political order, and the gender economics of the psychosexual order. This concern is shown, for example, in the recent interest in a more overtly politicized Lacanian psychoanalysis lying at the bottom of much feminist theory, as well as in those theorists who have maintained the sexual/political economic distinction through an insistence on the distributive nature of the categories: I am thinking here of Gilles Deleuze and Felix Guattari's work,[2] as well as some of the later work of Jean Baudrillard.

But while I make no presumptions to solving this apparent impasse, I think it might be instructive to shift the focus away from the conflicting teleologies of Marx and Freud and see, however imperfectly, both economic forces, the political and the psychosexual, at one particular moment of their apparent differentiation: the site of their production on the Restoration stage.[3] One possible key to understanding this double (or multiple) economy, I think, lies in the dual (or multiple) nature of the *fetish*—that highly invested object which so easily moves from materiality to ideality and back again.

I would like, then, to investigate the Restoration stage as the site in which the violent, metonymic chain of production was translated into money and capital through the creation of an economics of excess and expenditure. This economic system was constructed around a specific fetishized commodity[4] and its attendant system of signs, and moved almost imperceptibly into an exteriorized, discursive system of wit and gesture. The specific commodity that was produced, reproduced, and consumed on this stage was and is the gendered body of capital itself—that economy of alienation and production in which gender is manufactured and commodities are gendered.

It is important to remember, however, that this doubled[5] economics of desire represented by the fetish—the doubling through which the commodity takes on and signifies the aura of desire, while the self takes on the blank character of an object—represents a more widespread splitting and fragmentation of desiring economics that eventually develop along multiple and seemingly opposed theoretical axes, of which Marxist and Freudian theoretics are only two examples.[6] Taken together, however, the Marxist and Freudian conceptions of the fetish object, despite their apparent incompatibilities and contradictions, form a complementary circulatory system of the fetish, which now moves from an alienated, subjective desire, through desire's realization in material production, back into a reconstructed and estranged desire, and so forth.[7]

In this circulatory system of the fetish, it becomes clear that the opposition between idea and materiality (a non-Marxian opposition, I might add) is an Imaginary opposition. As one axis of the fetish folds imperceptibly into the other, both the materiality and ideality of the fetish meet, as Baudrillard, and Deleuze and Guattari, suggest in quite different ways, in the marketplace of the sign.[8] The sign comes to represent, in fact, the fragmentary (for *fragmentary* one might read *reified*) existence of the commodity-fetish as both object and idea.

This fragmented economy, as Michael McKeon points out, differentiates itself on the Restoration stage even as that same theatre mystifies the essential connectedness of the various forms (psychic, literary, philosophic, and political) of these economic (sub)systems.[9] The paradoxical differentiation and concealment of the various systems is paralleled in the disparate modes of differentiation and mystification by which the belabored sexual body is both further alienated from the self, and finally commodified in its fetishized objecthood.

This stage or marketplace of desiring production demonstrates its fetishist proclivities early and most clearly, perhaps, in early Restoration tragedies (and to some degree in the formal movements of tragedy in general). Such a play is Thomas Otway's *Venice Preserv'd,* a play that seems to suggest an entire reformulation of the Jacobean economics of desire away from death's exhaustion and toward death's deferral.[10] Indeed, the Jacobean plenitude of death that we see in Webster's *Duchess* already portends the economic reorganization that emerges in Otway. This morbid plenitude represents the hopeless binarism that has death as its resolution: the ceaseless oscillation of the fetish object from psychic terrain to socioeconomic field has an emptiness at its center, death at its core. This, again, is the fetish's link to its other appearance as phobic object, an object that comes to represent that absence of being *in* the binarism.

We can see, through the development of the drama in the plays of Otway, Congreve, Etherege, and Behn,[11] a preconscious concern with the flows of production, with *value* as the product of occupational energy (what Marxism might call "labor" and what Freud called *Besetzung*), which is both expended and created along the metonymic chain of (largely) male desire and production. Along these two axes, *fetish* is that which "rises" to (Marxist) exchange, and "falls" to (Freudian) repression. Thus repression forms a rough corollation with exchange through the continuous *displacement* or circulation of the fetish; surplus value (Marx) would then appear the corollary to a Freudian phobia or Lacanian lack—an effect that has no objective existence but in the symbol, either money (*that* mystification), or the fetishized dream image of woman's body.

The question implied by this explication remains only partially answered by Marxist theories of power and is generally submerged in the historicist writings of Foucault: what is the specific *unifying* force that organizes these object-bodies for their eventual socioeconomic exploitation? What might we call the social tendency that imagines the stages of economic exchange even as the forms of capitalism emerge? What *is* this circulatory system of the fetish, finally, but *theatre,* the very site of violent, fetish *production?* Indeed, we can read the Restoration theatre not merely as the reflection of these economic reorganizations, but also as the locus in which they are produced, exchanged, distributed, and consumed—the circularity of desire's object production, in and out of bodies, in and out of mind, defining the exchanges of the marketplace whose productions are predicated on a terror of loss, lack, and hungering.

Venice is precisely such an anorexic play, a "desiring-production" that feeds only on the desire to feed.[12] In *Venice,* this apparatus systematically consumes its participants as each plays out his or her own cravings. The play realizes these consumptions by translating the body—or more specifically the female body-as-object—into a *currency* that allows for its movement and eventual depletion through the systems of exchange. Ultimately, the fleshed body, exemplified in the character of Belvidera, experiences its disappearance into the economic order as a *terror of starvation* that is redeployed as a *terrorism of expenditure,*[13] which in turn empties itself in the systems of representation.

The play's references to starvation and hunger are epidemic: Jaffeir first describes honesty (a word used later by the rebels to describe their daggers) as a "damned, starving quality," and his friend Pierre responds by telling him that "honest men / Are the soft, easy cushions on which knaves / Repose and fatten. Were all mankind villains, / They'd starve each other."[14] Pierre goes on to decry political passivity and demands action in the face of this hungering, but Jaffeir, who senses that Pierre's craving is cannibalistic, deflects this demand, and identifies his own demon as "Want! worldly want!" (2.1.356).

Moreover, a larger conceptual famine seems to be the operational principle of the world at large. Priests are "starved" by prayer, and society's citizens "starved like beggar's brats in frosty weather" (1.1.279). On the domestic scene, Jaffeir describes his marriage to Belvidera in similar and decidedly parasitic terms: "My life feeds on her," he says to Pierre (1.1.78). And Belvidera invites his consumption: "Starve me with wantings," she beseeches him late in the play, invoking the most terrifying specter of suffering she can (5.2.94). Jaffeir becomes consumer, Belvidera his commodity.

Conditions and images of deprivation course through the play as well. Priuli has lost his daughter, Jaffeir his wife, and Belvidera her husband. Pierre turns away from Aquilina, whom he loves, and she in turn is deprived of her lover, Pierre, as a result of the economic necessity that impresses her as a courtesan. Antonio the senator, apparently loved by no-one, buys affection and abuse with the coins in his purse. Meanwhile Jaffeir, already without his wife, is further deprived of Pierre, her surrogate, on the scaffold. Finally, in a kind of judgement upon the entire system that would produce this deprivation as its most tangible product, the revolutionaries vow to deliver the city as a whole to "waste and desolation."

In its showings of hunger and deprivation *Venice Preserv'd* is very near the most primal impulses of the drama, in the recollection, regulation, and display of pain and desire articulated through the differentiating function of political and economic law, a law that is, in Nietzsche's words, "burned into the memory" by virtue of its terrorizing, specular excess. *Venice* begins in the memory of this terror:

> In your brigandine you sailed to see
> The Adriatic wedded by our Duke,
> And I was with you: your unskillful pilot
> Dashed us upon a rock; when to your boat
> You made for safety, entréd first yourself;
> The affrighted Belvidera following next,
> As she stood trembling on the vessel side,
> Was by a wave washed off into the deep. (1.1.31–38)

The remembrance is elemental, *mythic,* and is recalled by Jaffeir (up to this point Priuli's protégé) with a vividness attesting to its recollected force. It seems that during the annual celebration of the fabled marriage of Venice with the sea, Belvidera, Priuli's daughter, is washed overboard. Jaffeir, with little thought given to his own safety, leaps into the water and pulls her from the undifferentiated terror of the raging, mythic sea.

Following this episode, Belvidera and Jaffeir fall in love and marry. Jaffeir thus relocates Belvidera from the mythic order into the law and family through a marriage contract. But in the eyes of Priuli, Jaffeir has not taken her in lawful marriage but has "Seduced the weakness of my age's darling, / My only child, and stole her from my bosom" (1.1.25–26). Priuli is inordinately and pathetically outraged at the theft of his property: "You stole her from me; like a thief you stole her, / At dead of night; that cursed hour you chose / to rifle me of all my heart held dear" (1.1.49–51). He curses Jaffeir with "want" because he will not relent in his possession of the daughter: "Drudge to feed loathsome life; get brats and starve" (1.1.110). Jaffeir, however, asserts that Belvidera has not been stolen at all but has merely "paid me with herself" in return for her life (1.1.48).

The processes of exchange that develop later in the play begin here with the usurpation of the mythical father's (incestuous?) desire for the "stolen" daughter. The terror of deprivation and starvation follows this *imagined* crime—when we meet Jaffeir he is already feeling the pinch of want and hunger as Priuli's rejected protégé: "Home I would go / But that my doors are hateful to my eyes, / Filled and dammed up with gaping creditors" (1.1.112–14). The roots of the oedipal logic of wealth grow from this terror of loss.

Yet even though Jaffeir has "now not fifty ducats in the world" he is "still in love, and pleased with ruin" (1.1.116–17). He sleeps sated "with soft content about my head," glutted with Belvidera's "luscious sweets of plenty" (1.1.99). Belvidera is associated again and again with plenitude in Jaffeir's mind, the result of an accrual of value in her body through the remembered history of the play: she not only owes Jaffeir *her* existence, she has cost him "half his life" and more—all of the wealth that he has forsaken in order to take her as his wife (1.1.113–17). Love is thus inversely equated with power and wealth through the copulative and consumptive functions of Belvidera's body. The affluence and prestige that had been extended to Jaffeir in the *promise* of Priuli are reinvested in Belvidera, who can, of course, never hope to realize such a price. As an overvalued commodity "purchased on margin," she faces certain depression and eventual collapse.

The disparity between price and value localized in Belvidera produces an inflated sense of gravity that permeates her relationship with Jaffeir. His emotional overflow, and her own excessive erotic and emotional dependence, seem totally out of proportion to the actual perceptions of value that accrue to "normal" marital relationships. She strains under the weight of this overvaluation, and the distended excesses of her speech cover an emptiness of significance in her words:

> If love be treasure, we'll be wondrous rich:
> I have so much, my heart will surely break with't.
> Vows cannot express it: when I would declare
> How great's my joy, I am dumb with the big thought:
> I swell and sigh, and labor with my longing. (1.1.341–45)

In fact, the issue of her "labor" is a longing that is aborted in terror and death. As I will demonstrate later, the *sign* of her love—her swelling, sighing body—is gradually transmuted and dispersed into the murderous dagger wielded by the terrorist Renault.

The disparity between price and value exemplified by these emotional overvaluations is ironically heightened by the worthlessness with which Belvidera and Jaffeir speak of themselves. Jaffeir is constantly telling us how wretched he is, that he is "not worth a ducat" (1.1.251). Moreover, this worthlessness is a product of his own behavior, for he seems obsessed with giving things up: Priuli's promised wealth, Belvidera, the dagger that he has exchanged for her, his friendship with Pierre. He is filled with such ambivalence and moral turpitude that when he does make a moral choice, it is by necessity the wrong one and disaster follows, feeding his sense of worthlessness.

Belvidera, on the other hand, speaks in language typical of an anorexic; she sees herself as bloated, pregnant with desires she cannot satisfy, desires that seem to distend her flesh.[15] In addition, there is a gulf between this aberrant self-image and what she "should be." In an expression that seems to contradict her "swelling" appearance in the beginning of the play, she tells Jaffeir that he must "Look not upon me as I am, a woman, / But as a bone, thy wife" (3.2.116–19). As a means of rectifying the discrepancy between these two images, she asks Jaffeir to "starve me with wantings" as punishment for her vacillating faith in him, even though some fifteen lines earlier Jaffeir had prayed to "Feed her with plenty" (5.2.94, 79). This fasting and self-flagellation are carried into the larger context of the play. Belvidera is equated with the city of Venice itself through the imagery of starvation, want, and consumption suffered beneath the state/father that governs it. The revolutionary Pierre says of Venice:

> How lovely the Adriatic whore,
> Dressed in her flames, will shine! —devouring
>   flames,
> Such as shall burn her to the watery bottom
> And hiss in her foundation! (2.3.96–99)

Compare this to Belvidera's despairing exhortation late in the play:

> Oh, give me daggers, fire, or water!
> How could I bleed, how burn, how drown, the waves
> Huzzing and booming round my sinking head,
> Till I descended to the peaceful bottom! (5.3.136–39)

This equation between the self-starving Belvidera and the city destroyed by revolutionary desire gives us a clue to the political ramifications of the common "neurosis" of anorexia. The problems of self-image that are associated with this obsession are not created "in the family" (although they are often deployed there), or even in culture's obsession with certain types of body images, but rather in the organizational processes by which the political order creates and maintains women and men as coinage whose true value has nothing to do with the *signs* of value they carry on the surfaces of their bodies. The body, in this sense, becomes the location upon which violent sociopolitical *assignments* intersect and obliterate the body's "true" value, which is, of course, no value. Bulimia/anorexia becomes illness as a life and death metaphor for all of the struggles and counter-struggles between the body and the political order, an order that tries to discipline and reform the body through each of its consumptive/productive functions—eating, defecating, speaking/writing, sexuality. The problematic as we see it here is not merely the objectification of the body, which is probably inevitable in culture and certainly in the theatre, but the *way* the body is objectified within the web of specific socioeconomic relations.

In *Venice* we can see bodies being organized and aligned along the axis of production/consumption, an axis that is still shifting from an economy of symbolic exchange, emblematized in the figure of Belvidera, to an economy of desiring-production, emblematized in the courtesan Aquilina. Counterpoised against this we can see in the anorexic language and imagery of the play a critical *self-control* that is exhibited either as *withholding* production/consumption (through starvation or excess), or as self-induced *expenditure* (purging, aggrandizement, exteriorization—*katharsis*). Each becomes a strategy of resistance to the body's triangulation and commodification as a cultural fetish object. Ironically, though, the resistance that begins as an opposition to cultural determinism almost instantaneously reformulates itself in a binarism created between the coercive and specular image of the bloated/hungering body, and the image of the body as a fully articulated (lean and muscular) plenitude, the body as the reflex and extension of culture itself.

The mirror of that extension, the "striated space" that describes the organizational continuity of the body in time and space—the city-as-theatre—reflects and is reflected by grids and networks of discourse, the organized routes of exchange that localize and describe the body as an object *within* the city.

It is interesting to note here the significance of the city in the ideology of the revolutionaries. Pierre in particular seems to confuse the *city/body* of Venice with the *power of state* that governs it: what, for example, will the destruction of Venice accomplish? What will be left for the revolutionaries once the city is delivered over to the "devouring / flames, / Such as shall burn her to the watery bottom / and hiss in her foundation"? There is apparently a discrepancy or confusion in Pierre's mind as he conflates price paid (blood, in this case, or violence), and value obtained (power). But his confusion resolves itself when we appreciate the value of the city in the terrorist's plan. Its worth rests entirely in its spectacular possibilities *as a sign of terror;* price and value are seemingly identical because both will be *realized* at once when the city/body is consumed and disappears into blood and flames.

The inability or refusal to differentiate between price and value thus generates both the flow of dilated emotion, and later, the circulation of extremist violence in the play. There is, then, an equation established between sexual desire and political violence, as the actual value of each is concealed in different ways within the processes of exchange and later exteriorized through expenditure.

In fact, the sexual and political merge continually in the course of the play. We can see this in the ostensibly erotic relationship between Belvidera and Jaffeir, a relationship that has decidedly politico-economic overtones: she is, after all, an active issue in the marketplace of political intrigue. As such, she needs translation into moveable currency. Her exchange value is ultimately transposed into a more visible and easily manipulated coinage understood by the rebels—a currency that can flow easily through the semioeconomic network of the play. Her value, which had earlier been dispersed into a promissory discourse centered on her body, is now transferred to the dagger that Jaffeir offers as collateral to his loyalty—the dagger that will "buy" his wife's death should he betray the plot.

Indeed, all of Priuli's centralized power—power that is transmitted through his spoken promise of wealth and prestige to Jaffeir, then reinvested in Belvidera after she is purchased by him, and finally retranslated into the spoken promise of Jaffeir to the rebels—is finally objectified and localized in the dagger itself. We can see in this localizing process not only the objectification and commodification of Belvidera in the political marketplace, but also the degeneration of the power of the spoken word. Priuli's original promise of wealth to Jaffeir needed no collateral, but Jaffeir's promise to the rebels requires the certification of his loyalty in the exchange of the phallic dagger/wife.

We might compare the uncertainty of Belvidera's exchange value and her almost complete absence of *use* value to the set price of Aquilina, the courtesan. She too is bought and sold according to what the market demands, but she has little worth as a mere object of symbolic exchange. Her price is seemingly determined entirely by use value, but this use value is also made dangerously ambiguous in the confusion between price and worth. The senator Antonio buys her with the coins in his purse, but her former lover Pierre has, in Jaffeir's words, paid for her with his life, the "dearest purchase . . . of labors" (1.1.166). Though Aquilina may be cheaply "bought" she is expensively "purchased," and once again the confusion between price and value generates an expenditure that is located specifically in her body. In Pierre's case the play's erotic and political disbursement is represented in his disposal of Aquilina; in Antonio's case, in the exhaustion of desire through the theatricality of violence.

At both the sociopolitical level and the level of sexual desire, then, the economics of expenditure is born of the conflation of price and value in which the self-interest of the state is initially concealed. Price paid and value assigned seem to be identical, and objects appear to be perfectly represented by the signs of worth inscribed into them. Everything is in balance. But while state power seeks to maintain this apparent equilibrium, anti-state forces, the forces of pure expenditure, seek to shatter the seeming. These forces look not to production and its obfuscations of value in the generation of signs and their concomitant slippages, but to catastrophe or loss, as the basis of power and exchange. They look to the economics of terrorism in which value and price seem to meet in the act of violent disbursement.[16] George Bataille addresses this disbursement in a decidedly Dionysian, theatrical way:

> A human society can have . . . an *interest* in considerable losses, in catastrophes that, *while conforming to well-defined needs,* provoke tumultuous depressions, crises of dread, and, in the final analysis, a certain orgiastic state.[17]

Again, we can compare this to the rebel's description of the orgiastic blood bath that awaits Venice:

> Fire the city round in several places,
> Or with our cannon (if it dare resist)
> Batter't to ruin. But above all I charge you,
> Shed blood enough; spare neither sex nor age,
> Name nor condition. . . .
> If possible, let's kill the very name
> Of senator, and bury it in blood. (3.2.329–32)

The catastrophe of the rebellion is not designed to produce anything but terror—a lack or an absence to which an unimaginable, unrepresentable, and absolute value accrues. Terror is, in this sense, the means by which the empty and exploitative nature of surplus value is exteriorized. Paradoxically, however, through revolutionary terrorism, terror's "value" is, in turn, estranged from the enormous cost of *its* production through its repression in signification. This alienation finally *subverts* the very unrepresentability that terrorism seeks to communicate.

This is the impasse of revolutionary violence, but it is also the essential problematic of poetry—which Bataille says is "synonymous with expenditure," a "meaning . . . close to *sacrifice*"—and most especially of theatre, a phenomenon that is born, in the words of Artaud, in a certain "gratuitousness provoking acts without use or profit." Consequently poetry, theatre, and terror intersect in a pure, unrepresentable expenditure *(katharsis)* which is at every moment threatened by the repressive alienation of representation.[18]

In *Venice,* the impasse of unrepresentability is circumscribed by an *absence of references* to hunger in the middle portions of the play, references that re-

turn again in the final scenes. Although there is still a parasitic desire operating at the framing edges of the play, the abundant allusions to food and
feeding that course through the opening and closing scenes cease in the middle.
It is as if hunger silences itself at some unlocatible point because it cannot
identify its craving, or wills not to. Instead, attention is suddenly turned to
human butchery and intimations of cannibalism in the image of a sadomasochistic *pharmakos:*

> Come, lead me forward now like a tame lamb
> To sacrifice; thus in his fatal garlands,
> Decked fine, and pleased, the wanton skips and plays,
> Trots by the enticing, flattering priestess' side,
> And much transported with his little pride,
> Forgets his dear companions of the plain
> Till by her, bound, he's on the altar lain;
> Yet then too hardly bleats, such pleasure's in the pain. (4.1.88–95)

Not inconsequentially, it is when the hungering discourse ends that daggers
and swords and human sacrifice appear, signalling the metamorphosis of
craving into violence and terrorism.

   The catastrophic deprivation that initiates the mutation of hungering terror into terrorism is indicated by the loss of the dagger that Jaffeir hands over
to Renault. This dagger is, at the moment, the only real dagger in the play,
the only one that exists as a tangible *performative* object, an actual stage property. As such it exudes what Walter Benjamin would call an "aura"[19] in
which its particularity engenders a sense of infinite value that surrounds the
object itself, especially as it represents the ultimate prize, the lover Belvidera.
Although it may not be "worth" as much as she is, and although its value
may be somewhat indeterminate and partially alienated, it still maintains a
specialty: it is *the* dagger that Jaffeir has given over, the object that then
becomes the focal point of the exchange economy of the play. As such, the
dagger becomes the repository of the sexual, economic, and militant energies
that have been localized in it through speech and exchange. It has become a
fetish object. But it also serves to cover over the blank space of terror inasmuch as it represents the potential for pain, murder, and disappearance. It is
not only a fetish object, it is a phobic object as well.

   The murderous power of the dagger as fetish/phobic object is clearly revealed when Jaffeir turns it and Belvidera over to the rebel contingent. This
exchange works both as a threat of terror and death to Belvidera, and as a
symbolic castration of Jaffeir. When he makes the exchange, and more importantly, when he defines this action as a promise of loyalty, there is a
transference of power, another expenditure. He becomes increasingly effete
and disaffected after the exchange is made. The dominant Pierre suddenly
becomes the object of Jaffeir's overinflated emotional outpourings which he
expresses in the imagery of torture:

> O Pierre, wert thou but she,
> How I could pull thee down to my heart,
> Gaze on thee till my eyestrings cracked with
>   love,
> Till all my sinews with fire extended,
> Fixed me upon the rack of ardent longing. (2.3.228–32)

What we once might have thought to be great love on Jaffeir's part, now seems little more than a primary narcissism expressed as sadomasochistic desire craving itself to death, a death represented, once again, by the dagger: "A thousand daggers, all in honest hands, / And have not I a friend will stick one here?" (2.2.63–64).

The violent and sexual connotations of the dagger as fetish/phobic object are revealed again later in the play when Renault, the aging rebel, holds it before the cloistered Belvidera like some glistening, baroque penis. Here the dagger represents "the pledge of a false husband's love," or in Lacanian terms, a *phallus,* the free-floating copula or signifier inculcated with power like the body of Belvidera at the play's start. As phallic object, the dagger ultimately becomes the tool of political and sexual extortion as long as it is able to represent the *possibility* of the unrepresentable—the promise of terror, murder, and death: the threat of non-being, in other words. Here terror seems to become the mirror-image of life itself.

The promise of terror is radically undercut, however, by an antithetical movement of exchange in the play. Early on Pierre literally "buys" the use of Jaffeir's dagger with a purse of coins:

PIERRE.
> *[Gives him a purse]*
> Here's something to buy pins,
> Marriage is chargeable.
>   JAFF. *[aside].*   I but half wished
> To see the devil, and he's here already.
> —Well!
> What must this buy—rebellion, murder, treason?
> Tell me which way I must be damned for this.
> (2.2.33–38)

In this case the dagger is directly equated with use value as represented by money. Now the function of money is exactly that it is a uniform and easily reproduced token of exchange for given commodities. But in *Venice,* the function of money is by and large usurped by the dagger, which moves with much greater fluidity through the systems of exchange. The only time money is exchanged in the play is when it purchases a dagger. Pierre buys Jaffeir's, and Antonio buys Aquilina's. The dagger seems to be the preferred currency in the play, and functions almost identically to money. But whereas money serves to conceal the *violence* of exploitation and appropriation, the dagger marks, as I have already suggested, the precise location in which material desire reemerges as violence.

At any rate, the mechanics of valuation are the same for daggers as for money—like money for example, the value of the dagger becomes more and more dispersed as daggers multiply in the play. And multiply they do. As the hungering discourse ceases, there suddenly seem to be daggers and swords everywhere:

> PIERRE.   Daggers, daggers, are much better.
> JAFF.   Ha!
> PIERRE.   Daggers.
> JAFF.   But where are they?
> PIERRE.   Oh, a thousand
> May be disposed in honest hands in Venice. (2.2.58–60)

Not only are we are told that there will soon be a sword sheathed in every breast in Venice, but *textual* citations also abound. The word itself appears some thirty or more times, often in repetitive, incantatory exchanges like the one just cited.

But notice that *these* daggers exist only as discourse, as words. We never *see* them as we do the single dagger given in exchange for Belvidera. The immateriality of these "spoken" daggers ghosts the futility of the revolution that gave them birth, for as the number of "daggers" grows through the course of the play, and the descriptions of violence and mayhem increase, the real dagger, the fetish/phobic object, locus of power and terror, disappears entirely into discourse and diminishes in real potency—it literally disappears into the play and is never seen again. The diffusions of power localized in sword and dagger finally become so complete that no rebellion takes place, no widespread killings occur, because the violence that once resided in the dagger as pure, unimaged potential energy has been expended in language and theatre. The remnants of dispersed power reside only in memory once again, in a discourse that invests false value onto objects created by it.

The (im)potentialities that have lain beneath the surface of the plot degenerate even further as the symbolic value of the dagger continues to decay. Once the dagger was the objectification of (questionable) loyalty and (perverse) love; but its symbolism shifts to the manifestly pornographic, when the exhibition of the dagger/body to Antonio's illicit gaze by Aquilina is effected through the payment of money. Yet, ironically, it is now money that conceals the dagger's relationship to real violence; it is money that prevents the dagger from doing what it was created to do—killing the Enemy. The dagger becomes abstracted, a mere sign of itself—it becomes, in a word, theatricalized. Finally, in a kind of genetic anticipation, the dagger becomes a mere prop in the brothel scene between Antonio and Aquilina, a phobic/

fetish object in the psychosexual murder fantasy which Aquilina has been paid to enact, but an object whose real danger is held at bay by the true periapt, Antonio's purse:

> AQUIL. *(draws a dagger)* See you this, sir?
> ANT. O laud, a dagger! O laud! it is naturally my
> aversion; I cannot endure the sight on't; hide it,
> for heaven's sake! I cannot look that way till it be
> gone—hide it, hide it, oh, oh, hide it!
> AQUIL. Yes. In your heart I'll hide it. (5.2.181–85)

Once again the seeming phobic/fetish object appears and disappears with a dazzling ambiguity within the networks of exchange. Once again, the theater's complicities with that network are named in the play between Antonio and Aquilina; the dissipation of violence against the state (the dagger in the hand of Aquilina, the revolutionary's lover) is being effected through the economic power of the state (Antonio) displayed and executed *as theatre*.

This dissipation of revolutionary violence through the mechanics of capital flow not only strips objects of use value, it also reduces the Senecan brutality of the anti-state guerrilla forces to mere illegal activity:

> Can thy great heart descend so vilely low,
> Mix with hired slaves, bravoes, and common stab-
>   bers,
> Nose-slitters, alley-lurking villains? join
> With such a crew, and take a ruffian's wages,
> To cut the throats of wretches as they sleep? (3.2.160–64)

Indeed, through the medium of exchange, in this case the speech of Belvidera, criminal mayhem is reduced even further. Initially the vision of terror in Belvidera's description of the coming bloodbath is expressed in these terms:

>   . . . the poor, tender lives
> Of all those little infants which the swords
> Of murderers are whetting for this moment.
> Think thou already hear'st their dying screams,
> Think that thou seest their sad, distracted mothers
> Kneeling before their feet, and begging pity,
> With torn, dishevelled hair and streaming eyes,
> Their naked, mangled breasts besmeared with
>   blood,
> And even the milk with which they fondled their babes.
> Softly they hushed, dropping in anguish from 'em. (4.1.48–57)

But the power foaming in the doge's sea, the potency of the seminal terror that results in shipwrecks and "mangled breasts besmeared with blood / and

. . . milk," is transformed at play's end to a "sea of milk" skimmed by "ships of amber" (5.2.151).

In every case the transformation of expenditure into depletion is managed through the agency of representation: disbursing violence and desire as image, word, and coin; dispersing power into verbal threat; rechanneling the movements of desire in both Priuli and Renault into plotted intrigue and high-powered political exchange; and most significantly for our purposes, transmuting libidinal, political, and economic terror into an absurdist terrorism through Antonio's theatre of perversion. Ultimately, this dissipation of power through various modes of representation works to the advantage of the state, and in the final analysis, it is the rebels' insistence on assuming the significative functions of this terror and power that dictate their downfall. What little force they have is bled off into the rhetoric of conspiracy and ideological bombast.

In *Venice,* as elsewhere, terror is deeply involved with desire and the processes of commodification and exchange. This is especially true as desire is frustrated in the political and economic arena. The objectification of desire in the body-as-commodity may seem at one level a partial solution to the economic impasse of desire and demand that is exemplified by the antagonism between Jaffeir and Priuli over the affections of Belvidera. However, this "solution" is itself subverted by an opposing violence that also seeks to "free" the body/self by relocating it through the orgiastic excesses of anti-state terrorism.

Thus at some level, conscious or unconscious, terrorism aims at the destruction of the representational systems of power that hold the body in economic/political bondage. However, terrorism by necessity gives itself over to the bondage of the very representational systems from which it earlier sought liberation, because in order for terrorism to be effective it must *display* the unrepresentability of terror through the very systems that it seeks to destroy. Consequently Pierre's conflation of value and price in the destruction of Venice is terribly misconstrued, because the image of terror that this destruction produces must always be a product of the orders of power. This is, to a lesser degree, the same dilemma that theatre confronts in its ongoing historical ambivalence over the terror of thought. Even when it seeks to expose the tyranny, its truth is appropriated by the dictates of culture in the very reproductions of specularity-as-truth.

We see this problematic reappear again and again in the theatre. Much of the later Restoration theatre's attempts to flout the discipline of the Interregnum's Puritan zealotry by mounting seemingly decadent and "immoral" plays, while at the same time mocking the very culture that came to the theatre to see these plays, reveals a deep and troubled ambivalence about the formulations of power, authority, and its subversions throughout the period.[20] Yet what is most interesting and ironic in these plays is not merely the development of a specific kind of disciplining gaze and its concomitant strategies of dissembling and deportment, but the *movement* from resistance to "moral" capitulation through the period.

Indeed, what is perhaps most ironic is that the comedy of manners or wit finally accomplished what the Puritans could not—the reformation and control of the sexual body and its passions through the harsh discipline of derision, and the production, through the canons of dissembling and gesture, of "correct" manners and deportment.[21] These seemingly "decadent" and "immoral" plays literally set the stage for the later development of domestic and sentimental tragedy, which finally (and fictively) realized the puritanical virtues of family, morality, and stability.[22] Although this might seem a mere continuation of the old debate regarding the moral intention of Restoration playwrights, it really is more than that. I am suggesting a cross-penetration in Restoration drama between the production of discipline in a Nietzschean theatre of economized violence, and the subsequent theatricalization of that violence and humiliation in the civil war culture of the Interregnum.[23] The debate, in other words, is really no debate: whether the plays were flying in the face of Puritan morality, or whether they were punishing mockeries of decadent public behaviors, is moot; the theatre accomplished both goals at once. Restoration theatre, in fact, seems to have operated as a means of social control which was at once part of the social milieu and separate from it; it mocked both aristocratic and Puritan ideology and behaviors at once. Here, theatre's sociopolitical agenda seems, somehow, its own—an agenda that can be glimpsed in the Restoration's disruptive, discontinuous formulations of tragic and comic forms.[24]

What we see in the Restoration plays of wit, then, is not so much an *evolution* of the process of objectifying the body and its passions. Much of the Restoration comedic theatre was, rather, an asymptotic realization in which the body's passions were "flattened" onto a "surface" where they might be produced and reproduced as *mannerisms*—behaviors that could be constrained, controlled, and reformed through the gaze and the witty report of the tongue, and conversely, could also be mimicked, hidden, and deflected from the gaze and the witticism through dissembling or *acting*.

Thus while *Venice Preserv'd* demonstrates a tendency towards a more literal objectification and commodification in the tragedy, Restoration comedy of manners demonstrates a *performative* objectification by which pleasure might finally be extracted and reproduced precisely and self-consciously *as theatre*.[25] Taken together, the two different but complementary dramas demonstrate a process of commodification and "derealization" of the body that finally extends beyond both politics and economics, and represents a much broader historical process of redefinition and reorganization centered in and on the body. I would suggest that this reorganization finds its articulation through the body by means of psychic and physical torture and humiliation, a systematized abuse that exteriorized and economized the body in a Nietzschean theatre of morals: the Restoration stage.

Harriet, the strong-willed heroine *contra* rake of Etherege's *The Man of Mode*,[26] is having her hair done by Busy, her maid, when the following exchange takes place:

> BUSY. Dear madam! Let me set that curl in order.
> HARRIET. Let me alone; I will shake 'em all out of order.
> BUSY. Will you never leave this wildness?
> HARRIET. Torment me not.
> BUSY. Look! There's a knot falling off.
> HARRIET. Let it drop.
> BUSY. But one pin, dear madam.
> HARRIET. How do I daily suffer under thy officious fingers (3.1.1–10)

Harriet's supplication ("Let me alone; . . . Torment me not") seems on the surface merely the response of a petulant and impatient young woman chafing against the constraints of decorum and fashion. Even though her anguish is obviously the cumulative result of many such uncomfortable sessions with Busy, we are still likely to read Harriet's responses as peevish and exaggerated reactions to a rather ordinary situation. But if we read on, we realize that the torment to which Harriet reacts is only part of a much more pervasive and morbid social conditioning to which she is subject:

> BUSY. Ah the difference that is between you and my Lady Dapper! how
>   uneasy she is if the least thing be amiss about her!
> HARRIET. She is indeed most exact! nothing is ever wanting to make her
>   ugliness remarkable!
> BUSY. Jeering people say so!
> HARRIET. Her powdering, painting, and her patching never fail in public to
>   draw the tongues and eyes of all the men upon her. (3.1.11–19)

The threat of punishment and pain in the form of derision and humiliation is real, inasmuch as the desire to undergo the torments of cosmetic treatments is generated by the terror of "jeering people," most often men, who wait with honed eyes and whetted tongues to ridicule the slightest failure of deportment. This situation indeed constitutes the application of torture[27] as a means of correcting the body in order to produce in and on it the proper lineaments, the correct postures, the exact form of appearance dictated by a culture of appearances. When Dorimant suggests to Harriet that he take her to Court to "show her off," she replies:

> HARRIET. And expect to be taken in pieces, have all my features examined,
>   every motion censured, and on the whole be condemned to be but pretty,
>   or a beauty of the lowest rate. What think you?
> DORIMANT. The women, nay, the very lovers who belong to the drawing-
>   room will maliciously allow you more than that; they always grant what

> is apparent, that they may the better be believed when they name concealed faults they cannot easily be disproved in.
>
> HARRIET. Beauty runs as a great a risque exposed at court as wit does on the stage, where the ugly and the foolish, all are free to censure. (4.1.151–63)

This manipulation follows a familiar pattern in the theatre—the complete disarticulation and reformation of the body effected both in the Court as theatre, and in the theatre as court. But here the process is more stylized, more precise in its instruction.

Similarly, Busy's desire to set things right with "but one pin" suggests the instrumentation of a very real pain to insure that appearances are maintained at all costs. That "one pin" also signifies the keen and minute attention to detail that this discipline entails:

> DORIMANT.   I fear this
> restlessness of the body, madam, proceeds from an unquietness of the mind. What unlucky accident puts you out of humor; a point ill-washed? knots spoiled i'the making up, hair shaded awry, or some other little mistake in setting you in order? (2.2.146–51)

Here Dorimant seems to be suggesting that the disorder of the body directly impinges upon the vagrancy of "the mind" (or passions) and vice versa. Correcting one corrects the other. The means of correction, of course, is wit, and the protection against the terrorism of wit is dissembling. But before we discuss the counterstrategy of dissembling, let us first look at wit as the productive source of that counterstrategy: what, precisely, is the nature of this abusive wit, and how does it operate specifically as discipline?

Wit, Freud tells us, is of essentially two kinds. The first type of wit is generally nonaggressive and takes pleasure in the simple play of language and association. The second type of wit, however, is a highly aggressive, hostile exchange between two speakers that seeks the pleasure of cruelty at the expense of a third party who is the victim of the witticism. According to Freud, the intent of this type of witticism is the gratification of an unattainable desire through the exploitation and objectification of that desire in language.[28] At the individual level, this is the type of phenomenon we confront in Restoration drama; when Dorimant castigates Loveit with his witticisms, he is making a cruel attempt to control another through the sexual disposition and ambience of manners, an attempt that he enacts in league with an *audience*.

But the mechanism of wit is significantly more complex than this. The very otherness that calls wit into play underscores wit's function as protection. Wit, in other words, is not only an aggression, but also clearly a defense mechanism that is brought into play at the first hint of social threat. In this sense, the witticism is little different from, say, the racist or sexist joke—both emerge as the expression and repression of a perceived threat, namely the *aphanic* threat of one's dissolution *in* the Other, which is exteriorized as "witty" discourse. Indeed, the very operations of male wit proclaim at every step their terror of otherness in general, and in the comedy of manners, of female otherness in particular. Thus while wit operates as correction and control over the wit's victim, it also channels the frightening hostility and incipient violence of the wit himself—while women are terrorized by men, in other words, men terrorize themselves. The discourse of wit, then, functions much like Otway's dagger. It is the exteriorization of an incipient, controlling violence that moves through the play as a currency, carrying the weight of a menacing social *evaluation*.

Wit's aggression, like the dagger, is also at some level a self-directed aggression (we might remember Jaffeir's lament: "A thousand daggers all in honest hands / Have I not a friend will stick one here?"). It is the instrumentality of self-disgust, and as such serves to discipline both the Other, and the self *in* the Other. This self-disgust, which seems somehow at the heart of the comedy of manners, helps us to understand the deep and violent disaffection of its characters: why, for example, does Dorimant attack both Loveit, whom he has already seduced, *and* Harriet, whom he hasn't? What "unattainable desire" could Dorimant be pursuing through his witty attacks on Loveit when he seems to have already exploited her as the object of his desire? The answer is, in one sense at least, obvious; Dorimant attacks Loveit because the essential desire that drove him to her has not been satisfied, indeed, could never have been satisfied merely by exploiting another object-body.

Consequently, Dorimant vents the rage of his *impotence* upon Loveit, an impotence that signals a perpetual unsatisfied craving, a hunger that *will* not be sated but through the possession of the Other's desire. But this possession is, of course, impossible because the Other's desire is not an object to be possessed. Thus Dorimant characterizes his insatiable, corrosive desire and the discipline it entails as a sickness, a consumptive syndrome that seems to feed on itself—an anorexia. When he breaks off his relations with Loveit, he characterizes his feelings in this way:

> DORIMANT. When love grows diseased the best thing we can do is to put it
>   to a violent death; I cannot endure the torture of a lingering and con-
>   sumptive passion. (2.2.241–44)

The characterization might not seem unusual at first—the relationship between Dorimant and Loveit is ending, and Dorimant eulogizes the death of a passion. But then we hear him describe his newly found passion for Harriet in much the same way:

> HARRIET. You make me start! I did not think to have heard of love from
>   you.
> DORIMANT. I never knew what 'twas to have a settled ague yet, but now
>   and then have had irregular fits.

HARRIET. Take heed, sickness after long health is commonly more violent
and dangerous.
DORIMANT. *(aside)* I have took the infection from her, and feel the disease
now spreading in me. (4.1.168–77)

We must be careful not to fix the blame for this jaundiced perception entirely
on the character of Dorimant. The characterization of love as a sickness is
endemic to these plays. Moreover, it is often difficult to discern whether the
disease is attributable to the emotion of "love," or to the society of manners
that has disfigured it. Inevitably, "love" and "manners" (the discipline that
deforms and reforms love) become indistinguishable in the acting out. The
lovers Dorimant and Harriet:

DORIMANT.
That demure curtsy is not amiss in jest, but do not think in earnest it
becomes you.
HARRIET. Affectation is catching I find; from your grave bow I got it. (4.1.118–
21)

Indeed, many of the characters in these plays frame their complaints in the
language of disease: "I hate myself, I look so ill today," says Loveit, and Pert
responds "Hate the wicked cause on't, that base man Mr / Dorimant, who
makes you torment and vex yourself / continually" (2.2.3–6). The phobia
that forces Loveit to spend hours primping and repairing, that forbids her
the slightest lapse in social intercourse, finally shows itself as sickness and
self-loathing when she is no longer able to sustain the discipline of appearances. And the fact that Harriet feels that the "affectation is catching" makes
us realize that the instrumentation of manners ultimately operates like an
infectious and consumptive machine, or like a viral weapon detonated and
dispersed through the contagion of desire itself, a contagion that defines the
disciplining and self-defensive posturing of wit.

But while wit serves to discipline both the self and the Other, it produces
its own counterstrategy: *dissembling.* Dissembling is the employment of gesture and manners literally raised to the level of defensive art (or at least artifice). In Restoration comedy, this display is indistinguishable from beauty;
defensive posturing, beauty, and artifice become identical in the problematic
of appearances. The dissembling nature of appearance itself becomes the
commentary on theatre within the theatre, for if "Beauty runs as great a
risque exposed at / court as wit does on the stage," then beauty (or, as is the
case in these plays, the pretense to beauty) and wit become the definitional
terms for theatre, and in fact collapse into one another when they appear *as*
theatre (we need only think of all of those female and male actors in front of
their mirrors "making up" for the Grand Guignol). Dissembling thus emerges
as the material production-reaction of wit's aggression. The female body becomes a kind of Phobic mask upon which is inscribed the unspeakable terror

of male self-repulsion. In any case, wit, dissembling, and theatre are described as contrary to nature: "That women should set up for beauty as / much in spite of nature, as some men have done for / wit." Thus wit and its dissembling theatre—the key and central disciplining, controlling force of Restoration high society's "natural passions"—were themselves deeply suspect, and had to be controlled. The dialectical tension between passion and its controlling theatre was reproduced in the presumed incommensurability between "nature" and artifice, and between seen "reality" and its discursive (witty) manipulation.

The incommensurability between speech and seeing that we saw in the Renaissance drama, then, is not really resolved in the Restoration, but merely formalized into an economic binarism of opposed forms of aggression, each operating *through* the seeing. While, as has often been suggested, the Renaissance theatre deployed cultural power *as* theatre,[29] we can see on the Restoration stage the corollary of this proposition—that power can, in some sense, only come to be *in/as* theatre, that theatre must in some inexplicable way exist as a prior condition of perception in order to receive that power-as-spectacle.

Within this milieu of theatre spectacle, there was a predictable extension of theatre's perceptual terrorism and control into the Restoration audience itself, if we are to believe the theatre histories. Characters within the plays were oftentimes modelled on well-known public figures, who, it would seem, could not resist seeing themselves ridiculed on stage (if this is true—and the relationship between Restoration audiences and their plays is certainly open to some debate—it would only confirm my previous argument). The audience itself, one can imagine, would have been a very effective "field of coercion," its gaze finally turned back on itself, its seemingly shared derision replacing the whips and stocks of Puritan discipline. Thus *in the theatre,* Dorimant's play of wit reformed and was reformed in the audience-as-Other *through the agency of audience itself,* which, like Dorimant, desired and constituted itself through the double-bound cruelty. Moreover—in a kind of strange anticipation of Genet, once again—this theatre seemed to identify theatre's own site as the very locus in which this double-bound cruelty was produced as spectacle.

The purpose of this exploitation, then, is not only an individual attempt at gratification through objectification; it is also indicative of a larger political and social process at work by which individual bodies and *groups or classes* of bodies are reorganized and reformed according to the demands of a particular historical episteme. We can begin, then, to see where the Freudian analysis of wit falls short: by concentrating on the origins of wit in the individual psyche, and the desires that wit fulfills in the individual, we fail to understand the ways that wit operates as a political tool in the wider structures of social and political representation. Only by understanding the wider social implementation of wit as a *coercive economy of the sign*[30] can we understand the desire to reinscribe the body/self as its own surface in Restoration comedy, for when the body is thus reinscribed or rewritten as representation, the "true self" disappears "safely" beneath the artifice. Thus in Congreve's *The Way of the World* Foible, yet another cosmetologist, speaks to the aging socialite Lady Wishfort:[31]

> FOIBLE. Your Ladyship has frown'd a little too rashly, indeed, Madam. There are some Cracks discernable in the white Varnish.
> LADY WISHFORT. Let me see the Glass.—Cracks, say'st thou? Why, I am arrantly flea'd; I look like an old peel'd Wall. Thou must repair me, *Foible,* before Sir *Rowland* comes, or I shall never keep up to my Picture.
> FOIBLE. I warrant you, Madam, a little Art once made your Picture like you; and now a little of the same Art must make you like your Picture. Your Picture must sit for you, Madam. (3.1.155–66)

There is an undisguised appeal to representational mimesis here, a desire to imitate and equal one's perfected image so that the self can be re-presented as an object of desire, and "hide" behind itself, so to speak. One can then *become* what one "should be" in the self as Other. The self thus recreates itself "behind" itself, and the "romance of depths" and surfaces begins.

We detect not only the threat of a decaying alienation here, but also the threat of real violence: where exactly will the mimetic struggle end but in domestic abuse, or at the point of a pin or a Jacobean knife, as it does today beneath the "officious fingers" of numberless Busys in the theatres of countless plastic surgeons? Moreover do we not, in the continuous *violent* interplay of wit and dissembling, face the threatened end of social relations between men and women? How can the mechanisms of wit and manners operate once they are unmasked, as they are in these plays?

We might refer once again to Girard, who sees the solution to the mimetic crisis in the establishment of law through which the violence of the crisis is quelled. In the Restoration comedy, the violent discipline of wit and the defense of dissembling are themselves regulated through the implementation of a similar law, the marriage *contract*.[32]

In *The Way of the World,* Mirabell and Millamant, who themselves engage at length in the battle of wit and dissembling, each make a long list of demands pursuant to their marriage. The numerous demands and counter-demands of each outline the behaviors and domains of power that each partner may claim as his/her own. When each has outlined his/her stipulations, Mirabell speaks:

> MIRABELL.   These *proviso's* admitted, in other things I may prove a tractable and complying Husband.
> MILLAMANT. Oh, horrid *proviso's!* filthy strong Waters! I toast fellows, odious Men! I hate your odious proviso's.

MIRABELL. Then we're agreed. Shall I kiss your hand upon the Contract? And here comes one to be a witness to the Sealing of the Deed. (4.1.302–10)

The open battle of manners and wit retreats here into the cryptic contractual obligations of diplomacy and treaty. The larger issues of social power and sexual indoctrination are thus seemingly concealed within individual chamber theatres or courts of domesticity—in what Foucault might have called one of the "hundreds of tiny theatres of punishment" operating within the social warp[33]—while the "family" itself begins to construct itself around its own public form on stage.

Indeed, the later sentimental comedies of Cumberland, or even the "laughing comedies" of Sheridan, signal the gradual establishment of the family unit as the primary political cell into which the larger issues of societal control are displaced. This process of individuation and isolation continues well into the nineteenth century, where the concerns of Romanticism rechannel the process into the recreation of the individual psyche as imagination. The violence of discipline is then redirected through the doctrine of imagination, which begins to reform and recreate the oedipal *mind* as yet another site of social control through the agency of internalized guilt.

The gradual emergence of women playwrights out of the Restoration and into the nineteenth and twentieth centuries is, in light of this imaginary movement "from body to mind," a double-bound proposition. On the one hand the Restoration theatre was to date the most focused attempt to define sexuality and gender through violence as major categories of social control. On the other hand, it was also out of this repressive, definitional process, ironically, that women somehow found themselves able to enter the theatre as writers and eventually as directors. Where in the Renaissance we seem to have but a single extant corpus of work by a woman (Elizabeth Carey Falkland), out of the Restoration and into the eighteenth century we see the emergence of such dramatists as Behn and Susannah Centlivre, Hannah More, and Elizabeth Simpson Inchbald. Although many of these gains were wiped out by increasingly hostile male theatre managers, causing more and more women writers to turn, in the nineteenth century, to the novel as an outlet for their ideas, some women playwrights went on to write well into the nineteenth century, a century that produced a relatively large number of female writers—both novelists and playwrights. While most female writers, in the nineteenth century at least, produced "sentimental" plays in which questions of power and integrity were formulated more or less exclusively within the family cell, other, mostly male, writers (such as Keats, Coleridge, Shelley, and Byron) went on to develop yet another imaginary space/axis for the deployment of theatre's control, namely the "mind," a mind that emerged, predictably enough, with its male ethos intact.

This suggests a simultaneous development in which the public engendering of the body was augmented by another kind of discipline, which took the interiorized space of the psyche and the family as its corrective site. Thus there now began yet another cross-penetration—while the "private" family became, largely, the ideological and theatrical space of female writing, it was through the theatricalization of the family that the family itself became a public fiction, an "object" capable of being scrutinized and critiqued—a legacy that Ibsen and the realists inherited later on. Moreover, while the sentimental comedy/tragedy appeared in the theatres, the more "psychological" plays of the romantic verse dramatists seemed to exist in a different, "private" theatrical space, which eventually developed into the other, psychic-surrealist theatre of early modernism that began, perhaps, with Strindberg.

As I suggested earlier, the resistance of theatrical forms and practices is, no matter how rigorously deployed, eventually absorbed and neutralized by the homogenizing force of theatre itself—the suspect theatre that, in Brecht's terms, "resists any alteration of its function," a theatre that takes resistance and, in staging it, "theatres it all down."[34] Indeed, as I have argued elsewhere, this is precisely the double function of theatre: to institutionalize cultural violence, while at the same moment diffusing its resistances. All theatrical enterprises are prone to this double-bound appropriation, no matter how ideologically radical or Other they try to be. Theatre, the primary site of cultural violence, the place in which the violence of the perceptual cleavage that *is* thought *is* embodied—this theatre will, through its ability to "stage anything," transform all resistant ideologies into their Others.[35]

Thus for all of the power and strength of women dramatists like Aphra Behn—herself literally terrorized and embattled to death—who produced plays that dealt specifically with the position and positioning of women in culture, the plays themselves were still woven from the same fabric of theatrical wit and dissembling as the plays written by men. And of course there was no way Behn or anyone else could have hoped to do otherwise. Indeed, as I have said, this is the very potency of theatre, the thing that allows theatre to engender, and to neutralize opposition to its engendering violence.

So while male and female playwrights in the Restoration theatre tried, to varying degrees, to resist both Puritan and aristocratic tyranny within the tyranny of theatre, they unwittingly consolidated another kind of social control—women in the sentimental tragedy-comedy, male writers in Romantic verse drama. But the Restoration stage was the necessary prelude to the establishment of an escalating and ever more invasive and totalizing social control, a control engendered first in/as theatre of the most "private" kind. In the language of feminism, the private indeed becomes the political, or, as Dorimant says, "The deep play is now in private houses."

5 THE BODY'S REVISION IN THE THEATRE OF MIND

BYRON'S *MANFRED* AND SHELLEY'S *PROMETHEUS UNBOUND*

Dorimant's observation announces a kind of eulogy for the Restoration theatre that anticipates the new and profound cultural transformation of performative perspective in romanticism. Through this transformation the "truth" of social intercourse will now seem to reside somehow "beneath" or "behind" the gestural surfaces of the Restoration play of manners. The projection of the theatre into the "interior space" of romantic verse drama, emblematized in plays such as Byron's *Manfred* and Shelley's *Prometheus Unbound,* announces this identification of "truth" with what is "inside" the mind and imagination.

Indeed Charles Lamb's notion of what has come to be known as the "mental theatre" of romanticism—a theatre that best exists in the *mise en scène* of mind recreating play text—is in many ways quite emblematic of romanticism's definition of theatre. This displacement of "truth" or authenticity "within" implies a desire to extend beyond gestural, empirical, representational systems, and will eventually bore out those psychic spaces in which the idealism of the sublime appears to intersect with the fascinations of terror in the topography of the imagination.[1]

But this "displaced topography" also describes an emergent psychology,[2] a psychology that recuperates the terrorisms etched onto the Restoration's body surface[3] and redirects them back into the formative interior of the imagination.[4] If we compare (as does Lamb in his essay "On the Artificial Comedy of the Last Century") the plays of the Restoration theatre with those done on the stages of the romantic theatre, for example, we see a dramatic movement away from public sociosexual exchange and toward a more domestic, "sentimental" drama consonant with the seeming contractions of power from the social sphere and into the family.[5] Developing concurrently with this there is in the configuration of the poetic drama an apparent "interiorization" of theatrical forms consistent with the romantic *reinvention* of the mind as an internalized body surface effected through the creation of a *theatre of the imagination*.[6] Oswald, probing the mind of Marmaduke in Wordsworth's *The Borderers,* speaks as an emissary of this theatre:

> This Stripling's mind
> Is shaken till the dregs float on the surface;
> And, in the storm and anguish of the heart,
> He talks of a transition in his Soul,
> And dreams that he is happy. We dissect
> The senseless body, and why not the mind?—
> These are strange sights—the mind of man, upturned,
> Is in all natures a strange spectacle;
> In some a hideous one.[7]

Despite romanticism's abhorrence of any mind/body split, and despite its desire to reestablish an organic connection between reason and imagination, it ended by redefining the body *as* mind, and thus sustained the body/mind division that it tired so resolutely to resist. This redefinition allowed the mind, like the body in the Restoration, to be compartmentalized, disciplined, and "dissected."

So while we can feel the intensity of the "libidinal liberation" of energies that romanticism represented, and can recognize (as did Artaud in Shelley's *The Cenci*) the thrilling excess and force of romantic verse drama, we can at the same time perceive a reemergence of terror as the asymptotic principle of the imagination's desire for a sublime freedom. A play like *The Cenci* demonstrates this; the desire that is central to the play is Cenci's desire for the liberation of libidinal energy that, when actually released into the textures of the play, destroys the characters in an excess of violence. This energy is, moreover, guided and reformed at every step by a terrorizing psychological scrutiny that is absolutely bound up in the "powers and powerlessness" of thought *as language*. Thus Orsino observes:

> 'tis a trick of this same family
> To analyse their own and other minds.
> Such self-anatomy shall teach the will
> Dangerous secrets: for it tempts our powers,
> Knowing what must be thought, and may be done,
> Into the depths of darkest purposes.[8]

This "self-anatomy" is parsed out through specific words that both indicate and repress the terror that festers in the psyche: "That word, parricide, / Although I am resolved, haunts me like fear," says Giacomo, and Orsino replies that "It must be fear itself, for the bare word / Is hollow mockery" (3.1.340–43). What is of particular interest here is that this *word* mutates into silence because "word" is ultimately inadequate to the crime: the central infraction in *The Cenci,* presumably incest, is never spoken. The entire text of the play, in fact, operates as an attempted secondary process by which "the crime" is triangulated and approached asymptotically, but never apprehended. This *béance* suggest a crime that is indeed unthinkable—what may have been an unspeakable crime (incest) in the nineteenth century becomes emblematic for the very condition of unspeakability at the heart of the drama. Finally, the "unspeakable crime" is unspeakability itself, the unrepresentable that desires and repudiates its image at the heart of the play; this is, once again, the Phobic/Deimic interplay of terror at theatre's core, the silent core that Benjamin identified with the tragic hero, and we earlier identified as the repressed ideology of the political unconscious.

Here the Phobic/Deimic relationship between language and terror is essentially psychological, a relationship that ultimately allows terror and its power to be exploited by the Cenci. Terror is, once again, appropriated and used as the tool of a sociopolitical reformation of the status quo both in the play and outside the play through the very description/creation of the psychological. This, I would argue, is the critical "subtext" of romantic verse drama—the usurpation of imagination by the terrorism of the psychological, a psychological that awaits the appearance of the psychoanalytic to correct it.[9]

But while others have approached the romantic theatre from the vantage point of its existence as a "mental theatre,"[10] I am suggesting, as I have throughout these pages, something at once more troubling and more elusive: that the "mind" as it is treated in romantic verse theatre did not exist before the appearance of this theatre but was in fact composed by it. The "mind" of Cenci, or Prometheus, or Manfred is not a preexistent perceptual apparatus which was then investigated by romantic theatre. Rather the very scenic agency of "the mind" that is so emblematic of romanticism is the substance of romanticism's repressed theatre. Thus romanticism did not inhabit the "space" of mind with its theatre, nor did it recreate theatre as a mental activity—instead romanticism recreated its own particular mind space, the mind space of Imagination, *as* theatre. The appearance of this mind space, as Deleuze and Guattari have shown in reference to Freudian psychology, remained consonant with the development of capital and the circulation of its fetish/phobic objects, a consonance that was ratified by theatre and theatricality, and to which theatricality gave it its form: "the unconscious as a stage. A whole theatre put in the place of production, a theater that disfigures this production even more than could tragedy and myth . . ."[11]

We can see hints of this developing mythic psychologism in the romantic imagination's fascination with the Kantian idea of the Sublime.[12] Kant theorized the Sublime as an effect produced through the apprehension of limitlessness in nature. This apprehension initially produces an "unpleasantness" because of the inability of reason to assimilate what is unlimited, undefined, unbounded. But this experience of unpleasantness in turn produces a corresponding pleasure when the perceiving mind realizes its absolute affinity with the unlimited. As thought perceives that it, like nature, is unbounded, we experience the Sublime, according to Kant, as a phenomenon of mind, or *as the mind reconstituting itself.*

The idea of the Sublime was accompanied by an ecstasy which overflowed quite readily into romantic art.[13] But the Kantian sublime ecstasy has another more ambiguous and coercive side. The initial perception of unpleasantness, when the mind cannot properly represent the magnitude of nature to itself, is characterized at one point by Kant as "fear" and later on as "terror." Unless one possesses the proper "development of moral ideas" given to us by "preparatory culture," Kant wrote, we experience the magnitudes (or what might today be termed "slippages" or indeterminicies[14]) of nature not as sublime but as terrifying. The Sublime, then, far from being a perception of infinitude, is instead the result of "moral instruction," a product of culture. Thus while Shelley writes in the *Defense of Poetry* that "poetry turns all things to loveliness," poetry also "adds beauty to that which is deformed; it marries exultation and horror, grief and pleasure . . . its secret alchemy turns to potable gold the poisonous waters which flow from death through life."[15] Poetry, in short, has the power to make palatable all that is repugnant, and this is the precise function of ideology through which "the good affections are strengthened by pity, indignation, terror, and sorrow." Indeed, Shelley even goes on to invoke an Aristotelian *katharsis* when he provides that the desirable end of tragedy is to produce "an exalted calm" following this terror, a calm that is "prolonged from the satiety of this high exercise . . . into the tumult of familiar life" (1077)—precisely the aspect of *katharsis* that Brecht so despised.

This social disciplining aspect of the Sublime and its *kathartic* effect is perhaps best exemplified in Kant's philosophy when he suggests *humility* as a kind of sublime experience, in which the cultured mind voluntarily undergoes "the pain of remorse" in order to more effectively *eradicate* the source of its humiliation. Humility is sublime because it causes and reinforces the *internalization* of discipline and guilt; it creates, in other words, the very space of repression that characterizes the fiction of the modern preconscious/unconscious mind, what Deleuze and Guattari call "the Oedipal" mind, and what Foucault identifies as the emergent Oedipal consciousness in nineteenth-century capitalism. This is a consciousness marked by the coalescence of madness, guilt, moral sanction, and just punishment through the "psychological effect of a moral fault" which spread itself over the topology of psy-

chology and made the "scientific psychiatry" of the nineteenth century possible.[16] This mind, then, is not a real "mind" or minds that exist somewhere
as actual or essential "spaces of thought." Rather the very topographical metaphor of mind as a space of individuation is a result of romanticism's assumption of an imaginative interiority of thought, which was and is, in its
structuring of experience as alien difference, primarily and distressingly theatrical. This alienating mind turned back on itself is the terrorizing aspect of
the Sublime in perhaps its clearest manifestation.

The full *political grandeur* of this psychologic, self-inflicted sublime terror
is revealed when Kant elevates it to the level of the social, and reveals how
even "war itself . . . has something sublime about it" because it effects a
kind of purification and discipline of the social fabric, which in times of peace
becomes commercial, debased, cowardly, and effeminate. Ultimately, the
ideology of the Sublime (and that is exactly what it is)[17] utilizes the threat of
terror, which might be unleashed at any moment upon those who have refused or rejected the teachings of "culture" that will predispose them to perceptions of the Sublime. The equivalence between "truth" and *katharsis* that
we mentioned earlier is also, then, a correspondence between truth and terror: not only is truth enforced by terror, but also the truth of cultural violence is perfectly concealed in the sublimation of terror to imaginative thought.

This is perhaps romanticism's highest irony: that in spite of its resistance
to the constraints of neoclassicism, the romantic imagination was, finally, a
product of neoclassical discipline. As Kenneth Burke writes:

> Although the cult of the "imagination" is usually urged today by those who
> champion poetry as a field *opposed* to science, our investigations would suggest
> the ironic possibility that they exemplify an aspect of precisely the thinking
> they would reject. For our modern views of the imagination come to us *via*
> the idealist Coleridge from the idealist Kant—and we have already seen the
> strong scientist bias in the Kantian doctrines.[18]

Indeed, the creation of the Imagination in romanticism, the development of
an inner space apparently protected from the assault of the regulating gaze
and the machines of corrective wit, finally accomplished the opposite of what
it ostensibly set out to do. Instead of creating a space (or, to be more topo-
logically accurate, a closed, curved surface) "behind" or "beyond" the "pan-
opticon" of the Restoration stage, the theory of the imagination created for
the gaze and its disciplines a whole new dimension within which to operate.
The creation of this *seeming* "interiority" allowed bodies to be organized along
an entirely new axis, the axis of "mind," whose qualities, far from being
hidden, were exteriorized and objectified as the very condition of their enunciation.[19] Once again, we can see this process most clearly in the theatre of
romanticism, and most particularly in the verse plays of the romantic poets.[20]

The claim that I have been making for theatre—that theatre should be seen a the prior category in which the mind sees itself; that there is, in some sense, a theatre that precedes the "mental theatre"—should not be surprising when one realizes that psychiatry was itself casting its practice as theatre during this period of time. Foucault, in fact, identifies an opposite and complementary movement to theatre practice in early nineteenth-century psychiatry, in which "delirium" was treated in a theatre of the image operating "entirely in the space of the imagination," a theatre that intersected "with one of the major forms of theatrical experience" of the day—an emergent naturalism. This theatre operated in complement to another psychiatric technique, *fear,* and the two techniques were linked in the disciplines of psychotheory. Foucault quotes from a psychiatric treatise of the period when he writes: "It is all one whether the invalid's imagination is cured by fear . . . or by an illusion." He then goes on to elucidate:

> Insofar as it is of the essence of the image to be taken for reality, it is reciprocally characteristic of reality that it can mime the image, pretend to the same substance, the same significance. Without a break, without a jolt, perception can continue the dream, fill in its gaps, confirm what is precarious about it, and lead it to its fulfillment. *If illusion can appear as true as perception, perception in its turn can become the visible, unchallengeable truth of illusion.* Such is the first step of the cure by "theatrical representation": to integrate the unreality of the image into perceived truth. . . . It is within a continuous discourse that the elements of delirium, coming into contradiction, bring on the crisis. A crisis which is, in a very ambiguous manner, both medical and theatrical.[21]

To see the lingering effects of such an approach, we have only to remember the use of the asylum in the modern period as the place within which "false ideology" is cured through the long process of "deprogramming"—the "rehearsal" of true perception out of "false consciousness."

The creation of theatrical imaginative interiority, exercised concurrently in the asylum and in such verse dramas as *Manfred* and *Prometheus Unbound,*[22] displaced and reduced the usual social production of theatre into a very different space of representation. This representational space assumed a value that was inversely correlated to its refusal of the "real" dramatic space of the stage.[23] So while it is true that the verse plays of romanticism were rejected as theatre for reasons grounded in the very limitations of the romantic stage that those plays tried to exceed, and while it is also true that even today we are apt to find these same biases in theatre histories, the more compelling reason behind the presence/absence of the poetic theatre in romanticism lies in its (and psychology's) dramatic claims on the imaginary oedipal mind as the primal theatrical scene.

The refusal of the "real" theatre to acknowledge the essential theatricality of this newly articulated "mind myth," coupled with the refusal of the poetic theatre to acknowledge its own plays as a kind of "pure" theatre, forced the theatre of the imagination, within its own delirium, to return in the Real as the mind itself. This mutual expulsion occurred because the mythic theatre of the mind and the "real" theatre were, like the myth of science, like myth itself, different manifestations of the same repressive function: "Since madness is illusion, the cure of madness, if it is true that such a cure can be effected by theatre, can also and still more directly be effected by the suppression of theatre."[24]

I have chosen to discuss the poetic plays of the romantic period as its most significant theatre precisely because they delineate most clearly the development of this new phenomenological space for the play of terror (the coercion of fear/illusion in the oedipal mind), and because these plays represent the most interesting possibilities for current theatrical reinterpretation. The performances of romanticism, when posited against their own repressive function in the reproduction of the psyche, show most clearly, I think, the romantic theatre's link with modern and postmodern performance.

Finally, I should make it clear that while I am, in a sense, trying to "liberate" these romantic plays back into the theatre as *performance,* this is a very ambivalent strategy: indeed, what is most interesting about these plays, what makes them most significant, is their reformulation of the "Name of the Father" into a new and more malignant space. Thus the fetishism of incest, the reformulation of woman as hallucination[25] (another absence), the "privatization" of the personal, and the development of the bureaucratic violence of theatre/asylum in these plays, all represent the recuperation of an essentially "phallocratic" space, but a space that needs to be deconstructed if we are to successfully reposition our understanding of theatre's history in terms of its terror.

In Byron's *Manfred*[26] the reproduction of the psyche's terror appears in a host of dislocated articulations and dispersions of identity—the "phantoms" and interiorized voices conjured by Manfred's speech—objectified and fixed in a seemingly limitless, but ultimately constrained, imaginary space. This space of confinement is Manfred's own tortured imagination, which is in turn imprisoned within an alienated and objectified consciousness of itself—"The Castle of Manfred" that stands always "at a distance." Similarly, in Shelley's *Prometheus Unbound,* the mythic-imaginative space is "a Ravine of Icy Rocks in the Indian Caucasus," the bleak place of Prometheus' confinement in which the psyche is reconstituted in the dissemination and regathering of psychic forces designated as natural and divine energies: Earth, Moon, Phantoms, Furies. In both cases, the imagination is the locus in which a "recolonization" of consciousness occurs, a consciousness that eventually becomes the *mise en scène* of psychologic discipline itself.[27]

In each instance, the dispersion of identity occurs amidst ethereal landscapes and terrifying precipices whose dangers are beyond understanding or articulation; as Manfred stands alone among the cliffs he speaks this sublime and terrible recognition: "And you, ye crags, upon whose extreme edge / I stand . . . wherefore do I pause?" (1.2.13–19). The presence of such a land-scape marks a simultaneous obsession with the Sublime and a fascination with terror, as these indicate the conditions of a mind that forms itself against the limits of signification—limits that are inscribed in the mind as a "terror" that "survives the ravin it has gorged."[28]

The *articulation* of terror into a terrorism of psyche is in fact the articulation of the imaginary oedipal/phobic mind itself, a "regulating idea or principle of reflection (terror) that organizes the parts and flows into a whole."[29] Like the romantic imagination, this mind is defined by the limits that terrorize it. In both cases these limits are, as Kant tells us, proscribed by the culture into which that mind/imagination is born. This articulation of mind involves, as I have suggested in previous chapters, the necessary transformation and objectification of terror into an ism that can be represented as a spectacular truth—psychologism. As Foucault says of psychologic practice: "[Delirium's] confirmation in theatrical fantasy restores it to truth which, by holding it captive in reality, drives it out of reality itself, and makes it disappear in the non-delirious discourse of reason." This transformation into the "nondelirious discourse of reason," a kind of *"forclusion-inversion,"* is effected, as it was in Otway's *Venice,* by terror's passage through the economy of signification, by which its insubstantiality takes on form and *appears*—is *imaged* or *mediated*—as lethal force.[30]

In romantic verse drama, the passage of terror into terrorism often appears simultaneously as a passage into the Sublime. In *Prometheus Unbound,* the passage of the terrorizing memory of pain into imagination and language is presented as the prelude to a sublime cosmic salvation. In *Manfred,* the transformation of the terror of pain and remorse into apparition and performance signals, through the flames of a final *aphanisis,* the heroic embrace of tragedy as truth. The ontological and theatrical roots of this truth echo the death-as-life mythos of the *Quem Quaeritis:* "Old man," says Manfred triumphantly before he expires, " 'tis not so difficult to die" (3.4.151). In that death, death itself is apotheosized as the divine, *aphanic* end of imagination.

We see in this concern with heroic and stoic death the apparent return of Walter Benjamin's classical tragic hero—the alien god/man stretched taut to silence between the world of gods and the world of men. "He is convulsed," says one Spirit to another in *Manfred.* And the other answers: "Yet, see, he mastereth himself, and makes / His torture tributary to his will. / Had he been one of us, he would have made / An awful spirit" (2.4.159–64). There is in this death a return of tragic desire as well. The reclamation of tragic-heroic desire comes from an other, concealed, desire in romanticism, a desire to repeat the historical inscription of law as a function of myth, in this case the myth of mind. The authority of the mythological texts gives shape and substance to psychic forces, while at the same time it allows them to dissolve, eventually, into the pure representative function of language. This symbolic function is the structural "law" of psychoanalytic theory and practice into which, Lacan tells us, the analyst himself must disappear. In *Manfred,* as in Lacan, the "analyst" exists as a projection of the hero's desire into the locus of the Other who "knows":

> MAN.   Say on, Say on—
> I live but in the sound—it is thy voice!
>   PHAN. Manfred, tomorrow ends thy earthly ills.
> Farewell!
>   MAN. Yet one more word—am I forgiven?
>   PHAN. Farewell!
> [*The* SPIRIT OF ASTARTE *disappears*] (2.4.150–55)

It is worth noting that in both of these plays, the reinscription of the law is signalled by the return of the tragic and the mythic as theatrical forms, the very forms that recreate the law. But while in *Prometheus Unbound* the return of the mythic-tragic law is quite explicit in the choice of mythic material itself, in *Manfred* the return of mythic-tragic law is merely implied in the literary structure of the play and in the psychological character of the hero. Manfred finally emerges as the mythical function of his own alchemical incantations, which exist first as writing and then as speech. These incantations form a kind of dream text emerging in the "speaking cure": "I call upon ye by the written charm / Which gives me power upon you—Rise! Appear!" (1.1.35–36).

The tragic-heroic qualities of Manfred are also implied rather than explicitly stated. He is not named for any character out of mythology, but exhibits many of those characteristics that we have come to associate with tragic heroes; he is isolated, brooding, anguished, defective somehow, hiding within his inmost being the secret shadow of some unpronounceable crime. He is a "Man of strange words, and some half- / maddening sin" (2.1.31), the romantic hero in the most melancholic and perhaps most powerfully centralized and alienated manifestation. Finally, Manfred is as noble in spirit as he is in blood, and stands tragically apart from the world of men:

> MAN. Patience and patience! Hence—that word
>   was made
> For brutes of burthen, not for birds of prey;
> Preach it to mortals of dust like thine,—
> I am not of thine order. (2.1.35–38)

But Manfred's tragic persona is not merely a gratuitous, "baroque," manifestation of the melodramatic "martyr-tyrant," to use Benjamin's terms. Rather, his persona is formed in the battle against a remorseless fate that places him at the brink of some profound new reorganization of the social. He marks the disarticulation of the unified neoclassical voice into a new demotic dispersion, the demos of mind, the dissipation of the state's power into the "interior" spaces of a new "psychological man," the guilt-ridden neurotic:

> MAN.   Oh! no, no, no!
> My injuries came down on those who loved me—
> On those whom I best loved: I never quelled
> An enemy, save in my just defense—
> But my embrace was fatal. (2.1.83–87)

If psychically debilitated, Manfred's interiorized, *repressed,* and guilt-ridden identity is also the source and end of a potential multiplicity of powers. While seemingly the victim of otherworldly spirits, he is nonetheless the one who calls them up and has power over them: "Ye mock me—but the power which brought ye here / Hath made you mine. Slaves, scoff not at my will!" (1.1.153–54). The psyche of Manfred stands as the origin of the forces that assault him and marks the locus into which they seemingly disappear. Thus, while Euripides' Medea "stands mute" between the gods and the new society, Byron's Manfred stands between the old society of exterior forces of oppression and the new repressive society inscribed within:

> MAN. The mind which is immortal makes itself
> Requital for its good or evil thoughts,—
> Its own origin of ill and end
> And its own place and time; its innate sense,
> When stripped of this mortality, derives
> No color from the fleeting things without,
> But is absorbed in sufferance or in joy,
> Born from the knowledge of its own desert.
> *Thou* didst not tempt me, and thou couldst not tempt me;
> I have not been thy dupe, nor am thy prey—
> but was my own destroyer, and will be
> My own hereafter.—Back, ye baffled fiends!—
> The hand of death is on me—but not yours.
>   [*The* DEMONS *disappear*] (3.4.130–40)

Here then is a critical distinction between classicism and its romantic revisitation in the drama: the gods are now emanations of interior forces, and the hero will disappear, not into the new "open" democratic society, but into the closed pluralities of his own neuroses. Even though the hero possesses a potential power over his neurotic multiplicities, he is finally subjugated and destroyed by his insistence on the heroic status of "imagination" and on the teeming totality that it implies.

While the dispersion of voice and character in these plays might seem to be contradicted by the appearance of the force of romantic heroism, the strong presence of the hero is not at all antithetical to the dispersions of power and consciousness that he seems to represent. He is in fact the necessary complement to the fragmentation of consciousness that we see revealed in these plays. The romantic artist/hero—tortured by remembered crime, racked with unfathomable desires and guilt—appears as a synthesized locus for the apparently dissociated order of things. Manfred, out of whom the demonic elements of a dark consciousness seem to emerge, and Prometheus, who reassimilates them into himself through godly compassion,—both heroes in some sense reorganize the disparate elements of consciousness in and around the power of a synthetic and *provisional* "presence of mind." This is marked by a distinctly insubstantial identity and locality characterized in large part by the power of *voice:* "Now by the voice of him / Who is the first among you—by this sign, / Which makes you tremble—by the claims of him / Who is undying,—Rise! Appear—Appear!" (1.1.37–40). The corollary to this in the popular theatre was the appearance of the great romantic actors who also synthesized various elements of theatrical personae into an entirely new phenomenon, the luminescent and ephemeral theatrical "star."[31]

In *Manfred,* the stage upon which these syntheses take place is theatre itself. Theatrical ontology provides both the space and the metaphor for these transformations: "Appear! Appear! Appear!" cries the figure of Nemesis, invoking the phantom of Astarte to seeming corporeality in the court of Arimanes. This invocation to appearance is an invocation to the theatrical, a demand to *realize* the insubstantiality of desire in the apparition. But the demand to appear is precisely the problematic, for the *realization* of insubstantiality only occurs in the vision of its disappearance:

> PHAN. Farewell!
> MAN.   Say, shall we meet again?
> PHAN. Farewell!
> MAN.   One word for mercy!
>   Say, thou lovest me.
> PHAN. Manfred!
>   [*The* SPIRIT OF ASTARTE *disappears*] (2.4.154–57)

Here Manfred's demand for appearance is ultimately answered by an *aphanisis,* by the appearance of terror as *disappearance.*

The agency of disappearance is brought into being largely by the use of incantation or *repetition.* This invocation of the return exteriorizes and objectifies forces that are, according to the commentaries by Byron, the elements of Manfred's own interior struggle that he attempts to contain in the writing:

> Mysterious agency!
> Ye spirits of the unbounded universe!
> Whom I have sought in darkness and in light—
> Ye, who do compass the earth about, and dwell
> In subtler essence—ye, to whom the tops
> Of mountains inaccessible are haunts,

And earth's and ocean's caves familiar things—
I call upon ye by the written charm
Which gives me power upon you—Rise! Appear! (1.1.28–36)

However, the "written charm" fails to force the apparitions, and Manfred must resort to a more powerful spell, which has its origin in a literal black hole of self-consuming desire, a "star condemned, / The burning wreck of a demolished world, / A wandering hell in the eternal space" (1.1.44–46). Manfred's conjurations finally succeed through the power of this *image* of cosmological presence/absence. The mediation finally forces the exteriorization and apparition of "the thought which is within me and around me," the thought that literally terrorizes him to death.

But here is a paradox: the sublime thought that has its origin not in a "written charm" but in a terrifying "power deeper than all yet urged" is finally effected *through writing and speech,* through the incantation and the order, so apropos to theatrical alchemy, to "Appear!" A hidden power, seemingly deeper than all others, is projected into that single word, which itself appears again and again in the text. This word in turn disperses itself into the incantatory multiplication of words that appear and disappear as the condition of theatre/performance itself.

The invocation to appear, to take on form and substance in the act of enunciation, identifies the space of Manfred's performance as a space of production. It is, however, a space of production in which the insubstantial is objectified not as commodity but as *ideology.* The truncated processes of objectification in Restoration drama are here reclaimed and rerouted through the psyche, where they take on the lineaments of a psychic tyranny: "We are the fools of time and terror," says Manfred, "Days / Steal on us, and steal from us; yet we live, / Loathing our life, and dreading still to die" (2.2.165–67). Indeed, the creation of the romantic imagination represents yet another stratification or lamination in the history of the body's terror.

The mechanism of this assault is bound up, again, in the idea of the Sublime, but a Sublime that shows itself not as an ecstatic perception of affinity between imagination and nature, but rather as the recognition of the failure of signification when faced with seemingly limitless force. Thus Manfred and Beatrice Cenci are unable to pronounce the crime, not because of its heinousness, but because the crime is *the failure of speaking-consciousness itself,* which can only be expressed as silence. This is, as I have suggested, the silencing lack of the political unconscious, a Lacanian space of repression in which the social continuously recreates itself. Thus Manfred's silence, like the silence of Beatrice or Prometheus, whom I will discuss later, is closely aligned with Benjamin's notion of heroic silence—the space of a concealed social production, which is what the silence of the tragic hero represents. Thus the contrast in each of these characters (Beatrice, Manfred, and Prometheus) between eloquence and silence comes to represent in each case a passage from something like a gestural and "social" language to the silenced language of the political unconscious, and to the *genetic* "crime" of insufficiency that inhabits and informs it. The apparent silencing of the voice, in other words, reproduces the seeming interiorization of the unconscious that romanticism represents.

In another seeming paradox, this interiorized insufficiency resurfaces, as it does in Otway, as excess. In both *The Cenci* and in *Manfred* nature appears not in its usual romantic mode as a healing or energizing power, but as congestion, an alien and alienating malignancy impinging on the mind. Moreover, this predicament does not lead Manfred to seek redemption either in nature or in the spirit, but instead leads him back to significatory systems. Even though he throws out the "written charm," he still uses the spoken word (at least in the text) as his last invocation of power. And when Manfred finally dies, his "liberation" is effected as a refusal to speak, a refusal to *pray* for redemption, a classical-heroic silence that implies, as it does in Beatrice's silence, a plenitude of language *unspoken,* "all things swim around me, and the earth / Heaves as it were beneath me" (3.4.147–48).

Thus the Byronic ontology of the Sublime, although obsessed with the limitless, is itself defined by the bounds of signification. The acute pain of Manfred is best characterized by the torture that this closure generates. The *authoritative power* of Manfred's language, in fact, is rooted in a phenomenology of pain whose origin *is* the seeming mind. At play's end, Manfred is able to repel the spirits of death by the sheer force of words only because he invoked the power of his suffering:

> SPIRIT.   But thy many crimes
> Have made thee—
>   MAN.   What are they to such as thee?
> Must crimes be punished by other crimes,
> And greater criminals?—Back to thy hell!
> Thou hast no power upon me, *that* I feel;
> Thou never shalt possess me, *that* I know:
> What I have done is done; I bear within
> A torture which could nothing gain from thine:
>   [*The* DEMONS *disappear*] (3.4.122–28)

The Byronic Sublime, if indeed such a thing exists, is the recognition of an excess of *pain* produced by the "deconstructive" techniques of torture deployed through the limiting conditions of thought; this pain eventually becomes associated with the terror that is madness, and with the terror of going mad.

The outward show of this internalized and invisible torture is remorse, the remembrance of a prior crime that seems still to exist in the striations of the imagination which had sought to transcend transgression. As Manfred summons the celestial Phantom of Astarte, with whom he has presumably had unspoken incestuous relations, and who exists in the play as yet another incarnation of desire located in an absent/present body, he responds with an outpouring of guilt and anguish.

Yet we can hear, ironically, in his expressions of remorse a specific inversion of an earlier, *remorse-less* discourse—the social relations of the Restoration and their cruel plays of wit, which culminated in physical restraint and implications of torture. Manfred's response seems to come as an apology and act of contrition for these earlier practices, whose disciplining effects Manfred has now internalized:

> Astarte! my beloved! speak to me:
> I have so much endured—so much endure—
> Look on me! the grave hath not changed thee more
> Than I am changed for thee: Thou lovedst me
> Too much, as I loved thee: we were not made
> To torture thus each other, though it were
> The deadliest sin to love as we have loved.
> Say that thou loath'st me not—that I do bear
> This punishment for both—that thou wilt be
> One of the blessed—and that I shall die; (2.4.118–27)

This speech stands as an almost perfect (and opposite) complement to the speeches of Dorimant in *The Man of Mode,* right down to the characterization of love as disease and death. The kinds of exterior social constraints operating on an unrepentant character like Dorimant have been transposed, and now exist as a more fully developed *social conscience,* whose primary violence upon the body operates out of mind as guilt.

Certainly guilt does not appear first in romantic drama, but it appears there as a central and critical force. We see it again and again in the internalized penitence, regret, and anxiety of the romantic hero, which is conceptualized in Byron's drama (as it is in other romantic arts) in the repetitive thematics of darkness, perilous depth, concealment, disappearance, fragmentation, and madness carried within the hero's consciousness throughout the temporal course of the play. These thematics appear with notable regularity as the form and substance of the Other, the concealed watcher, the "spirit of the spell":

> Though thy slumber may be deep,
> Yet thy spirit shall not sleep;
> There are shades that will not vanish,
> There are thoughts thou canst not banish;
> By a power to thee unknown,
> Thou canst never be alone;
> Thou art wrapt as with a shroud,
> Thou art gathered in a cloud;
> And forever thou shalt dwell
> in the spirit of this spell.

Though thou seest me not pass by,
Thou shalt feel me with thine eye
As a thing that, though unseen,
Must be near thee, and hath been;
And when in that secret dread
Thou hast turned around thy head,
Thou shalt marvel I am not
As thy shadow on the spot,
And the power which thou dost feel
Shall be what thou must conceal. (1.1.203–22)

The fragmentation of the Byronic world into dark and demonic forces, and the disarticulation of the Promethean world into myriad demiurges, demons, and gods, demonstrate in each case a kind of sedimentation by which specific indices of consciousness are created, and in which the mind of the hero can then be "read" and "understood." In a kind of alchemical table of psychic elements, the minds of both Manfred and Prometheus are parsed out into their separate forces and elements—both material (air, earth, water) and psychic (demons, furies, destinies). Moreover, the presence of each is enunciated, in many cases, as a disembodied voice, the voice of the authoritative Other, or as Foucault might say, as a pure "enunciative modality."

The psychic and elemental forces exist in these plays as words floating on the air, as moments of signification by which a specific operation of mind is categorized. We detect echoes of the morality play here, but those forces were moral, or seemingly "always already" codified: they seemed to move in an already exteriorized realm. They appeared to roam the cosmos at large as phenomena separate from the hero, and controlled by God or Satan, waiting to be summoned by that objectified and fully codified Other (God or the devil).

In the romantic verse plays, the moral has finally infected the body and has produced the hallucination of a "private" aesthetic vision—the moral axis is dispersed as the internalized a(n)esthetic of the hero/artist. Thus in both *Manfred* and *Prometheus Unbound,* crime itself is sublimated and dispersed back into the play as poetic discourse. This anesthetic exists, like the *Quem Quaeritis,* as yet another sort of theatrical apotheosis of crime characterized as a spectacle of the legal/theatrical: "Let others flatter Crime," says Prometheus, speaking like the prosecutor, "where it sits throned / In brief Omnipotence" (1.1.400–402).

The romantic mythic hero, emblematized in Manfred and Prometheus, expresses the end and origin of his being in pain and terror: "In each human heart terror survives," says Prometheus. This pain and this terror are generated by an unspeakable crime, which is not named but is continually spoken *about*. In this, both heroes remind us of the Greek Medea, who speaks so often *about* silence that she eventually entombs silence in the word itself. Thus while Manfred's crime exceeds words, it also exists as a pure language sign: "that which is within me; read it there— / Ye know it, and I cannot utter it" (1.1.138–39). Similarly, Prometheus demands the utterance, the rearticulation and remembrance, of the crime that has condemned him to pain and torture. Both heroes, then, try to locate crime in the words that name it, and both eventually come to identify crime and the ambiguous causes of suffering with the catastrophe of language itself. The crime, finally, is not spoken; it is speaking itself: "A spirit seizes me and speaks within: / It tears me as fire a thunder-cloud" cries the Phantasm of Jupiter, as he feels the words of prophecy rise in his mind and threaten to obliterate him (1.1.254–55).

We confront the crime of language most especially in Shelley's *Prometheus,* in which the desire to realize the disappearing presence of language is associated with a primal curse that has kept truth (in the persona of Prometheus) terrorized: "there is a secret known / To thee . . . / The fear of which perplexes the Supreme: / Clothe it in words, and bid it clasp his throne / In intercession" (1.1.371–76).

Shelley's *Prometheus* is predicated upon this crime, which is speaking itself. The movement of the disremembered crime through memory and into language is the crucial dramatic movement in this play. Just as Byron's *Manfred* operates in terms of performance—the insistence, again and again, that the insubstantial appear and take form—so *Prometheus* operates in terms of enunciation: what is not spoken, what can never be said, what was once spoken and forgotten, what is spoken in different tongues, what must be spoken again and perhaps again. These are the critical turns in the play as it tries to rearticulate the Nietzschean primal crime as both blessing and salvation.

This is an impossible task. Language itself seems to rebel against such idealism. Prometheus summons the Phantasm of Jupiter and beseeches him to reveal the curse that Prometheus spoke eons ago, and has now long forgotten. The Phantasm responds:

> PHANTASM OF JUPITER. Why have the secret powers
> of this strange world
> Driven me, a frail and empty phantom, hither
> On direst storms? What unaccustomed sounds
> Are hovering on my lips, unlike the voice
> With which our pallid race hold ghastly talk
> In darkness? And, proud sufferer, who art thou?
> PRO. Tremendous Image, as thou art must be
> He whom thou shadowest forth. I am his foe,
> The Titan. Speak the words which I would hear,
> Although no thought inform thine empty voice.
> THE EARTH. Listen! And though your echoes must
> be mute,
> Gray mountains, and old woods, and haunted springs,

Prophetic caves, and isle-surrounding streams,
Rejoice to hear what yet ye cannot speak.
      PHAN. A spirit seizes me and speaks within:
It tears me as fire a thunder-cloud. (1.1.240–55)

Language speaks *through* the Phantasm. Located in the authoritative Other (Jupiter) a memory, language precedes the Phantasm and enunciates its desires before the Phantasm (or even Jupiter himself) can apprehend them. Language, in Artaud's words, "steals" desire before desire can be realized. It leaves the voice *phenomenally* empty. This is the condition and substance of language as it reproduces itself *through the experience of pain*. Yet if one goes on to demand that language *heal* the pain it produces, one realizes a paradoxical impotence of language. Within this paradox broods madness; this particular problematic of language, so powerfully enunciated in Shelley and so much a part of later modernist thought, anticipates Artaud's particular maddened genius:

> No precise information can ever be given by this soul that is choking; for the torment that is killing it, flaying it fibre by fibre, is occurring below the level of thought, below the level that language can reach, since it is the very union of what creates the soul and holds it together spiritually that breaks down at exactly those times when life summons them to consistent clarity. No clarity is ever possible concerning this passion, this sort of cyclical and fundamental martyrdom. And yet the soul lives . . .[32]

This segment from "Fragments of a Diary from Hell" was written by Artaud to try and exorcise a mental anguish that stemmed in part from his perception of the incommensurability of language and pain. But we might just as easily read this segment as one of the most incisive commentaries to date on the particular agony of Shelley's play. And while we may see, in the romantic project, the very formulation of this "pain" as the formulation of a power that the system keeps secret and thus controls, and while we may decide that this *wordless* pain is, in effect, an illusion, the refusal of pain's enormity when it is experienced *in extremis* seems to me a peculiar postmodern obscenity (I am thinking here, for example, of Baudrillard's absurd contention that even pain belongs to the order of the hyperreal). What is torture, after all, but the systematic attempt to elicit the body's pain before it *can* be formulated or "thought" as language? What is terror but the very wordless response to this enormity? It seems to me that this pain of extremes, of torture, is what both Artaud and Shelley are trying to circumscribe in all of its unspeakableness as something like *pure consciousness*.

Both the phantasm of Jupiter (because he is only a phantasm, a vessel through whom language speaks, a ghost) and Artaud experience the agony of an infusion of consciousness fully formed, complete with words and images, complete with discursive formations and psychological objects, that enters the mind in a rapacious torrent of pain, usurping desire and placing it in the service of sociopolitical control. Both Artaud and the Phantom are figuratively raped by "their" minds, minds that in fact come from without as constructs of the sociopolitical order. This is the essence of the tragic Promethean *subjectivity* in Shelley's play, in which Titanic desire is subjected to and enslaved by the demands of representation when Jupiter commands the prophecy *be told* to him as the condition of Prometheus' freedom. The articulation of the prophecy would install Jupiter for ever as tyrant-king, but in Shelley's play, Prometheus refuses to speak the "secret" that would deliver the human race to final tyranny. Once again the *secret* power is the Unspeakable; it is the theatre of thought, submerged in the unutterable substance of history grounded in the reality of pain, "the slow years / Which thou must spend in torture, unreprieved" (1.1.422–23).

The romantic imagination, which paradoxically is both the product and the source of the "fully ripened" oedipal mind, is born and sustained by a grand ontology of pain, an ontology that was, some one hundred years later, more fully excavated by Artaud:

> From the pain mined from the bone
> something was born
> which became what was mind
> to marinate in the driving pain,
> of pain,
>   that womb,
> a concrete womb
>
>   and the bone,
>   the bottom of the bedrock
>   that became bone.[33]

There is a dialectical movement here by which pain and imagination create each other through mutual inscription ("From the pain . . . something was born"). It is as if pain were the necessary by-product of the creation of the imagination, or as if imagination were generated by the action of pain on the body through time (duration), by a "monotonous crucifixion," in the words of Artaud, "in which the soul destroys itself without end."

Indeed, Prometheus and Manfred do not merely *experience* pain, they *endure* it, welcome it, and even work to produce it in themselves. Though one hopes for release and the other does not, both heroes find their liberation *in* the endurance, which allows them to recreate the world through the pain of remembered time. Both Manfred and Prometheus seek liberation through the power of imagination-as-memory, by which the past and present are reconstructed in a visionary power expressed either through moral defiance opposed to the torment of the remembered crime (*Manfred*), or through the agency of cosmic love that transcends the agony of torture and cruelty *(Prometheus Unbound)*. In either case, *imagination* and *pain* seem necessary complements. Both playwrights locate the worst kind of pain *in* the mind/imagination, and both seek to work out their liberating visions specifically through the imagination *of* pain.

Elaine Scarry constructs an ontology of pain in the body along similar lines. Scarry sees the interdependence of pain and imagination in these terms:

> The only state that is as anomalous as pain is the imagination. While pain is a state remarkable for being wholly without objects, the imagination is remarkable for being the only state that is wholly its objects. There is in imagining no activity, no "state," no experienceable condition or felt-occurrence separate from the objects: the only evidence that one is "imagining" is that imaginary objects appear in the mind. Thus, while pain is like seeing or desiring but not like seeing x or desiring y, the opposite but equally extraordinary characteristic belongs to imagining.[34]

Although Scarry is not speaking specifically about the romantic imagination, and is talking more expressly of physical pain (physical torture, in fact), the linkage between pain and the imagination is striking for several reasons. Scarry recognizes the peculiar placement of the body in history, a placement that necessarily subjects it to pain and disappearance through violence. She also recognizes that the re-creation of the body-as-object is crucial to its reformulation within the systems of power. Although she does not privilege pain, she is quick to point out pain's unique place within the "fabric of psychic, somatic, and perceptual states," where it seems to be "the only [state] that has no object" in the world:

> Though the capacity to experience physical pain is as primal a fact about the human being as is the capacity to hear, to touch, to desire, to fear, to hunger, it differs from these events, and from every other bodily and psychic event, by not having an object in the external world.[35]

However, as I have suggested throughout this work, at least one other of these "psychic, somatic, and perceptual states"—namely fear—shares with pain its lack of an object-relation *when it (fear) is perceived in its extremity as terror*. Following Lacan's understanding of the phobic object as a kind of iconic displacement of the terrorizing possibility of *not being,* the phobic object becomes a mere "patch" covering nothingness. There is thus no *necessary* relation between terror and its object; the phobic object is expropriated by consciousness (the imagination) precisely *because* terror has no object in the world.[36]

Scarry sees the creation of literary works through the experience of pain and violence as the means by which we are able to understand the "deconstructive" force of pain and thus "reconstruct" the world as a product of the imagination. This seems specifically Shelleyean in its liberal and utopian presumption. The literary object, moreover, bears no *necessary* relation to the pain that generates it, but stands instead as a kind of provisional object in the world to which pain refers. As such, we are left to wonder how this literary object can reflect on that to which it only accidentally refers. In the history of drama, this phobic object, this "ill-fitting patch" that covers the rent in theatre's consciousness, is the romantic *play text itself,* which comes into being through the tortured imagination as the documentation of terror's consciousness coming into history as poetry, as *spoken writing.*

Consequently, the ideology of the romantic art misreads its repressive self-referentiality as truthful commentary upon "reality" or life. Thus when Shelley, in the *Defense,* sublimates the art object to history, he represses the art object's historical specificity beneath its presumed "universal" qualities ("A poem is the very image of life expressed in its eternal truth"). That life itself should be a historically conditioned category of thought is of course beyond the ken of romantic sensibility, and it is only in the modern period that the art object's absolute alienation from life is perceived as its (perhaps) greatest truth.

We see again and again in the corpus of romantic literature as a whole this focus on interiorized pain and torture as the inversion of the romantic preoccupation with the Sublime. Thus as Jerome McGann suggests in the afterword to *The Romantic Ideology,* there is a kind of final irony in the radical Shelley's participation in the attempted creation of a globalized ideology of mind, a coercive idealism that the poet articulates, even as he exults in the bliss of imagination (the very invocation of Kant in the *Defense*[37] sets up this irony) and exalts the function of poetry as the creator of "new" and reified "materials of knowledge and power."

The links between ideology and terror are made even more explicit in Shelley's play when Prometheus describes the attendant gods of Jupiter as "thought executing ministers" who trample down the beloved human race. At the head of these faceless minions, he creates Jupiter, the tyrant par excellence—he who murders desire by consuming all desires within himself, and who demands the subjugation of all forces by sheer force of representative power grounded in the threat of real pain. The oppositional political sensibilities of Shelley appear quite clearly delineated against this image. He seems to see the complete reinscription of sociopolitical repression in/as imagination haunted by the absence of the god/king in the external world (thus *the Phantasm* of Jupiter).[38] Here is Foucault, describing the reinscription of the theatre of punishment at the turn of the nineteenth century in France:

> [the legal code of 1791] provided, in effect, by means of the theory of interests, representations and signs, by the series and geneses that it reconstituted, a sort of general recipe for the exercise of power over men: the "mind" as a surface of inscription for power, with semiology as its tool; the submission of bodies

through the control of ideas; the analysis of representations as a principle in a politics of bodies that was much more effective than the ritual anatomy of torture and execution . . . [in which] *despair and time eat away the bonds of iron and steel*.[39]

In transposing the myth "back" into the imagination from history, where Shelley would "heal" its violations, he aids in the recreation of political repression as semiosis, psychic inscription, and oedipal psychology. What might have stood as a political allegory now becomes an imaginary landscape crisscrossed and defined by the forces of representation; as a result, the political world becomes a dreamscape, and all questions of political or social coercion are referred back to the "elemental" forces of consciousness (Jupiter, Earth, Fury) from which these neo-Hegelian "Idealisms" emerge.

The irony is that Shelley, through the committed, reforming vision of his poetry, unwittingly begins to reconstitute political repression as psychological repression, and in so doing abets the very process of oppression he most despises. Even as he acknowledges in his play the impossibility of representing what is most crucial to human beings (a crucial failure in romanticism, as I will show), even as he comprehends the futility and violence of cloaking desire in a language that is designed to subjugate it, Shelley engages by necessity in that same violence in its most acute form when he serves as midwife to the birth of a psychic logic begotten in the imagination and utilized as a new technique for directing the forces of repression. These are the forces that operate, in the words of Deleuze and Guattari, as internalized "microfascisms" sustained in the *mise en scène* of mind/family as reflections of the political tyranny within which they find their being.

The interiorization of the political/social,[40] which provides for the grand sense of community through imagination in Shelley's critical work, sets the direction for the coming collapse of the social in modernism. In modernism, the romantic belief in a curative, transformative Imagination collapses beneath the weight of a growing alienation and solipsism brought on by the terrorizing disarticulations of the economic and sociopolitical sphere. Modernist drama begins at the point where psyche and family begin to collapse as a symptom and reflection of much deeper crises of political, social, and cultural terror, crises that are bound up with the disintegration and dispersal of meaning and authority, a dispersal that is perhaps nowhere more clearly emblematized than in the emergent terrorist act of the postmodern period.

As terror is performing its "psychic curettage" in the English romantics, in romanticism's Germany, political terrorism emerges thematically on the stage for perhaps the first time in Buechner's *Danton's Death*.[41] In this play appears for the first time the double inscription of terrorism/theatre, which insinuates itself as a central motif in the "pan-modernist" theatres of the next century.

Buechner's play represents the very moment that terror "from below" begins to rearticulate itself and move more resolutely away from tyrannicide toward the *egalité* of modern terrorism. Thus as the provisional authority figure of Robespierre tells us th. 'terror is an outgrowth of virtue," and that "to punish the oppressors of mankind is a kindness," so the pre-modern practice of terrorism, some twelve years after Buechner's death, redefines itself in similar terms in the terrorist writings of Karl Heinzen, and a little later in the ideas of the Russian Terrorists Bakunin and Nechaev.[42] In these writings, the moral issue is the same as it is for Robespierre—the elimination of corrupt oppressors—but there is a fundamental shift as terrorist rhetoric begins to organize itself more and more around a lack, as power and oppression become increasingly dispersed and impossible to locate.

Similarly, Buechner's play marks in another, rather rough, way a specular reversal of state and anti-state violence. At the historical moment of the play's appearance, the violence of terrorist secret societies and tyrannicides becomes increasingly publicized and theatricalized in the productions of anti-state terror (the original spectacle of the Reign of Terror itself). At the same time, the spectacle of state terror begins to submerge itself in secrecy and silence as a means of economizing and dispersing its threat in the image of terror as an absence (also, ironically, an aspect of the Reign of Terror, which eventually interiorized terror as paranoiac self-suspicion)—the secrecy of its violence designed to reveal its presence *as* secrecy or absence.[43]

Moreover, with the actual removal of the king during the Reign of Terror, the king and his violent, authorial gaze is, as Foucault would say, eventually "reinscribed" (as in English romanticism) as an interiorized surveillance, in which "the sovereign" (language, authority, law) now observes and corrects from the "heart . . . of . . . representation," as a reflection that is alien and "deeply buried in an unreal space . . . foreign to all the gazes being directed elsewhere."[44] The paradoxical impotence of this elusive "sovereign," this Jovian Phantasm, exemplifies both the anxiety of romanticism's growing conviction of the inadequacy of representation to experience, and the simultaneous rage and guilt that this impotence engenders. This guilt and rage lead, eventually or inevitably, to the revolutionary fervor of the age, and later, to a kind of anti-intellectual "interior beheading" in the writings of Nechaev, Bakunin, and others. Nechaev, for instance, writes a tract entitled "Catechism of the Revolutionist" in 1869. Part Medea, part Byron, part Beckett, part Arthur Bremer, Nechaev exhorts the revolutionary through the dramatized life of the terrorist:

> The revolutionary is a doomed man. He has no interests of his own, no affairs, no feelings, no attachments, no belongings, not even a name. . . .
> In the very depths of his being, not only in words but also in deeds, he has broken every tie with the civil order and the entire cultured world, with all of its laws, proprieties, social conventions, and its ethical rules. He is an implac-

able enemy of this world, and if he continues to live in it, that is only to destroy it more effectively.[45]

Hence tyrannicide is reborn, this time without a king. The terrorist must now kill from the inside out. He must, like King Ubu, destroy thought, emotion, and intellect in order to function; he must "repressively desublimate" desire and thought in order to murder, thus preserving and concealing power in the very dis-organization of the psyche itself—a perfect reflection of the reordering of society after the king's execution. The actual movement of terror's dispersion in France is recreated, finally, across the seeming psychoglobal landscape of the coming modern period. As the king is removed from the tyrannicide, anti-state terrorism takes on the unanimous character we see in it today.

Georg Buechner enunciates this emergent, proto-modern, solipsistic terror *in* the theatre *as* theatre's terror in *Danton's Death:* "Have you seen the new play?" asks The Second Gentleman on the street:

> A Tower of Babylon! A
> maze of arches, stairways, halls—and it's all blown up
> with the greatest of ease. You get dizzy at every
> step. A bizarre idea! (He stops in embarrassment)
> First Gentleman
> What's the matter?
> Second Gentleman
> Oh, nothing! Your arm, sir . . . it's the puddle—
> there. Thank you. I barely managed it—that could
> have been dangerous!
> First Gentleman
> You weren't afraid?
> Second Gentleman
> Yes, the earth is a thin crust. I always think I'll
> fall through a hole like that. You have to walk
> carefully—you might break through. But go to the
> theatre—take my advice. (2.2)

The image of the puddle, a literal and oxymoronic "filled-up hole" in the text, is arresting: as the two men are discussing theatre, one of them stops in terror before the theatricalized rupture, and exclaims his ontologic Phobia of falling through this *béance* into the very truth of the illusion itself. His admonition immediately following, "But go to the theatre," thus takes on an ambiguous resonance: is he admonishing his companion to escape from truth into illusion, or to escape from the illusion of truth into the truth of illusion?

The sense here that theatre's dreadful illusions are somehow a refuge from a Phobic and ontological danger are both underscored and complicated in the next lines of the play, as Camille condemns the sensibilities of the "masses" who respond more readily to the fabrications of theatre than to life:

If they aren't given everything in wooden copies, scattered about in theatres, concerts, and art exhibits, they'll have neither eyes nor ears for it. Let someone whittle a marionette where the strings pulling it are plainly visible and whose joints crack at every step in the iambic pentameter: what a character! What consistency! Let someone take a little bit of feeling, an aphorism, a concept, and clothe it in coat and pants, give it hands and feet, color its face and let the thing torment itself through three acts until it finally marries or shoots itself: an ideal! . . . Take people out of the theatre and put them into the street: oh, miserable reality! (2.3)

The condemnation, articulated in the theatre, accuses the very audience watching it of the same misplaced awe and sympathy that repel Camille, when he exhorts Danton to "take people out of the theater and put them in the street!" (3.1) The complications are brought to an even more harrowing acuity when we realize that the revolution is *in every sense* theatre: it is theatre operating as "the site of violence" in the celebratory songs around the guillotine, and it is also Buechner's play text itself, the shadowy emanation of an actual historical pain.

The play, then, looks in two directions, and this is precisely the double vision that delivers it to its historical moment and beyond. While *Danton* may be seen as the mere reformulation of the events of 1789 and after, in a more important sense the play, as shown in the ambiguity of the Gentlemen's exchange, is an extension and prolepsis of the terror of "guillotine logic" into the modern period [46]—a kind of psycho-logic of absence, in which the internalization of the absent king (or, as in Genet, the Queen) generates a kind of raging, libidinal backlash that vents itself in the victimization of the absent king *as* an absence through the self-destructive urges of terror in and out of the theatre. Thus the formulation of the terrorist victim as simply anybody—the "democratic" anybody who exists as the very function of the king's death—and thus the final lines of the play:

A Citizen
      Hey—who's there?
Lucile
      Long live the king!
Citizen
      In the name of the Republic!

Circulating together, these lines secrete the very lymph of theatre's power play in history: Who's there . . . long live the [dead] king . . . in the name of the republic . . . who's there? . . . long live the king . . . This is the prefiguration of that circular terrorism that emerges in modernism, in which stable authority and identity are, at every turn, both repudiated and (secretly) longed for. This is a logic in which, as emblematized in *Danton,* terror/revolution becomes theatre, and theatre appears as revolution/terror, the dream's navel of terror's production: "We have not made the revolution," says Danton, sounding like Irma in Genet's *The Balcony;* "the revolution has made us." Finally, it is only death that resolves the blurring, by transposing theatre/life into each other in the reproduction of the same. As Danton says:

> What's the difference if they die under the guillotine or from a fever or from old age? As long as they can walk offstage nimbly and can make pretty gestures and hear the audience clap as they exit. (2.1)

The stage is set for the further smearing of the theatre/life distinction in the seeming disintegrations of the modern theatre, disintegrations that deliver us to the "real" theatre of fundamentalist terrorisms, "our theater of cruelty, the only one that remains to us, perhaps equal in every aspect to that of Artaud or to that of the Renaissance."[47] The spectacle of cruelty and terror afterward begin to take on their peculiar hyperconsciousness, the hyperconsciousness of a self-disgusted and self-terrorized world whose theoretical midwives, Nietzsche, Marx, and Freud, bring to final articulation.

6 TERMINAL STAGES

MODERNISM AND TERROR

Here is one of the current truisms: the modulation from romanticism to modernism initially appears in the theatre as a series of faults or fractures in the continuing excavation of the romantic psyche. These fissures are the epicenters of later modernism's sense of its final collapse, and they signal the apparent disintegration of the psychosocial. In these reverberations we see the seeming end of the imaginary human community, the eventual "end of humanism" itself, and the implementation of a different mode of terror—the digitalized terror of madness, radical alienation, solipsism, and cultural "molecularization."[1]

This, at least, is the sense of the modern period that we seem to have inherited from the modernists themselves. But it is an ambiguous inheritance, indeed an illusion; for the fragmentations of the modern period, modern alienation itself, are also the bare appearance of what the theatre has been suggesting all along, sometimes in spite of itself—that the "whole" represented by culture, identity, law, and propriety has always been multiple, fragmentary, and contingent. When Foible discerns the "cracks in the white varnish" as Lady Wishfort sits before her vanity mirror, she is literally reading the effects of a culture/self that is "always already" disintegrating. The Restoration stage, like theatre before and following, found in the make-up of mere appearances yet another Phobic mask that both concealed and revealed this seeming perceptual decay. Similarly, Manfred's "multiplicity of selves" conjured through his theatricalized spells, suggests a theatre that has always recognized the multiplicity of identity and the shifting terror of its uncertainty.

The terror of theatre, then, cuts both ways; while struggling to cement social relations with the illusion of the unitary, theatre at once activates a vision which sees "in the cracks" the falsehood of unities. Theatre is, in other words, a *dialectical* space, and any truth function brought to it is at once transmuted into its negation.[2] While we might imagine within this seeming function some possibility for a theatre that would operate as a field of sociopolitical resistance, we should also recognize that in this same apparently negating function, the bare appearance of disintegration on the modernist stage also conceals and reveals another, profoundly hegemonic function—performance's consolidation with/in the power networks of postindustrial capitalism, networks that operate *as* the mere appearance of disintegration and fragmentation, that operate, in a word, as *theatre itself.* For as Jameson has pointed out, the fragmentary universe of disparate and isolated consciousness that has given rise to poststructuralist theory presumes a concealed, a priori totality operating in the interstices as the "political unconscious" itself.[3]

But the unconscious is, by definition, an inscription that is necessarily concealed. So initially, at least, we are faced only with the symptom and the seeming—with the apparent transposition from romantic neurosis to modernist schizophrenia appearing in the postmodern period (as it did in the medieval Church) as a theatre cast into the Real by the disintegration of the social. But in modernism, unlike other periods, the very theatricalization of power's dispersed and ubiquitous violence operates, paradoxically, as power's principle mode of concealment. Thus as the mediations and images of power and violence seem simultaneously more pervasive and more unlocatable, confrontation and resistance become harder to formulate, and we are faced with a theatre—both the theatre-in-culture, and theatre-as-culture—that is marked, more and more, by a reactive violence, by discontinuities, and by a subtle metamorphosis in which desire for the terrifying Sublime is transmuted into a desire for terror *as* the Sublime—for violence as transcendence.

This metamorphosis forms an apparent continuum between two extremes, each of which stands at the edges of a broad-ranging theatrical ontology: the tension between the extremes of life and "the mere appearance of mere appearance," to use Nietzsche's term once again—the tension between the Real, in other words, between *history,* and the illusion that is its theatre. Thus some modes of theatre and performance have become increasingly obsessed with the tyrannical practice of theatre raised to a frighteningly intense degree; I am thinking of the rigors of Grotowski's work, or the blatantly authoritarian work of auteur directors like Robert Wilson and Samuel Beckett, or the frenzied and self-consciously "colonizing" theatre pieces of Richard Foreman. At the same time, other forms have become fixated on the terrifying appearance of actual violence on stage, as in the work of body artists like Vito Acconci, Marina Abramovic, Stelarc, and Chris Burden, discussed below. Meanwhile in political culture the terror of oppositional violence—anti-state terror, or what has been called "terrorism from below"—becomes more and more dramatized on the stages of various international "theatres of terrorism."

Consequently, the appearance of political violence—of terrorism—in the modern period ultimately emerges either as the often hidden, tyrannical desire to preserve the seeming orders of power at all costs, or else as the sublime desire to obliterate limits (Jameson's "untranscendable horizon" of history inscribed in the limits of representation). Thus while political hegemonies often work to conceal their terrorisms, or to reveal them only *as* concealment,[4] disaffected political groups and artists alike have sought to pull away the Phobic mask and articulate (or try to) the terrorism concealed by state representational silence through the spectacles of theatricalized violence. This reactive violence, this violence of *ressentiment,* seems more and more to define the terrorized condition of solipsistic, postmodern perception itself. This perception represents, then, the theatricalized effect of state terror's very consolidation and secretion.

These conditions are reflected back into the "real" theatre again in a kind of imaginary tension or continuum between a "conventional" and largely bourgeois theatre of relatively stable theatrical forms (still naturalism and realism in most cases), and another, more overtly violent theatre of "the new"—theatres of ever-shifting forms and uncertain content, theatres of disjuncture, conceptualization, and experiment. This imaginary opposition between order and chaos, between "the fragmentary" and "the totality," is, moreover, carried within individual forms of performance and theatre as the very condition of their existence. Thus the debate between "experimental theatre" and "performance art" in the seventies, or the nervous adoption of new performance techniques in the more traditional regional theatres in the eighties, seems to reflect (albeit weakly) the larger tensions between bourgeois and anti-bourgeois theatre, between theatre and life, between theatre and politics.

At any rate, the changes and oppositions, Imaginary or not, have operated against a background of presumed identity. That is, there seemed to be, somewhere, a "world of the theatre" that was a definable, and in some ironic sense, stable world that needed to be either preserved, radically altered, or obliterated, depending upon one's cultural proclivities. Thus the tension between perceived forms and "anti-forms" in modernism's theatre have paralleled, in a peculiarly modernist way, the tension between hegemonic and democratic power in Western cultures. The debate between tyranny and anti-state violence, which has been an ongoing theme in the theatre, has, in the modern period, shifted in a quite self-conscious way from a didactic debate to a formal one; even as "realistic" or "naturalistic" plays express didactically the terror of dissolution, loneliness, and alienation, other, more "experimental" plays express a kind of terrorism in and through their own shifting forms.

As Jameson and Foucault tell us, it may be impossible to see the oppressive lineaments of our present episteme; it may be impossible to uncover the contents of the political unconscious, in other words. Nevertheless, we might look at the more overt and changing forms of terror's theatre for some hint as to the particular strategies of the concealed hegemonies.

If, for example, we focus our attention for a moment on the truism, on the apparent "spectacular" appearance of terror's effects on the modern stage in the forms of fragmentation and solipsism, we might begin to define modernism's hegemonic terrorism provisionally as the negation or inversion of terror's fragmentary image on the stage. We can follow the romance of modernist theatrical disintegration, then, as the inversion of postindustrial, multinational capitalism's consolidation of power—a consolidation effected through the decentralization and displacement of power and capital accumulation (multinationalism, corporate diversification, mergers and acquisitions, and so forth).

In the movement of these final pages, as we bring together the fragmentation of modernist perception, and the fragmentation that I have posited as the basis for theatre itself, it becomes clear that the present project takes as its point of departure the very ethos of the postmodern for its rereading of theatre history. The fragmentation that is thought is here reinscribed in the hyperconsciousness of the postmodern as the object and effect of its own history. The divisive fragmentation of thought, then, stands as the sign of its own unknowability, and for the unknowability of the hegemonies that have deployed it. This fragmentation becomes its own *kathartic* function, in other words, displacing the pain of the division with the discourse of displacement. This is the reification: the fragmentation of thought transformed into the thought of fragmentation.

We can already begin to discern terror's displacements from imagination to social disintegration in early Ibsen. *Peer Gynt,*[5] for example, not only bridges a chronological gap between the drama of late romanticism and early modernism, but also provides a conceptual transition. Although formally a play like *Peer Gynt* belongs more properly to the mythic, quasi-psychological world of the romantic verse drama, it represents at the same time the gradual reformulation of a new cultural consciousness, the political consciousness of modernism operating in the guise of the mythic and ironic and now working through its ideologic function *as theatre production.*

In spite of the play's modernist ironic timbres, Peer's travels, for example, are usually discussed in terms of an interior quest through a terrain of imagination, where he meets the monstrous and bestial forces ("Witches, Gnomes, Goblins, Elves, *etc.*") of his own dissolute spirit. Moreover, like *Manfred* and *Prometheus Unbound,* the play seems, at some level, to promote the virtues of endurance in the face of pain and terror, as Peer wanders the mythicized, desolate landscape of mind with the determination—if not the mettle—of the Byronic hero. At the play's end, as he is about to return home to his love Solveig, he speaks of this interior desolation in distinctly Byronic terms:

> Is there no one, no one to hear me even—
> No one in darkness, no one in heaven—!
> So unspeakably poor, then a soul can go
> Back to nothingness, in the misty gray. . . .
>   let me be covered by drifting snows;
> Scratch on a rock, "Here no one lies." (5.10)

Although we may think at once of Manfred's heroic desire for, and terror of, obliteration, we are not, alas, reminded of Manfred's courage in the face of this nothingness. In the final scene Peer cannot screw up the courage to enter Solveig's hut, and stands before the door in an agony of hesitating, muttering, existential indecision:

> Forward and back, it's just as far.
> Out or in, it's a narrow door.
>   (Stops.)
> No! Like an endless, wild lament,
> It tells me: return, go in where you went.
>   (Takes several steps, but stops again)
> Roundabout, said the Boyg!
>   No! this time
> Straight through, no matter how steep the climb! (5.10)

Through the course of the play he produces within himself the hesitating prototype of a later modernist hero, something like Beckett's Clov—a paralytic and oddly bankrupt figure lost in a grey and hollow landscape of dissolute self. Yet in spite of this, the textures, though ironic, still remember and invoke the myths of romanticism.

In the period following *Peer Gynt,* we see an interesting development in Ibsen's vision. In his "middle" or "modern" phase, the evidence of cultural decay is no longer revealed through the historico-mythic structures of ironic heroic quest, but rather through the corrupted traditions of love, marriage, and family, which are now depicted "realistically." Yet as different as his earlier plays may seem from such plays as *A Doll's House* or even *Hedda Gabler,* what we see in Ibsen's changing forms is merely the final transposition and compression of monstrosity from the mythic-ironic into the psycho-political and eventually solipsistic sphere of modernist consciousness, where the felt impoverishment of romantic interiority is clearly revealed in the *realization* of the mythic character as absurd and banal. The insatiable, monstrous, troll-like desires of Hedda Gabler, for example, when revealed within the cultural poverty that drives her to excess, seem even more mean and pathetic than they would in the landscape of *Peer Gynt*. Similarly the mythic monstrosity of Krogstad's actions in *A Doll's House* are greatly reduced when subjected to Ibsen's sociologic apology. The demonic energy of his evil is effectively repressed in his "salvation" by the love of a good woman.[6]

Eventually, though, as Ibsen's exploration took him deeper into the mechanisms of psychic desiring in plays like *The Master Builder* and *When We Dead Awaken,* "scientific" realism and naturalism no longer seemed sufficient devices for inquiry, and his plays began to touch more upon the techniques of symbolism and expressionism as a means of presenting the psychic forces of the collapsing ego.

Yet as much as Ibsen eventually struggled with the limiting conditions of naturalism and realism that he inherited from the popular theatre of the nineteenth century, his drama was still constrained by the "classical" conventions he sought to surpass. The logical development of the Ibsenian "well-made play," in fact, suggests an Aeschylean juridical structure operating beneath the smoothly formed surface. In a great economy of language, for instance, Ibsen constantly *legislates* a past that is the necessary condition of the present, and he does so in a way that suggests that the past exists as evidence that can be brought more or less intact before the judicial eye.

These revelations of character in society are delimited by the conditions of a nineteenth-century positivism in which the events of the past, though perceived differently by each character, are nonetheless presumed to exist empirically. In Ibsen, all the disparate facets of memory are reconstituted as *truth* through the forensics of dramatic investigation. Yet this action presupposes a communal consensus that the deeper strata of Ibsen's plays often seem to deny: "all our spiritual sources are poisoned," says Thomas Stockmann in *An Enemy of the People,* and "the whole of our vaunted social system is founded upon a cesspit of lies."[7]

Although the complexity of Ibsen's plays belies any easy analysis according to simple cause and effect, the surface structures often seem to support the traditions of categorical knowledge, causality, and empirical evidence. Thus while we can certainly acknowledge the genius of Ibsen's achievement in the well-made play, we can also see that by exposing psychic terror to the light of nineteenth-century "knowledge"—in sublimating terror to dramatic structure and "psychology"—Ibsen, like any number of playwrights before him, effectively *repressed* terror by consigning it to the systems of representational power through the agency of dramatic mimesis.[8]

In his later work Ibsen seems to have struggled against these constraints, as his dramatic forms began to approach various anti-realistic techniques. But he was unable to fully explore these new forms before his death in 1906. What is most significant for the present study is that Ibsen, as the seminal figure of modern drama, who moves from the mythic to the psychopolitical, seems to have located the collapse that characterizes modernism in the dual fragmentation of the social and psychic, a fragmentation that seemed to exceed the explicative power of realism and naturalism.

August Strindberg interceded where Ibsen could not. What we see in Strindberg's plays isn't so much the objectification and displacement of psychologic terror in "realistic" or emblematic characters or naturalistic plot devices, as it is the movements or oscillations of psychosocial catastrophe itself. Terror is no longer just an effect of theatre in modernism, it is also its subject/object. The disintegration of family and class-centered society,[9] and the destruction of the individual psyche,[10] expose an exhausting, solipsistic terror at the heart of culture, a terror that seems categorically causeless and empty.

In *The Dance of Death, Part I*,[11] for instance, the fatigued or stressed textures of the play (a fatigue that belies the tremendous energy of Strindberg's dramatic composition) are conveyed in an almost hyper-realistic dialogue that approaches the absurdity of Beckett:

> THE CAPTAIN. Isn't it time for mackerel soon? It's fall, isn't it?
> ALICE: Yes—it's fall. . . .
> THE CAPTAIN: Both inside and outside! But no matter! Apart from the cold that comes with autumn—inside and out—a grilled mackerel with a slice of lemon, and a glass of white burgundy, is not to be disdained.
> ALICE: The thought of that promptly made you eloquent, didn't it?
> CAPTAIN: Have we any burgundy left in the wine-cellar?
> ALICE: I didn't know that we have had a wine-cellar for the past five years.
> (1.1)

The repressed violence that comes to the surface again and again in the dialogue between Alice and The Captain, the violence that has caused "twenty-five years of misery," is often ascribed by critics to Strindberg's own unhappy marriages and tumultuous life and to his resulting rejection of social proprieties and institutions such as marriage. But it is never so simple in Strindberg. To approach the terror and pain in his work at an autobiographical level alone is to describe the play from the inside out and to reduce Strindberg's complexities to simple cause and effect. As I have already suggested, Strindberg seems to be after exactly the opposite of cause and effect. Even at his most bitterly self-indulgent, his plays seem to circle a noncausal center; it is as if terror and pain were self-perpetuating and not produced by any person or thing or condition.

Thus when Strindberg's characters are emblematic, it is in a wholly indeterminate sense: if a character "causes" conflict—like Laura in *The Father*[12]— she appears less a villain than the terrorized victim of a society that is collapsing into itself. As the Father says to Laura after her "crime"—which is precisely no crime—is revealed:

> And where does the fault lie? Perhaps in our spiritual, Platonic marital relations. One used to marry a woman for love; but nowadays one enters into

partnership with a business or professional woman—or one shares one's bed and board with a mistress! And then one has illegal intercourse with the partner—or one casts a stigma upon the mistress! But what becomes of love—healthy, sensuous love? It dies as a result! And what happens to the offspring of this sort of love in shares, payable to the bearer, without any mutual responsibility? And who is the bearer when the crash comes? Who is the physical father of the spiritual child? (54)

Although marriage is here condemned as a "cause" of discord, the origin of the problem is located at a much deeper level, in the history of the economization and *incorporation* of body, passion, and mind that characterizes Western history and its theatre.

In *The Pelican,* one of Strindberg's later plays, the familial and the political again seem to disappear into one another. Although the play ostensibly take place within a particular family, many of the expressionistic intonations of the play suggest political allegory, but political allegory that is itself dismantled by the schizophrenic intensity of the action. Here there are master-slave relations that seem at once invasive and pervasive. In a scene late in the play, the twisted psychopolitical gaming of Jean Genet is suggested in the oscillations of power between Mother and Daughter:

THE DAUGHTER: . . . From now on I'm going to be in charge here!
THE MOTHER *(furious)*: You mean I'm going to be your maid?
THE DAUGHTER: I, yours; and you, mine. We'll help each other.[13]

There is no simple resolution of the master-slave complex here. One does not, as Genet knew, merely overthrow power; social oppression cannot be dismantled in the political arena, nor within the family or psyche. Each character indeed seems bent on his or her own self-destruction in the other, despite each one's pathetic claims to power in an entropic universe of diminishing resources:

THE SON: It's hopeless, isn't it?
THE MOTHER: Yes, there's no hope at all.
THE SON: That's right . . . No hope at all!
        He leaves.
. . .
THE MOTHER: Close the window, Frederick!
        A flowerpot is blown down.
Close the window! I'm freezing to death and the fire is dying in the stove!
. . .
        Don't turn off the lights!
THE DAUGHTER: We have to economize. (3)

This enunciation of hopelessness and impoverishment is not merely an expression of existential depletion, it is also a psychopolitical awakening; as each of the "sleepwalkers" in the play comes to consciousness he or she realizes that there is no categorical solution to be found for the circumstances of history. This impasse is reached again and again in particular Strindberg plays, and is reflected in the entire corpus of his work, which moves in and out of various approaches to the problems of power: the psychological, the political, the spiritual, the scientific; all are investigated and ultimately found inadequate as sources of knowledge.

Ultimately, the destruction of humanity evident in Strindberg's drama is not merely the result of faulty social conditions, flawed human nature, bankrupt spirituality, or impotent science. Rather, it is the result of the very *disintegration* of formal knowledge within society, a disintegration that neither is preceded by nor follows from the disintegration of the individual, the family, or the social.

Strindberg moves into more and more highly individualized crypto-political texts, texts that seem always at the edge of solipsistic excess. This movement reflects a condition of dissolution into the pain and terror that is history, a history that Strindberg plays out as theatre. Indeed, the very sonata-like structure of *A Dreamplay*—theme, variation, recapitulation—suggests the eternal return that *is* history in the continuous reappearance of images in ever-changing contexts; what is repeated is also never the same. In the ending of *The Pelican,* the dispossessed Son tries to shatter the impasse of re-presentation when he resorts to a terrorist act, as a way out of the historical prison of return and repetition: he burns down the parental home. This single act of violence results in a kind of sublime bliss in which history *seems* to be swallowed up in a violence that *seems* ahistorical:

> THE SON: It was the only way!
> THE DAUGHTER: You did this!
> THE SON: Yes, what could I do?—There was no other way.—Was there any
>   other? Was there?
> THE DAUGHTER: No. Everything had to burn up, otherwise we could never
>   get out of here. Hold me in your arms, Frederick, hold me tight, dear
>   brother! I'm happier than I've ever been before . . . (3)

The bliss of history's end in the obliteration of memory is a critical impulse behind Strindberg's drama, and seems to hinge on his own need to exteriorize the violent desire to end history—personal and political—in the writing and staging of these intensely visual plays.

The terror and pain in Strindberg, then, is perhaps not so much a result of his own personal and domestic turmoil as it is the acutely-felt agony of humanity's disappearance into a history that Strindberg experienced in the collapse of his own domestic relations.

This disappearance of humanity into history is also, as I have already suggested, the critical moment of the emergent terrorist act. Whereas Ibsen's work seems intent on investigating the behavior of the subject under certain

kinds of social conditions, Strindberg seems to sense an apparent fragmentation of the entire social fabric, both public and personal, subject and object,
that is the seeming full-blown historical condition of modernism. Yet even
Strindberg, in his post-romantic attempts to reaffirm, however weakly, the
social institutions of marriage and family (such as the minor-key reconcilia-
tion at the end of *The Dance of Death*), does not fully comprehend the terror
and psychic destruction of the coming catastrophe that *is* modernism, a storm
that is located in the seeming destruction of the *self/family* and of the social
community at large.

There are moments when Strindberg seems close to such a realization,
and these are the moments when he seems the closest to terror and madness.
During his periods of wandering and experimentation, in his life as *flaneur-
cum-Parisian-street-person*, during *The Inferno* years themselves, Strindberg
glimpses the psychosis of the modern, and then withdraws. In 1893, for example, during a particularly troubled hiatus in his theatrical career, he se-
verely burns his hands while performing alchemical experiments in Paris. His
perplexed friends and acquaintances urge him to return to the theatre and
give up these distractions. He eventually goes back to writing and working
in the theatre, leaving his alchemical work behind him. But the interval seems
to have energized his playwriting, and he generates many of his best plays
after this return.

It is left to Antonin Artaud, some forty-five years later, to complete the
alchemical investigation from within the modernist crucible, and to describe
the affinities between theatre and alchemy that Strindberg had discovered on
the modern stage. Between 1931 and 1936 Artaud details these affinities in a
chapter of his manifesto, *The Theater and Its Double*, entitled "The Alchemical Theater":

> Now these [metaphysical] conflicts which the Cosmos in turmoil offers us in
> a philosophically distorted and impure manner, alchemy offers us in all their
> rigorous intellectuality, since it permits us to attain once more to the sublime,
> *but with drama,* after a meticulous and unremitting pulverization of every in-
> sufficiently fine, insufficiently matured form, since it follows from the very
> principle of alchemy not to let the spirit take its leap until it has passed through
> all the filters and foundations of existing matter, and to redouble this labor at
> the incandescent edges of the future.[14]

Indeed, the things that are "insufficiently fine" in Strindberg—his ready faith
in psychology, his desire to salvage somehow the family unit and the social
contract in the face of their apparent disintegration, his lingering faith in
reason and intellect—are absolutely atomized in Artaud's thought.

But Artaud goes much farther than this. He not only rejects the family
and its repressive violence—"Don't believe in father / or mother, / don't
have / papa-mama"—he refuses the entirety of Western onto-politics that has
given him over to pain and confinement: "don't have . . . nature, / mind /

or god, / satan / or body / or being, / life / or nothingness / nothing that is outside or inside."[15] This absolute refusal of the rational and categorical is the critical difference between Artaud's vision and the experience of cultural breakdown in the work of earlier modernist playwrights. While Ibsen and Strindberg fear the fragmentation, Artaud welcomes and develops it as a strategy to obliterate culture, science, and art—all collaborators in the assassination of life through the violence of representation, a violence that Artaud felt preceded thought and stole it away. For Artaud, finally, alchemy is the means by which thought might be imagined in a "pure" state, before the systems of signification and representation can steal and enslave it.

Clearly, "thought" for Artaud was far more than empirical knowledge, logic, or representation. It was "a vitality more precious than consciousness," an excruciating activity both of brain and body, "a wholeness that includes all of consciousness, and the secret pathways of the mind in the flesh." This thought is total: physical, spiritual, mental. It far exceeds the meager energies of mere reason:

> The day will come when my reason will have to accept them . . . these forces which from outside have the shape of a cry. . . . intellectual cries, cries born of the *subtlety* of the marrow. This is what I mean by Flesh. . . .
>
> For me, the word Flesh means above all *apprehension,* hair standing on end, flesh laid bare with all the intellectual profundity of this spectacle of pure flesh and all its consequences for the senses, that is, for the sentiments.
>
> And sentiment means presentiment, that is, direct understanding, communication turned inside out and illumined from within. There is a mind in the flesh, but a mind quick as lightning. And yet the excitement of the flesh partakes of the high substance of the mind.
>
> And yet whoever says flesh also says sensibility. Sensibility, that is, assimilation, but the intimate, secret, profound, absolute assimilation of my own pain, and consequently the solitary and unique knowledge of that pain.[16]

Thus theatre is the space of absolute potential, in which thought as pure *apprehension* desires its *being materialized into flesh* before reason and its representations can intervene and kill it. But theatre is not only the space in which thought is given flesh, it is also the space within which the fallen, tortured flesh of the body is *de*materialized back into thought, into the immediate apprehension of its own pain as a history that exceeds representation. Indeed, what Artaud envisioned was no less than a complete reunification of body/ thought realized in performance: "I imagine a system in which all of man would participate, man with his physical flesh and the heights, the intellectual projection of his mind."[17]

This reunification of body and thought in Artaud operates as a double inscription. Not only is the tormented body understood as the site of a "social inscription," but inscription itself is utilized as a weapon against the body's usurper. In his last days Artaud took to drawing and writing alchemical texts with feverish intensity. These texts were, in Artaud's mind, the literal flesh of the Other. The pieces that survive are fragile, almost relic-like, in a state of distress, "grated, furrowed, ground, and labored by his hand."[18]

These pieces were not mere representations of Artaud's fevered thought. To him they were the actual bodies of friends, enemies, and acquaintances. When Artaud attacked the paper with the ferocity of his vision, when he burned it and tore it, he believed himself to be burning and tearing the body of the receiver. Sometimes the burns and tears were directed to the receiver as a punishment, sometimes they were meant to be curative, sometimes they were executed and sent as a warning. But in all cases, the paper itself was transmuted in Artaud's mind into flesh and blood. The representation that Artaud had refused in the Imaginary/Symbolic indeed returned to him in the Real.[19]

In this late work of Artaud we have the completion of the dramatic inscription that we saw emerging in *The Spanish Tragedy*. Not only is the body the text, but the text is at one and the same time the body. The tenuous distinctions finally collapse. But for Artaud this collapse was not a disintegration; it was a reunification that signalled the promise of conquest over the seemingly endless processes of the body's redeployment and reformation by culture through "theatre's double."

I should reiterate: the reunification of body and thought was for Artaud infinitely more profound than a mere rejection of the Cartesian mind/body split. It spelled out a desire to absolutely obliterate both the theatre of state and its "present" body (which exists as its inscription, text, or wound in history: the law), in order to discover the absent, stolen body beneath its inscriptions. Artaud privileged the theatre as a form of thought precisely because, as the site of aboriginal violence, it is the only place in which the body can discover itself in this way precisely *as disappearance*. As Derrida writes, "the theatre of cruelty is born by separating death from birth and by erasing the name of man." Thus the theatre, like the fragmented body-thought displaced in order to be reformed in the image of the Other is, in Derrida's words "born in its own disappearance," in its *aphanisis;* and it was in this disappearance that Artaud sought, paradoxically, the "appearance of life itself."[20]

We are looking once again at the perceived origins of Western theatre. In the disappearance of theatre and man, and in the "appearance of life," Artaud desired the *erection* of the body and its thought prior to its death in representation/*resurrection*. He wanted the body's being/thought superior to materiality, in the Flesh of thought *before* the Word, before the Flesh's extortion into systems of signs and power. He wanted to present this body before it was subjected to the torturous inscription by the state, before its disappearance in the legerdemain of presence/absence through which power is established and maintained. He wanted theatre at the precise instant in which it passes from the terror of its own radical contingency into the sign systems

of terror*ism, before* the "monotonous crucifixion" of abstraction and its seeming finale in the empty tomb. He wanted theatre to appear as a kind of inverted hallucination, an anti-matter Mass that would annihilate the historical
movement of catastrophe-as-life outlined in the theology of the *Quem Quaeritis*. The theatre of cruelty would then reclaim and present the *actual* body
"stolen . . . at birth by the thieving god"[21] and concealed in the locus of the
Other before its torture, inscription, and secretion beneath the signifier. In
the theatre of cruelty we are at the very edges of the ontologic problematic
upon which theatre is based and in which we, and it, have our being.

Artaud knew that this appearance of the body, of *life* as present and not
"re-presented," was an impossibility; it exists only as pure potential. Yet,
paradoxically, although Artaud desired this potential, in Derrida's words he
also "desired the impossibility" of it. Although he realized that "the theatre
of cruelty . . . is already within representation," and thus impossible to produce as *life,* he thought that the existence of this theatre of cruelty as poten-
tial/impossibility might permit us to "conceive its origin, eve and limit, and
the horizon of its death." It would allow us to see, once and for all, that
through representation, humankind and its theatres are born simultaneously
in/to disappearance, in/to terror.[22] It is tempting to think that Derrida, also
seeing the impossibility of Artaud's project, desires it as well.

Artaud is part of that lineage that sees the possibilities of theatre in the
very subversion and impossibility of the theatrical itself. But unlike others in
that tradition, he is a theatrical epoch unto himself: Artaud and his writings
represent a historical and performative *béance* that is *articulated* as theatre, but
lacks, for the most part, actual theatrical being-in-production. Locked within
his thought, Artaud's theatre lapses into the silence of a Lacanian *"forclusion"*
that is, like the theatre of the romantic poets or Foucault's "suppressed theatre," the very condition of its existence.

Unlike the romantics, however, Artaud rejected the ability of representation, of language, to properly articulate (or at least suggest) what was outside of representation; like the romantics, he rejected the contemporary stage.
But unlike them he also rejected the traditions of thought and word that kept
the stage in place as an institution of repression. Thus while the romantic
poets ultimately deposited their dramatic works—riddled as they were with
béance, silence, *forclusion*—in the Symbolic (in language), Artaud's complete
rejection of the Symbolic and its Imaginary supports identified theatre in its
entirety as *béance,* and cast it into the Real, where it returned with all of the
hallucinatory force of cruelty and terror that one might expect.[23]

That Artaud's writings contain, in this one sense at least, the whole of
modernist and postmodernist ontology (or rather its anti-ontology) would
explain why his work continues to be so influential today. We can see how
all other theatrical enterprises after Artaud are, in some sense, implicit or
explicit attempts to resuscitate theatricality in the face of seeming cultural
dissolution. They are projects that try to understand and *recoup* the loss of

community or communality that Artaud pointed to in the black hole of his alchemist's crucible. Thus some of the most pessimistic voices of our age—Pinter or early Genet, for example—reflect in their very pessimism a latent desire to reconstruct the social after the burning vision of Artaud had reduced it to conceptual ash.

Derrida points this out when he lists the various kinds of theatres that "fail" to understand Artaud's vision, and thus fail to understand the nature of the postmodern crisis: "All non-sacred theatre. . . . All theatre that privileges speech, or rather the verb, all theatre of words. . . . All *abstract* theatre. . . . All theatre of alienation. . . . All nonpolitical theatre. . . . All ideological theatre."[24] Derrida indicts each of these forms because they fail to understand the depth of the cultural violence and oppression that supports them, lives through them, breeds in them. Even Brecht in his highly politicized "theatre of alienation" did not entirely grasp the root of the oppression that he so desperately wanted to overcome. By the same token, the seeming radicalism of some of the "happening" and agitprop performances of the late sixties dissolves beneath the light of Artaud's incandescent vision, inasmuch as it "substitutes political agitation for the total revolution prescribed by Artaud."[25]

Beckett's theatrical impoverishments do not fare much better in this particular essay.[26] Although never referring to him by name, Derrida dismisses Beckett when he dismisses "what is still called the theatre of the absurd" because of its "self-destructive speech" and gestures of "hopeless recurrence," which signify an existentially *"negative* relation of speech to itself," thus a "theatrical nihilism," which can never be, "in the sense understood by Artaud . . . an *affirmation.*"[27]

Indeed, for all of Beckett's compassionate resonance with alienation and hopelessness, for all of the raging pathos of his characterizations, his productions move silently and inevitably into a theatricalized terrorism, a "theatre of torture," which surreptitiously recreates the torture chambers of state in the agony of waiting and the pain of being bound. As H. Porter Abbot writes in a recent article on Beckett:

> Beckett is famous for his exactitude, for the precise realization of his will on stage. One should keep in mind, moreover, what Beckett does to his actors. He ties ropes around their necks and crams them in urns. He ties them to rockers. He buries them in sand under hot blinding lights and gives them impossible scripts to read at breakneck speed. The word for this is torture. . . . If one still needs to be convinced one can listen sometime to Billie Whitelaw describe the experience of being completely bound down with straps and braces for a performance of *Not I.* "Oh, Billie!" Beckett cried, when he gazed upon his immobilized creature, "what have I done to you?"[28]

What is most surprising—and most disturbing—about this insight is that Beckett, perhaps more than any other modernist playwright, seems at critical points closest to perceiving terror's origins in the thought of disappearance: "long hours of darkness . . . now this . . . this quicker and quicker . . . the words . . . the brain . . . flickering away like mad."[29] We would think him to be so appalled at the directorial tyranny of his work that we might wonder what makes him go on. The intense pathos of Beckett's work suggests that he is not doing it for the mere pleasure of its violence.

That is sometimes the sense we get in Pinter's work, however, where violence emerges as overt thuggery in plays like *The Birthday Party*. And while the plays of Genet move a great deal closer to an explicit equation between theatre and its tyranny—in *The Balcony* for instance—this equation is played out more as sociopolitical degradation and perversion than as ontological terror and collapse. In Beckett, however, violence is rarely overt, and is always grounded in a metaphysical necessity. The violence of tyranny that emerges in Beckett's plays appears because theatre *is the place* of that specular violence:

> VLADIMIR: Look!
> ESTRAGON: What?
> VLADIMIR: *(pointing).* His neck!
> ESTRAGON: *(looking at the neck).* I see nothing.
> VLADIMIR: Here.
> > *Estragon goes over beside Vladimir.*
> ESTRAGON: Oh I say!
> VLADIMIR: A running sore!
> ESTRAGON: It's the rope.
> VLADIMIR: It's the rubbing.
> ESTRAGON: It's inevitable.[30]

Indeed, the rope knotted around Lucky's neck in *Godot* is a real rope, and, we assume, really does chafe and burn through the endless, precise *rehearsals* (lit. "reharrowings" or reinscriptions) of a typical Beckett production; the real violence of Beckett's theatre irrupts immediately from the terror of its thought in practice.

Beckett confronts the relation between tyranny and theatre directly in *Catastrophe*,[31] in which the theatre that gives birth to tyranny, and the tyranny that supports theatre, bleed almost imperceptibly into one another.[32] Indeed, even the relations of power in this play are fused: is the figure in the chair—concealed, constructed, formalized—the victim of domination, or the formal representation of tyranny? We come to realize that the fusion itself emblematizes the absolute and pervasive tyranny of the theatrical ontology, in which each of the participants in the theatrical spectacle is alike victim and victimizer (it is, in fact, through Beckett's *Catastrophe,* with its endless readjustments and subtle, exact control of deportment, that we begin to understand the fine lineaments of terror in, for example, the details of deportment on the Restoration stage). This insight might seem at first to belong more specifically to Genet, but Beckett infuses his insights with a deep sense of *metaphysical* brutality through which he tries to address the very issue of theatre's terror, and thus point to theatre's *origins* in Deimic terror. In failing to recognize this, Derrida, in his earlier essay at least, does Beckett a disservice.

Thus in Beckett we can see how theatre's previous fascination with terror's effects in performance shifts to terror as the object/subject of theatre. We see this in a very different way in Genet. Whereas in Beckett we have the theatre's history replayed as an ontologic terror (see, for example, *Krapp's Last Tape*), in Genet, terror's history is played as theatre, indeed *is* theatre. In *The Balcony*,[33] for example, nearly every permutation of terror we have thus far discussed is replayed and "emptied out" in the theatre/brothel: from the flagellant terror imposed by the figure of the judge through his executioner emanation—the terror of the *Quem Quaeritis*—to the modern, psychosocial terrorism of surveillance and collapse, in the figures of Irma or the Chief of Police.

In each case theatre is represented as a lack that implies a terror—a hole within the various roles and discourses, which can find no substance to fill it; the "minus something" that makes a "true image . . . of a false spectacle," (75) a hole that is in fact the substance of theatre itself. Thus Genet ultimately identifies theatre as a sort of lack-production that generates culture. Like the myriad cultural authorial roles played out in the tiny theaters of punishment, the reality of power and authority itself is merely a function of the theatrical, as when the Chief of Police has his image "detach itself" from him, and go through the endless multiplicative functioning of the brothel's hall of mirrors. This endless mirroring of the role or image, the Chief of Police tells us, is what will ensconce him forever in power as a culturally internalized authority, which, like the absent Queen, operates only as a lack. And where does this "detachment" and mirroring have its origin?—in the theatre. Cultural power is thus *born* in theatrical lack. Danton's exclamation that "we haven't created the revolution, it has created us," is transposed—the characters in Genet's play haven't create the revolution, theatre has. As the Chief of Police says to Irma, the Madame and *regisseur* of the brothel's grand and minute theatricalizations: "Let them try [to penetrate reality]. I do as they do, I penetrate right into the reality that the game offers us, and since I have the upper hand, it's I who score." But Irma refutes him, speaking as the voice of theatre itself: "It was I who did everything, who organized everything" (50). And indeed within the theatre/brothel, culture and its rebellions have been produced and orchestrated through the endless warpings of desire and attendant costume changes. *Danton's* revolution as theatre becomes, in Genet, theatricality as revolution. We can glimpse in this reversal the potential theoretical proximity of Brecht to Genet, and even to Artaud—for if political culture emanates from, or *can be made to emanate from* theatre, theatre as a form has profound political possibilities as a tool for subversion and "true" revolution, *if theatre can find a way both to accept and resist itself.*

Here we should especially remember Brecht, who is indeed the most chastening example of theatre's power to conceal its deepest repressive and terroristic powers. As early as 1931, Brecht understood that poised against the subversive potential of theatre was the fact that theatre did not wish itself to be subversive, except in its own (status quo) cause:

> Theatre itself resists any alteration of its function, and so it seems desirable that the spectator should read plays whose aim is not merely to be performed in the theatre but to change it: out of mistrust of the theatre.[34]

Brecht, whose concern about theatre has been absorbed at each turn of thought throughout these chapters, saw perhaps more clearly than any theorist, before or since, the tyrannical potency of the theatre's ability to produce repressive social practices and conditions, not merely through its concealed ideological agendas, but also through its ability to neutralize all resistance:

> Today we see the theatre being given absolute priority over the actual plays. The theatre apparatus' priority is a priority of means of production. This apparatus resists all conversion to other purposes, by taking any play which it encounters and immediately changing it so that it no longer represents a foreign body within the apparatus—except at those points where it neutralizes itself. The necessity to stage the new drama correctly—which matters more for the theatre's sake than for the drama's—is modified by the fact that the theatre can stage anything: it theatres it all down.[35]

But Brecht seems, finally, to have underestimated the power of theatre, which, like Irma, always retains "the upper hand" of a status quo silence and silencing power. How else can we explain the reception of Mother Courage (in a production that Brecht approved) not as a war profiteer, but as "the irrepressible mother" whose presence all but obliterated the deeper strivings of the play?[36] We should, perhaps, recall Adorno's response to Brecht's didactic and formalist aesthetics, in which he warned that, in an age in which genocide has become a mere theme in art,

> works of art that react against empirical reality obey the forces of that reality, which reject intellectual creations and throw them back on themselves. There is no material content, no formal category of artistic creation, however mysteriously transmitted and itself unaware of the process, which did not originate in the empirical reality from which it breaks free. . . . It is this which constitutes the true relation of art to reality.[37]

Adorno seems to be suggesting that the real theatrical inquiry in the present age ought to focus its attention on the theatrical itself, that is theatre's relation to "reality." But it is dangerous to enter the theatre with such a political aim unless one fully realizes the power of theatre to reduce that aim to its own ends. Thus the production of a "message in art, even when politically radical, already contains an accommodation to the world." Theatre, "the stance of the lecturer," conceals "a clandestine entente with the listeners, who could only be rescued from deception by refusing it." This is the problem of political art, which not only "preaches to the converted," but also, more importantly, continues to "play along with the culture which gave birth to murder." [38] If we recall our original thesis—that theatre (re)produces culture without end—we realize that we are indeed dealing with a form that "gives birth to murder" in its own way, a way that is "always already" intrinsic to the performative.

So for all of Brecht's correct suspicion of the tragic form, we can still see in his theatre the ghosts of tragedy's power, a power that would displace fate with history, *hamartia* with false consciousness, and catharsis with socio-ideological correction through displacement by another, "enlightened" ideology/consciousness. The same charge can, unfortunately, be leveled against much political/performance theory today, theories that still operate according to the lineaments of tragic form, a form that at base seeks to affirm the displacement (catharsis) of one system of power and ideology with another, while maintaining its rights according to some notion of "fate" (that which is irresistible, an "untranscendable horizon") at the expense of the downfall of an Other (the locus of power and law—the patriarchal "hero"). The "rightness" of the displacing ideology is not what is at issue here, but rather the continuation of a concealed tragic impetus or form amidst claims to the contrary. The issue, finally, forms itself around our approach to tragedy—is the tragic to be defined primarily in terms of form, or in terms of concealed ideology? Perhaps the tragic is precisely that which conceals ideology as truth.

This question raises some complex issues. The nonlinear forms of, say, Adrienne Kennedy's plays *(Funnyhouse of a Negro, A Rat's Mass)* suggest a kind of anti-tragic structure that some theorists would see as a remedy to patriarchal conceptions of theatre as tragedy. Similar claims can be made for other kinds of performance art by women. The endurance pieces of Marina Abramovic, with their emphasis on objectifying violence, come most readily to mind, as do the cultural-historical critiques of Rachel Rosenthal, the essentially patriarchal history of tragic theatre is critiqued in the work of such playwrights as Caryl Churchill *(Cloud Nine)* or Marie Irene Fornes *(Fefu and Her Friends)*. [39]

Penetrating as these works may be on a didactic, formalistic, or even deconstructive level, they sometimes seem, in the context of feminist theory, to repress an important aspect of their existence as performance: the simple obscenity of their appearance *as* theatre. Fornes's play, for example, for all of its professed desire to realize intimacy between its characters/actors, does not seem to be aware of the corrosive influence of the audience on that intimacy. Thus while Emma and Fefu try to communicate their affection at some "authentic" albeit "theatrical" level, the audience watches anxiously "in the dark" as it were—empathetic, repelled, fascinated, distraught—voyeurs in every sense of the word, exuberant partakers of tragedy's pity and fear.

Similarly, in Churchill's play, the lurid relationship between the explorer, Harry, and the boy Edward (who is played by a woman) is both politically revelatory and consciously titillating. The politics of gender are brought into high relief through the luridness of a theatricalized "gender deconstruction." To ignore this aspect of the play, or even to repressively sublimate it as "the point of the play," is to ignore crucial political questions: to what degree does "the creation of theatre [spring] from the condition of unfulfilled desire in the male subject," to quote Sue-Ellen Case,[40] and to what degree does theatre emerge from the unfulfilled desire of the *human* subject? To what degree can human consciousness, male or female, ever hope to extricate itself from the Symbolic (which Case seems to equate almost exclusively with male desiring-production)? To what degree, finally, is the desire to elevate a new ideology to displace the old *by necessity* a *tragic* desire? I state the problem in these terms not merely as a criticism of feminist positions, but because it seems to me critical to confront the issue of theatre's essential and unredeemable corrosive power if feminist art, among others, is to survive "the ravin it has gorged." At some level, it is necessary to hate the theatre, and not merely the "male gaze" in the theatre.

The distasteful irony here is that a writer like Genet, for all his abominable cynicism and apparently repugnant attitudes toward women and politics, shows us an uncensored glimmer of corrective vision that sees the corrosive power of theatre in its rawest, most unredeemed form. Through each of its twisting, jaundiced permutations of psychopolitical desire, the transubtantiations of power in the theatre/brothel are both brutal and repugnant, a true testament to theatre's most unsavory alliances, and more profoundly, to theatre's proleptic and *concealed* productions of terror and coercion. When Irma says that each of her customers/costumers wants "everything to be as true as possible. . . . Minus something indefinable," she is pronouncing theatre's most powerful and "true relation with reality," as well as theatre's subtle intercourse with psychic terror. When the Chief of Police says, "I'll make my image detach itself from me. I'll make it penetrate into your studios, force its way in, reflect and multiply itself . . ." (48), he is likewise enunciating what is most essential and exact about culture/power's very creation in the panoptic tiny theatres of punishment and death that the theatre/brothel represents.

In fact, theatre in Genet appears, as it does in the present work, as a *kind* of origin, as the practice/site of a violence that is, as it is in Nietzsche, *essentially* theatre. It is clearly upsetting to hold up someone like Genet as an ideal of theatrical perception over and against writers whose aspirations I admire much more. But there is something in Genet that most deserves attention from those working in the theatre—the knowledge that all theatre is, at some fundamental level, repugnant. That theatre is deserving, perhaps, of our admiration, but also, as Artaud says, of our hatred. Whatever our political intentions, it would seem good advice to remember that hatred.

Before leaving Genet, however, we should note some crucial and insurmountable problems with his vision of theatre. Apart from his repellent attitudes and his cynicism, there is his misperception of theatre's material production. What is perceived by Genet as theatre's proleptic function (its anticipatory production of modes of coercion and terrorism in the *mise en scène* of psychosexual violence), is too often conflated with simple violence—as though terror and violence were identical. This conflation comes about because Genet seems to slip past the deeper problematics of ideology in the theatrical production and its violence. Ideologies and power plays abound in his work, to be sure, but they seem, by and large, to operate at the individual, psychosexual level, or when they do not, they operate reductively as pure political thuggery. As Mme Irma, theatre's voice and demigod, begins to shut off the lights of the brothel, and all the theatre-goers prepare to go home, the political cynicism and jaundiced sensibility of Genet emerge clearly:

> It took so much light . . . thirty-eight studios! Every one of them gilded, and all of them rigged with machinery so as to be able to fit into and combine with each other . . . And all these performances so that I can remain alone, mistress and assistant mistress of this house and of myself. . . . Bolt the doors, my dear, and put the furniture-covers on. . . . In a little while, I'll have to start all over again . . . put all the lights on again . . . dress up. . . . *(a cock crows.)* Dress up . . . ah, the disguises! Distribute roles again . . . assume my own . . . *(She stops in the middle of the stage, facing the audience)* . . . Prepare yours . . . judges, generals, bishops, chamberlains, rebels who allow the revolt to congeal, I'm going to prepare my costumes and studios for tomorrow. . . . You must now go home, where everything—you can be quite sure—will be falser than here. . . . You must go now. You'll leave by the right, through the alley. . . . *(She extinguishes the last light)* It's morning already. *(A burst of machine-gun fire.)* (95–96)

The implications are clear, and seem to align themselves with the general argument I have been making about theatre in history, namely that theatre is not an artifact of culture, political culture is an artifact of theatre. Even the revolution against culture is formulated as theatre, and usurped by it. If we think, again, of Irma as theatre em-bodied (a rather simplistic approach, I realize), her words are indeed chilling, but also a bit ambiguous—what after all is her, or theatre's, desire? Merely to "be left alone"? Is that *really* theatre's desire? Are we to assume a kind of ideological vacuum in her words? If so, Genet's eye is perhaps not jaundiced enough.

I think, in fact, that Genet's ambiguity is symptomatic of a deeper problem—a material conception of a theatre that is not sufficiently materialist. For if we attend to Genet carefully, we sense at every turn the suppression of thought's terror (anontologic terror) not into theatre, but into "mere" theatricality—that is, into an activity of performance that appears as the (reductive) moment of theatre itself, a moment of the purest artifice.

Now, in opposing theatricality and theatre, it might seem that I am opposing a materialist view of theatre with an essentialist view, but this is to miss the point. In pushing theatre's materiality past the moment of production, either as actual production or as writing/thought, I am trying to suggest a conception of theatre that is not a mere "desiring-production," but a moment, an instance of the possible, a "line of escape" charged with the certainty of its own (eventual) failure. This "line of escape," by virtue of its pure artifice, becomes, paradoxically, more than artifice. Theatre becomes a *condition of perception,* a condition whose shadow must be perceived before its emergence into materiality or material production. This, it seems to me, provides the only theoretical opportunity for theatre to escape both its inevitable absorption into patriarchal capital production and its inevitable neutralization as material/production. Facing Genet, then, I am not suggesting an anti-materialist theory of theatre, but am rather suggesting a recasting of thought's terror as a materiality that precedes production, which precedes its formulation as material*ism.*

The point here, however, is not to install Genet, or Beckett, or Artaud and through him Derrida, as the theatrical saint of the postmodern. The point is instead to show a certain lineage, a certain development in modernism, in which an attempt is made to turn terror, the terror of solipsism and isolation, back on itself as a strategy against the force and violence of representational systems that seem to obliterate the real presence and substance of the body.[41]

Predictably then, this strategy is employed in its most extreme forms on those stages that mark the very edges of the theatrical itself. Recently, this strategy has appeared most savagely in the work of those performance artists who have employed the surfaces of their bodies as the "last frontier" against these forces of control, commodification, and objectification. In this case, the body is perceived not as an object within a power grid, but as a surface that lies *between* the mechanisms of authority and the internal systems of control (thought and perception). While the body on the Restoration stage may have been the locus upon which the forces of social control were applied, for example, it is now not the body per se, but the body as membrane or reticulum drawn between the subjective self and the violence of the body's commodification. In the contemporary images of body art, the body, which presently seems in continuous danger of disappearing altogether into the economy of signs and information, is inscribed and mutilated by the artist in a last-ditch effort to locate himself though pain in real time and real space, beyond the surface economies of culture and art.

The appearance of actual violence in this type of performance demonstrates the breaching of an impasse concealed within the modernist/postmodern project. After conceptual art tried to "de-objectify" the art object by displacing it within the subjective perception of the artist and viewer, performance and body art has tried, in some sense, to "re-objectify" conceptuality by inscribing it in and on the body of the artist in an attempt to frustrate (once again) the circulation of the commodified art object within the economics of the art world.[42] In turn, this attempt to return art to the control and province of the artist has been called "transgressive," inasmuch as the sheer impact of the present, brutalized body calls into question the very lineaments of propriety and perception in art and performance.

This transgressive potential was still generating discussion and apology some twenty years after its first appearance in the exploratory work of such artists as Vito Acconci, Dennis Oppenheim, Bruce Nauman, and others.[43] A 1983 article in *Artforum* magazine, for example, explored some of the more disturbing kinds of body art as phenomena, which though not necessarily peculiar to postmodern performance, nonetheless marked a transgressive limit, a perimeter of resistance against status quo theatre and art.[44] Indeed, the excesses of these artists often do challenge the staid and safe specular distance of "mainstream" theatre and art events. The shock of seeing and affirming by our presence and commentary the literal mutilation of the body, the horror of standing witness to great and real pain, call into question many of our most cherished platitudes about the "liberating" effects of politically conscious art.

Indeed, by bringing into relief the essential ruthlessness of performance/art before an "enlightened" and consenting audience, such pieces seem to frame the precise problematic I have been articulating. Even when employing violence in a "shamanistic" or "curative" mode, many of these artists have unconsciously succeeded in framing and underlining the inescapable terrorism, brutality, and repressive effects of culture and art, especially theatre and performance, that demands of the artist the objectification of the most intimate details of their personal pain. We see this process operating in different ways, and at varying degrees of intensity, in the work of different artists.

In 1978 Linda Montano did a piece at a performance art festival at the University of California in San Diego which was based upon the "self-inflicted death" of her husband, Mitchell. The piece, *(Mitchell's Death)* employed personal narrative, mixed media (videotape, tape-recordings, live performance), and religious symbolism to effect a catharsis of the guilt, pain, and confusion brought about by her husband's death. This death occurred under very ambiguous circumstances: " 'He shot himself. Joe says, no it was an accident.' . . . She wonders if Mitchell committed suicide."[45]

While Montano read a text that chronicled the events surrounding her husband's death, a videotape was shown in which she appeared "with grey make-up inserting acupuncture needles into her face."[46] Montano appeared before her audience wearing the same acupuncture needles that she wore in the videotape. The doubled image of the needles piercing her skin represented a rich and multisurfaced image in relation to her monologue—both as symbols of phobic pain and self-inflicted guilt/punishment, and as curative fetishes as well.

In commenting on her work, Montano was careful to emphasize its "spiritual"—specifically Catholic—influences and meanings. The efficacy of the piece just mentioned rested in part, according to Montano, on the use of specifically Christian imagery and symbol—the cross, for instance ("I use it a lot when I am in trouble"), or the bereft virgin mother motif, suggested in the description Montano gave of her confrontation with the deposed body of her husband moments before he was cremated. She described how she caressed and touched and held him in death, creating a Pietà or *tableau vivant* of life, eros, and death in her performance-as-narrative.

The performance was deeply personal, confessional, alienated, self-mortifying: "At the end of the performance there was silence in contrast to the applause that had followed each of the other performances at the festival."[47] There is in this more than a passing reminder of theatre's origin in the *Quem Quaeritis* trope. The fixation upon death and pain seems, as it does in the Easter trope, to stand in contradistinction to the abstract and less pointed pain of what we might think of as a specifically political or social art. Indeed, there is very little here that might be called political at all. Even Montano's attempts to focus her feminine identity in the piece stand notably detached from any sort of feminist discourse. In this piece, at least, she seems largely unconcerned with "the social."

The power of the performance—even, we might add, in its secondary form as a document of performance—lies in the vicarious sense of bereavement and violation we are invited to experience in the tactile grief of another human being. The performance is sensual, almost obscenely intimate. Yet although we may experience Montano's abandonment as our own, it is not so much shared as it is privately consumed. We feel the decay of voyeurism as we read about her pain; her grief invades our own bodies like Artaud's metaphysic, "through the skin," or like those videotaped needles that describe her own desire for punishment and healing. Her grief and guilt are not being dramatized, they are being enacted.

In contradistinction to Montano, Vito Acconci has documented two performances that are strikingly similar to one another visually, as well as conceptually. The first piece, done in 1970, is entitled *Applications*. In it, a woman applies her lipsticked mouth to Acconci's body, leaving behind the marks of her provocative but dispassionate kisses. Acconci's body thus becomes a literal "text," a surface that records an obscured narrative of sexuality and latent violence—the lips suggesting bite marks, or the impression/expression of a long tradition of spoken and written language that has mutilated both the absent corporeal body and the textual, informational body that has superseded it.

The same idea is suggested later, in a different but related piece in which Acconci inflicts actual bite marks on all the parts of his body he is able to reach with his mouth. In this piece the "writing" surface has been inscribed more deeply, and with a higher degree of actual violence. The performed narrative, and the desire of performance as narrative, is more urgently impressed in the skin. The oral and the oracular combine to define the disappearance of the body beneath the myriad violations of writing/utterance. In this performance, personal history literally mutilates the skin. The equation between violence and narrative-as-history is not unlike the equation in one of Montano's early pieces, performed in 1973, in which she tells the story of her life while walking a treadmill. But Acconci's narrative, though linked to violence in a similar fashion, is also radically different. It is, most notably, silent, and it seems to highlight pain rather than cure.

In Acconci's work, the application and the bite mark appearing on the same body at different times—the "trace" disappearing and reappearing through history—serve in part to illustrate the history of the self, from the kiss and penetration of conception, through the fevered teething of infancy and separation from the mother, to the repressed violence and self-mutilations of later adulthood. The surface that separates the "outer world" from the "inner world" is more and more seriously threatened. Between the two pieces, the lapse from sexuality into violence and violation becomes a mere matter of degree, a question of logistics and economics.

Performance artist Chris Burden pushed that limit even further when he forced two crossed, live electric wires into his chest, which subsequently exploded in his flesh and burned him. The piece was called *Doorway to Heaven*. In another well-known performance *(Trans-Fixed)* Burden repeated the self-persecution motif when he had himself crucified to the rear end of a Volkswagen before the car was rolled onto Speedway Avenue in Venice, California, with the engine revved at high rpm. In yet another performance *(Shoot)* Burden arranged to have himself shot in the shoulder by an assistant with a small caliber gun.

In *Shoot* and *Trans-fixed* Burden took the precaution of x-rays and research on basic anatomy to insure that he would not be seriously injured, and would not suffer undue pain. Nonetheless, Burden's work seems to mark a new stage in the penetration of the body by violence in performance. In the work of Montano and Acconci, this violence is allegorized. The affliction of the body, though real, is in each case secondary to other conceptual concerns. In Burden, however, it is the image of real violence, the body undergoing its own pain and inscription, that provides the conceptual ground for other oscillations of meaning. Indeed, the work of Burden, probably the most overtly violent of those mentioned, is also the most clearly political, inasmuch as its message—that the aesthetic of terror is not, or should not, be a saleable commodity—is consciously directed at the political and economic dictates of the art world.

It is important to realize that the aesthetic of terror implied in these performances is not unique to the work of Montano or Acconci or Burden.

Several performance artists in the seventies and eighties have used physical mutilation, pain, and peril as the central image and focus of their work. Gina Pain, Stelarc, Abramovic/Ulay, to name but a few, have at times either inflicted actual violence upon their own bodies, or submitted their bodies to potentially lethal danger.

Moreover, the impetus to self-inflicted violence that we see in body art erupts in other modes of performance as well. Some of the pieces of choreographer-dancers Pina Bausch and Kei Takei, for example, or the work of the Japanese performance troupe *Sankai Joku,* have at time demonstrated the aesthetic of terror not merely as an image or idea, but as a dangerous fact realized in performance. Indeed, the impulse to terror has infected nearly every type of theater and performance to some degree. The reality of the peril was underscored in 1985 in Seattle, Washington, when a member of *Sankai Joku* fell to his death from a building after the rope from which he was suspended broke during a public performance.

Each of these performers delineates in a different way a fine but critical difference between the image of violence, and violence as image; between representations of terror in the theatre, and terror(ism) as representation. For although images of violence are certainly endemic to theatre and performance and proliferate throughout theatre history, the appearance of *real* violence on stage seems to mark a new phase of representation in the postmodern theatre.

Yet this novelty is deceptive. As I have suggested throughout the present work, the utilization of *actual* violence *as image* in theatre and performance perpetuates a long tradition in drama and performance that has been, and still is, responsible for the most repressive kinds of sociopolitical conditioning. It begins in our own tradition with the appearance of the *Quem Quaeritis,* and ends, almost predictably, with the mutilated bodies of performance artists.

As I stated in an earlier chapter, in the very act of identifying the *Quem Quaeritis* trope with the reappearance of European drama, theatre in the West (re)asserted itself as a political force in maintaining the status quo. It is a force that establishes its primary threat in the image of a *real* tortured and mutilated body that virtually disappears beneath the inscriptions of violence. Ultimately this image becomes saturated with the incipient threat of discipline and brutality. Even those forms, like body art, that try to use it subversively often fail, because the *image* of actual violence (if we can add yet another lamination) ultimately points only to itself, and signifies only what it appears to be, and does little to elucidate the mechanisms behind the appearance of an essentially political violence in history. The images of real violence, in other words, mystify the connections between theatre and law.

There have been artists—Valie Export and Stuart Brisley, for instance—who have investigated this very impasse in their work. Yet even these inquiries haven fallen short, because when actual violence is mediated in performance, when actual violence becomes "present," it inevitably shifts the emphasis of the problematic onto the *inaccessibility* of real, but mediated, pain.

Thus even when the body artists have tried to expose the relations between theatre, violence, and law, they have sometimes ended up accomplishing the opposite of what they set out to do. Pain and terror become seemingly less real—even, in their repugnance, more easily dismissable—as they are anchored in the Symbolic and become purely codified and commodified.

These images of commodified violence become, consequently, images of a constructed death—the death of feeling, of thought, of response. Although the images of violence may initially challenge our capacity to absorb them, absorb them we do, at first with trepidation, but finally with complacence, and even oblivion, as their very "reality" seems to distance them from us through repetition—either the repetition of documentation, or the seeming repetition of specific performances.

These repetitions cloak a critical paradox. We are told, on the one hand, that what we are seeing is real, and yet we are brought to a mediated disbelief simply because the image seems so exquisitely reproducible or detached that it loses the impact of *real* violence. Real violence always exists as a singularity, as a unique moment in history that can never be reproduced or repeated. The very immutability of the violent image seems, finally, to generate a *disappearance* of violence, a disappearance that operates in much the same way that the disappearances of state violence do. Both empty themselves in a *katharsis* of terror, a terror displaced into the future as threat, but a terror that eventually, through history, becomes less and less experiential and more and more a habit of thought, but a habit of thought that hungers for the experience of real violence in the coercive ambience of its endless reproductions.[48]

What is crucial in any study of theatre and its violence is to clarify the links between that violence and the theatre it appears in: the violence of threatened social chaos in the late Renaissance, the violent disciplining of the body in the Restoration plays of wit, the excruciating internalization of guilt in the theatre of romanticism, and the terror of solipsism and psychosis in the modern theatre. All of these forms of performance point back to *real* bodies that are suffering the *real* pain of history and acculturation. The body artists, for all of the political problematics of their self-inflicted violence, should remind us at least of that.

Yet we should not forget that there *is* a problematic. The appearance of these inscriptions may point to real afflicted bodies, but it also signals the moment of culture's complete control over the body. The violence of body art is hardly a transgressive act when the state no longer inscribes its laws into the flesh but incites the artist, like Kafka's jailor, to write them there himself. Far from resisting the systems of information and representation that confine and brutalize her body, the artist is eventually absorbed into the fictions of myth and law, this time by her own hand. And while it is true that body art, now perhaps passé, represents only a small fragment of contemporary theatre and performance, it also represents a larger capitulation to the spectacle of pure, self-referential violence, which seems to signal the self-destruction of a culture devoid of the political and historical sensibility that could halt, or at least slow, its inevitable self-annihilation.

Paradoxically, even while they have struggled with the inexorable violence of status quo values, theatre and performance in the modern period have expressed again and again a deep nostalgia for the sense of community and shared culture that they felt was being lost. Even as the convulsive, explosive violence of the avant-garde was counterpoised against the suffocating familial and psychopathic plays of early modernism, even as this violence moved into the post-apocalyptic theatre of Beckett and the schizo-familial work of Pinter or Shepard, the entire movement of theatre in modernism and postmodernism began to betray a pathos that seemed to grow out of the attempts to rediscover a sense of unity amidst the ruins, either in the family group, in the artistic/aesthetic community, or within the individual herself. It is the failure of this attempt that in part defines the age.

The certainty of this failure, a failure orchestrated by theatre's concerted effort to re-present a sense of the social—even as ruin—in turn defined a terror that was peculiarly modernist: a solipsistic terror, a terror of representation and objectification that eventually mutated into the terror of alienation, loneliness, separation, and disconnectedness. This terror was subsequently deployed, through modernist theatrical ontology, in the production of alienation, which was, in part, the result of romanticism's failure to define adequately the "individual" within the newly-created space of the "psychological man."

This modernist condition of failure, this production of the alien, has led to violence in rather explicit ways: within the theatre we have seen the appearance of more overt gestures of violence in Pinter, barely restrained rage in Beckett, and psychic extortion in Genet. Meanwhile, in society we have seen the emergence of the "guerilla" theatres of confrontational politics, whose latent violence first appeared in street theatre, sit-ins, and demonstrations, and later on exploded in various kinds of theatricalized and mediated acts of violence.

As much as various countercultures have tried to deflect their own sense of alienation through these acts, or have tried to turn alienation back on the social, it is perhaps the genius of modernist and postmodernist culture that it has found a way to deploy the incipient violence of alienation and fragmentation as yet another means of social control. As the individual recognizes his isolation, he is led to "correct" this predicament, either through the implementation of "counter-cultural" social empathy and communality—a new form of social engineering—or by living out the very perversity of the alienated condition, a condition that becomes a mere seeming perversity as more and more alienated individuals live it out. In either case, the solution to the condition is an enactment or showing, a performative and essentially theatrical enterprise.

We see this process in the drama and its relation to society, in the assault upon the audience in plays like Peter Handke's *Offending the Audience,* as well as in the attempts to break down entirely the "barrier" between audience and actors in the work of Grotowski, for example. We see it also in the cultural experiments of the sixties and seventies that took the theatre as their model: the "Happenings" and their dissolute relations, the "Love-Ins," and finally, at a further edge of social experimentation in the face of alienation, the theatricalized pseudo-communities of extremist politics, such as the cells of the SLA and the Weather Underground in the United States, the Red Brigades and Red Cells in Europe, and at the final, extreme precipice of perversity, the Manson clan living out its various incarnations at the Spahn movie ranch. These cultural experiments tried to re-produce a sense of the communal either through performative activities, such as demonstrations, or in the creation of a carnivalized and almost mystical identity *as an audience* (Were you at Woodstock?).

While the relation between these various groups and the disintegration of modern life assayed in its theatre may not be immediately apparent, it is important to note that in each case a community or *audience* is posited in the face of a lack. In each case, the activity of *performance* is employed to bridge the dissolving links (links that were perhaps never there) between self and community, self and family, family and community. In each case the means by which these ideologies of communality are communicated is essentially theatricalized, brought consciously into the realm of theatre and performance as a primary means of transmission. Guerrilla theatre and "street" theatres are perhaps the generic link between the Happenings and the highly stylized theatre of violence in which Patty Hearst rehearsed herself as Other and finally became a star, but the strategies of counter-alienation and group performance laid the groundwork.[49]

R. D. Laing and D. C. Cooper, in their collaborative book *Reason and Violence,* an explication of Sartre's ideas, state the political side of the predicament in these terms: in the face of a modern aporia of communality, group dynamics operate in one of two distinct ways, the *pledged group* or the *group-in-fusion.* The group-in-fusion is a group that experiences real danger from the outside, and whose sense of cohesion is based upon that real and immanent violence. The pledged group, on the other hand, which often grows out of the group-in-fusion once the danger that formed it has passed, senses danger *as a result* of danger's *disappearance* or lack. When actual danger ceases to threaten, the group feels the threat of its dissolution, and substitutes this fear for the other *real* fear—it externalizes its internal terror of *aphanisis* as external threat and then demands that the violence of the group be directed against it. This is not unlike a Lacanian phobia operating at the group level; the group is not merely replacing one terror with another, it is re-creating terror as an external object in order to cover up a lack of being.[50]

This cover up, it seems to me, is the critical movement of terrorism *in and out of the theatre*—the creation of a sense of community through the creation of an externalized terror that finds its objectivity in a *performative mimesis*. Terror is transformed through representation into a terror*ism* that depends upon a demonstration of "love" and "loyalty," of empathy or *pity*, enacted by each member for the others within the group through violence. Sartre speaks of the lynching as such a performance, but we see the theatricality of violent praxis raised to a much higher level of self-consciousness in the contemporary terrorist act, an act that "has always been designed theatrically."[51] We see it again in the horribly grotesque "body art" of the Manson clan, which depended upon staging and performance documentation (words written in blood, engraved corpses, cameras, news stories) for its full effect. At this point, the psychic and ontologic differences between certain modes of experimental theatre, and terrorist praxis, seem to blur.

Back on the side of leftist politics, Martin Jay commented on this tendency of the left to "aestheticize" itself when he wrote in 1971 that

> much has been made recently of the growing appetite for political histrionics in some sections of the New Left. . . . There has been a confusion of realms in which the traditionally separate worlds of art and politics have been merged, to the detriment of both.[52]

On the other hand, in Stephen Sloan's book, *Simulating Terrorism,* the terrorist act is *literally* theatricalized in an attempt to produce a "simulation" for counter-terrorist training purposes (chapter titles: "Writing the Terrorist Plot,""Writing the Terrorist Script," "Acts of Terrorism, or a Theatre of the Obscene"[53]), while also underscoring the ways in which the real terrorist act is a kind of theatre:

> The terroristic violence that we witness . . . becomes a grim play in which the terrorists, the victims, and a broader audience both consciously and unconsciously play out their respective roles. In this form of theater the individual acts appear to be characterized by high drama and uncertainty, but the total terrorist scenario often takes on a level of unpredictability that desensitizes those who watch the various incidents unfold . . . The level of drama of the obscene play depends upon a number of factors, including the setting, the actors, the media, and the audience.[54]

In one of the appendices to this book Sloan in fact recommends that those participating in the "simulation" be trained actors, and that the production follow closely the techniques of theatrical production of the naturalist/realist school. The final products of some of these counter-terror theatre training exercises were videotapes that, but for the *seeming* absence (and if one reads closely, it was only a *seeming* absence) of real terror, might have passed for "real" incidents. This, coupled with the fact that we the audience are often "desensitized" to the real terror in the first place, would seem to render these videotapes, and "authentic" videotapes of "real" terrorist acts, virtually the same.

But this simulation is only the by-product of a much more distressing obscenity, the obscenity of the theatrical enterprise itself, which, while trying to "educate" anti-terrorists by institutionalizing (or, to use Edward Said's term, "orientalizing") The Terrorist as a necessary element of political action, is partaking of the perverse and vicarious ecstasy of the terrorist power play. Again and again in Sloan's book, participants speak with awe of the passover into "reality" once the scenario is enacted, a reality that must, to some degree, provide a scandalous, Nietzschean pleasure to those who seemingly seize power.

Finally, we have to ask to which kind of terrorist theatre the word "obscene" in Sloan's quote refers. Indeed, we can clearly see in the production of Sloan's terror simulation yet another, "legitimized," nuance of a state terrorist theatre, which posits itself *between* theatre and "real" terrorism in order to extract from terrorism *and* theatre the maximum perverse pleasure of each—and all of this in the pursuit of a power/knowledge. The simulated terrorist act of the eighties, like the psychiatric theatres of the last century, reveal the continuum between terror, terrorism, and their essential theatres.

Understanding the essentially theatrical/ontologic problem of theatre/terror, and the blurring of the theatrical/political in this way, it should come as no surprise that the contemporary social phenomenon of terrorism (both "state" terrorism and terrorism "from below") would operate along fundamentally theatrical lines. But there is this critical difference: while state terrorism depends upon the spectacular concealment of its violence—the true apparatus of performance-as-power is hidden behind the flats and curtains, and the *image* of its concealment operates as an implied terrorism (as when the Disappeared become "visible" only after they vanish)—anti-state terrorism depends upon the spectacular qualities of a *visible* violence. The performance-as-violent-resistance can only occur in the incandescence of the floodlights, after all, with all of its mechanisms apparent in a kind of Brechtian appeal to performative/political *truth*.

Yet the final irony remains: this anti-state resistance still occurs in a performative space defined by theatre's ontology and history. It is still a space conceptually framed and contained, as Blau says, by the tormentors and teasers sustained by the state and its law; it is, therefore, a space that can never be subverted adequately to the overthrow of tyranny. As such, the resistance to social decay comes more and more to represent the ideals of a decaying status quo. The images of what was once, somewhere, real violence—whether as news event or performance—lose their meaning through repetition and become more and more saleable and entrenched in the symbolics of art or media. The great critique of social disintegration that begins the modern period in the work of Ibsen is effectively neutralized in the incessant repetitions of terrorist violence in the video image, until modernist disintegration itself now seems to dissolve into self-parody. This, as I see it, is more and more the ethos of the postmodern. As for the "concealed" hegemonic force behind the seeming fragmentation of modernism and its corollary, the constructed sense of community-as-audience, we need only refer to Charles Krauthammer's words, given in the opening paragraphs of the present work. What terrorism tends to be about, finally, is what theatre tends to be about: the means of circulating power and its currency as spectacle.

7

CONCLUSION

HISTORY AND THE STANDARD DEVIATIONS OF TERROR

In reversing the usual ontological hierarchy between writing and speaking, Jacques Derrida has demonstrated the ways in which that reversal reveals an entire problematic of being and absence underlying Western philosophy. Lack of being, dread, nostalgia, lack of authenticity, loss, are all shown by Derrida to be, at least in part, functions of a language that presupposes a spurious originary presence as the condition of its existence. Through this reversal of terms, Derrida has been able to "deconstruct" the entirety of Western metaphysics and philosophy in a wholly new and critical way, and has also taught us to be suspicious of any system of thought that insists on positing an "origin" as the cause of history's effects.

We have often supposed that the theatre in history appears as a manifestation of the culture that precedes it—a culture founded on ritual and religion, according to some, and appearing whole, like magic, as an entire system of customs and laws by which the "life of the tribe" is organized and maintained. Yet if we follow this presupposition, culture appears as an origin, a necessary prelude to the survival of the individual and the group; and cultural institutions like art, religion, customs, seem to appear derivationally as the means by which cultural cohesion is maintained.

I have, in the preceding chapters, suggested a Derridean, heuristic reversal of this hierarchy, and have posited theatre, or at least the theatrical ontology, as the condition that generates culture and its objects. Theatre, in other words, supplants Derrida's notion of "writing," and in so doing, allows for the possible reappraisal of such issues as "presence" and "speech" both in and out of the theatre.[1] I have, moreover, suggested that the breach and multiplicity within the self that *is* perception, and the projection of that multiplicity into the world as separation, alienation, and difference—the theatrical ontology itself—in turn generate the myth of culture as the seeming means by which that breach might be healed. This presumed healing takes place, in part, through the illusive exorcisms, purgations, and displacements of theatre-as-object—a cultural *pharmakos* or scapegoat, whose existence paradoxically precedes the formulation of culture in ritual.

I have suggested this heuristic reversal not simply to replace one originary category (culture) with another (theatre), but to superpose them in order to show, among other things, that the economics of ocularity and perceived violence are not merely "postmodern" concerns, but seem to form the ground of culture itself. Indeed, in this sense theatre is far from being simply the shadow of cultural indoctrination; it is both the instrument and the lens through which the breach of perception is formalized and objectified as a means of social control. Thus while I would agree with Guy Debord's assessment of the spectacle (or theatre, in my terms) as that which is "at once unified and divided," as that which "hides under the spectacular oppositions . . . a *unity of misery,*" I would extend this assessment back through the entire history of theatre—back to thought itself, whose abstractions are precisely the "common language" of separation and the "circular production of isolation."[2]

Indeed, the enacted repetition of the breach that we have come to know as theatre—the performance of an infraction—appears again and again in the drama as an ambiguously revealed crime, whose revelation seems to define the very condition of human "desiring consciousness" itself. Thus theatre—the apparition of "desiring consciousness"—and culture appear simultaneously in history, each the necessary condition of the other, each at once preceding and following from the other.

I have posited a theatrical split that appears before the institutional theatre—in the works of Hesiod, for example—and that remembers a specular, performative violence begetting culture. I have done this because this position suggests the existence of two very different theatres, a theatre that seems to precede and determine the *faculty* of perception itself, and a theatre that exists as the projection of that perception into culture: a Deimic theatre, in other words, and a Phobic theatre, or theatre's double.

The Phobic disguise represents the tension between these two theatres: the tension between theatre and its double, between chaos and law, between ideation and materiality, between mind and body, between absence and presence. But inasmuch as the shield represents this *tension,* and not merely the binarism by itself, the shield also comes to embody a certain dialecticism, ghosted, once again, in the relationship between the brothers: Phobos and

Deimos are twins, genetic equals, and we cannot say who precedes whom in the birth as *mise en scène*. While we may want to place the unseen Deimos as the originary terror, and Phobos as the mere showing, we also recognize that the showing is what, in effect, dialectically produces the "interior" of terror, its seeming "substance." Thus the *material production* of "real" terror is as much an action of the Phobic as it constructs "the interior," as it is the action of the Deimic, which—in seemingly negating the materialist moment of the dialectic—constructs Phobos as the agency of Deimic terror.

If the present work seems unrepentantly dualistic or even polyvalent, then, it is because the many splits, oppositions, and reversals intrinsic to the Phobic/Deimic dialectics of production/perception are not, and cannot, be resolved. While this painful impossibility may be the very effect and definition of the dialectic, the pain and terror of perception also produce the dialectic, the *thought* itself, that ponders those oppositions. The dialectic of pain, in other words, seems to be self-generating.

Indeed, some theorists have recently seen a partial antidote to theatre's coercion-production in the abolition of dialecticism itself.[3] Dialecticism comes to represent the static, phallocratic world of concept-ideology, which must be subverted by the dynamic world of "becoming," a "becoming" that seems to align itself quite naturally with various forms of liberation politics.

But this solution to theatre's tyranny is not without its own mystifying dangers, and is finally quite naive, for it is in the dizzying whirl of becoming that we first glimpse chaos, terror's first moment, the moment of perception dissolving into itself. And in the half-life of terror, seemingly outside time and outside history, a mere instant suffices for that terror to find its objective case and become an ideologic weapon once again: in other words, when the "remedy" of "becoming" is viewed *as* a remedy, when the becoming becomes *being* (which it must), the anti-dialecticism of the "in-between" becomes objectified once again as ideology.

Thus theatrical attempts to sublimate "slippages," or "nomadism," or "becomings," or indeterminacies of gender, class, or race, are all prone to failure because it is the (Phobic) theatre's function to neutralize and institutionalize such "anti-categories," and, as Adorno reminds us, this institutionalization is inevitable as long as thought thinks itself, as long, in other words, as there is theatre. This is, finally, the central significance of the Phobos/Deimos opposition—the inescapability of the oscillation between the remembrance of pain and the pain of remembrance, the inevitable objectification of and submission to the circular and repressive trauma of consciousness released into theatrical structure as ideology. The brothers are terrifying, and the relentless agon of objectifying consciousness that they represent is inescapable.

Theatre thus deploys terror's objectifications—its release into structure—by materially (re)creating terror in the image and act, while continuously reforming it as an idea, as the moment of thought itself. But in order to accomplish this, theatre must always maintain its link to terror's unnameable pain, a pain that exists in the Real, which always *seems* radically and spectacularly *un*dialectical even as it enters upon the objectifying space of the stage. Thus the dialectic of theatre production begins anew in the seeming fragmentation of each thought, each moment of perception.

But the dialectic of pain is not the real issue of this study: rather, my interest has been the way that pain is *seemingly* isolated and deployed as an agency of threat and coercion. Thus while the pain implicit in the dialectic may delude us into thinking that the major *philosophical* problem is with dialecticism itself (this seems to be the position of Deleuze and Guattari), we can also see how the dialectic of pain is not necessarily negative in principle. Indeed, while the implicit dialectic of the stage (presence-absence) is more often than not self-concealing, and while that oxymoronic, self-concealing dialectic serves as the ideological weapon of status quo power, dialecticism can also try to resist alienating pain from its causes and its uses. It is, or can be, *deconstructive* in its action, in its production-meaning.

Thus theatre production—the oscillation between idea and materiality, between thought and "real" production, between the dialectics of concealment-appearance and the *revelation* of those concealment strategies—suggests that it is impossible to set any single agenda as a first cause of either oppression or its staged spectacles: not the dialectic, and not gender, class, race, or economics. Indeed, while the orders of exchange (i.e., economics, gender, race, class), as Nietzsche tells us, depend upon an a priori specularity in order to emerge in the first place, and while those orders also depend upon the continuous production of new forms of the specular in order to maintain and exercise power, that specularity, that theatre, is itself double-voiced and indeterminate. Just as pain and terror both cause and effect each other, so, in its articulation of terror, theatre operates as both cause and resistance to that terror and oppression.

This oscillation between idea and material production is not really so different from Marx's own recognition that alienation-production not only is part and parcel of the capitalist order, but also generates it. We might even suggest that this alienation, born of specular division, marks the very inception *of* the political and economic order, or at any rate appears much earlier than the sixteenth century, where Marx places the beginnings of bourgeois capitalism.[4]

Consequently, the "condition" of theatre that I am suggesting is certainly determined by economics—by forms of production—but these forms of production do not necessarily conform to the metonymic chain of production that Marx describes. Accordingly, while theatrical production is often the means of comprising a fictive sense of bourgeois community and "common sense" truth, it is also at moments disjunct, metaphoric, and schizophrenic. Theatre production articulates, at times, the myth of a unified, shared culture, and at times the tortuous, ungrounded, and decentered production/forms of Nietzsche's *Genealogy*. The crucial point to remember, however, is that it is impossible to say a priori which forms of theatre are *necessarily* or intrinsically repressive and politically false. Sometimes the myth of fragmentation and paralysis is more debilitating and treacherous than the myth of the great society, sometimes the "slippages" of postmodern performance are more reactionary than the social realism of the regional theatres, sometimes, as Herbert Blau says, the most radical thing we can say in the theatre is "long live the king."

The Phobic repetition or remembrance of the infraction that is the Deimic theatre of consciousness is the remembrance of the *terror* of it. This terror is redefined and rearticulated in each age as a new mode by which culture—emanation of theatre—re-members and supports itself as a seeming "origin": its first impetus to desire possessing itself in its own image. In this way, theatre recreates culture in each epoch as a system of laws by which the theatrical remains intact; by which, in other words, desire can maintain its unending pursuit of itself through the performative images that it creates before its watching eye. Thus the term "theatre," which may seem to suggest an anti-historical essentialism, in fact indicates the opposite: theatre represents the very historical mutability of terror production as it is enacted.

The displacement of terror into ever changing modes, into new systems of laws, produces at performance's "end" the sense that terror *has* been displaced, that it exists as an absence. The curative *feel* of *katharsis*—which will again be cancelled in terror's inevitable return—is produced when terror's force and threat seem to be expelled. But this is only an illusion, for in reality terror is merely *being projected* into a future time and place where it waits to reappear as a new objectivity, a new instrumentality of violence. The terror that precedes its own displacement or *katharsis* is a terror of the *endurance* of violence, pain, death, disappearance; what always returns will return, and the momentary lapse or dislocation of terror into an unknown future time and place produces only a momentary sense of harmony or stasis—an immediate emesis and cleansing emptiness, or in today's terms, a *displacement* that enlightens and reveals truth "deconstructively" as an absence—the absence of terror's history.

The emergency of terror, then, is life's inversion, its mirror, the "negation of life which has become visible."[5] Terror, the threat of non-being, is what calls life into question and so gives it its reality. Terror is what, in the *katharsis* of danger and pain, re-presents life *as* life. When theatre casts its eye back to its Deimic origins, it is not merely looking for the traces of some real terror; it seeks the life that terror, in its unsignifiability, paradoxically signifies as an absence. Finally, then, it is terror's theatre that rules and encompasses life. These *katharses* are mere momentary flights from the rigor of theatre's memory, which waits for us in the agon of *aphanic* perception. When we look back in memory, representation and terror's theatrical mimesis keep terror's image unrelentingly before our eyes. We are, like Jason, seemingly accosted by that threat on all sides.

The perception of the split within and without that recollects the terror "disseminated" in thought, redistributes it along the many axes of the culture that theatre creates, namely: body, gender, text, mind, family, society; and finally today, through the reflexivity of the present period, in the genre of "terroristic" critical theory that characterizes itself as performance.[6] Each of these culturally-created objects becomes a new fragment, a new facet in which the face of Phobos is reflected, and "beneath" whose surface is concealed Deimos, the "nameless, wordless terror." The creation of these vehicles or objects by which terror is remembered is, as I have said in the recurring theme of this work, the implementation of terrorism. Terror as an unrepresentable is aboriginal in theatre/consciousness; terrorism in/as performance, on the other hand, is not—it exists as the product of thought and not as thought itself.

It becomes clear in the light of this heuristic reversal that the fragmentation of both society and psyche that we see in theatre's history is at once the cause and the effect of a terror that is concealed and formed in the very moment of consciousness itself. Such consciousness exists as an enacted separation through which the world *can* be perceived: indeed, the many reflections in history on our alienation from objects, self, world, others—our disappearance into the locus of the Other caused by our necessary capitulation to consciousness—are all generated by the moment of thought, the moment of terror, the opening of the breach, the raising of the curtain, the silence broken by speech, the first movement of the body in space before the parabolic eye.

The objectification that transforms the movement and force of an unpresentable terror into a representative terrorism demands the "vanishing presence" of an actual body existing in history, a body whose wounds testify to the real effects of terror and exist as secondary inscriptions that point back to what is unseeable, wordless. This explains why, in each new phase or mode of recollection, the theatre so often seems to remember a *dis-figured* body, a *real* body, in other words, that feels its pain, that is *watched* feeling its pain within the forensic spaces of history, culture, and law.

Even when that real body disappears, or seems to disappear, beneath the inscriptions of history and culture, the necessity of its (imagined or imaged) presence remains. The reason that I have sanctioned theatre more than the other arts as the space within which culture is generated, is that the theatre is by definition the space within which a real body's pain is *being watched* and is *being (pro)cured* in the watching, as power itself is *being exercised* in the intensity of the gaze. Theatre is, in short, the space and time in which the ontologic split of thought is most acutely perceived *in/as the body,* and in which the body is itself simultaneously thought in the mind's eye of the watcher.

The apparent ability of theatre to translate the terror of thought into flesh, as well as its seeming capacity to translate the unpresentability of physical terror into thought through representation, define its unique political and cultural power to reform actions and behaviors. This accounts, at least in part, for the current collapse of perception in culture of the difference between actual theatre, which embodies the terror that is thought, and "the theatres of terrorism." The latter are performative phenomena that do not so much objectify terror in performance as translate the physicality of real violence and pain into the "mere appearance of mere appearance" as a *mediated image,* a third level of abstraction that eventually empties itself entirely of terror and exists only as pure abstraction, a discourse of threat and coercion that continually seeks access to real bodies and their pain.

This collapse of difference between theatre's terror and the "theatres of terrorism" describes an important crisis of representation in performance that threatens to subsume and neutralize all possible resistance to state or cultural coercion in performance. We are told, for example, by political conservatives and "radical" performance theorists alike, that mediated terrorism *is* performance or theatre—not merely "designed as theatre" as Blau says, but *is* theatre. Jean Baudrillard, for example, observing from the province of the simulacra, sees mediated terrorism as "our theatre of Cruelty, the only one that remains to us, perhaps equal in every aspect to that of Artaud or to that of the Renaissance."[7]

Although modern, mediated terrorism may be *designed* as theatre, although it may be a simulation, a hyperreality, it is not theatre. Neither is it installation, performance art, or any art form that selects the living/dying body—a real body, even if "de-realized"—as its material. For us, mediated terrorism may be the documentation of some performative act that occurred somewhere once. Perhaps it is also a horrific theatre/performance for those bodies pierced with steel and lead, burnt with napalm and Semtex, violated with electric cattle prods, broken by psychic brutality; but we never will know, because it is not *our* theatre, since we, with extremely rare exceptions, were not there. For us, the *terror* of mediated terrorism does not exist, because it has been obliterated by the repetitions of its own abstracted image. This repetition deadens the initial impact, and finally blurs the distinction between immediate violence, and the mediated images of violence, between the terror that exists within the mind and within the theatre, and the "theatre of terrorism," which exists only in the media.

And if we reverse the terms we arrive at this sticking point: even if we admit the difference between the terrorist act and the theatrical performance, do we not still have to concede that much theatre might indeed be called a kind of terrorism? After tracing theatre's long history of terroristic practice, and if terror is indeed become so ubiquitous, how can we possibly deny its reality as actual terrorism on the stage? Perhaps we cannot; but it seems a kind of obscenity, once again, to equate what goes on in the interrogation cells of South Korea and South Africa with what happens, no matter how violent, on a SoHo stage. In the final analysis, we are still faced with a theatre whose violence, no matter how "real," still exists primarily as a sign of itself, while the violence of the interrogation cell is precisely that which is unsignifiable. (It is also worth noting that the theatrical ordeal, no matter how intense, is undergone voluntarily, while the very terror of torture rests in part on the victim's absolute lack of control).

Moreover, the conflation of such terms as "theatre" and "terrorism" that we have seen in recent years suggests a conceptual collapse that has had profound consequences. In terms of the contemporary phenomenon of mediated terrorism, perpetrators and victims of sociopolitical violence become indistinguishable from one another as the images of their pain and disaffection become smeared in the replication of images, as real rage and its agonies move into the "hyperreal" of pure representational function—as victims and perpetrators become, in other words, "mere" film actors. In this venue politicians, ideologues, anonymous citizens, government figures, family members, mercenaries, business associates, intellectuals—all are equally capable of becoming either fatigued performers or potential victims of the rage for order that is tyranny, or of the sublime passion for dis-ease that is anti-state terrorism.[8] We are facing in this the threat of a last reduction and dispersion of terror into the absolute terrorism of an isolation whose paradoxical hallmark is its absolute commonality. We see an anonymous victimization in a perfectly democratized war.

This collapse must be resisted at the level of difference. The differences between terror and terrorism itself, as well as the differences among the various kinds of terrorism, are differences that give meaning to—and thus allow the possibility of resistance to—political and cultural violence, if not on a global scale, then at least locally. For no matter how irrational they may seem, terror and terrorism have their meanings, and those meanings, which become intelligible as difference, must be read before resistance can become possible.

But, as I have already suggested, reading the meanings is no simple matter. For one thing, the seemingly immediate threat of violence in mediated terrorism, though characterizing quite well the paradoxical plight of the situationist victim in a world of "simulated" (mediated) violence, obscures the fundamental historical development of a terror/terrorism that is rooted deeply in our theatrical, cultural past. The historical roots of the "theatre of terrorism" reach much deeper than the current preoccupation with film or video or other mediated images and "simulacra." Indeed, Baudrillard's world of simulations is itself caught in the weave of this history—the simulacrum is, after all, only the most recent apparition of a theatrical ontology that must still, despite its denials, implicitly try to posit a "real" corpus "behind" the simulation, a corpus whose sole purpose it is to become a sign in order that it may assume the *character* of violence, either as giver or receiver. Far from obliterating the theatrical, the simulacra in fact help to conceal the violence of the theatrical that is still the necessary foundation of cultural and state power.

Certainly at the level of real pain there is no simulation. The very appearance of mediated terrorism—even as simulation—indicates that the reality of pain and terror survive, if not in terrorism's mediations, then *somewhere else*. This survival allows terrorism to continue to appear, for if pain and terror could ever become merely "hyperreal," they would no longer concern us. Talk as we will of a dematerialized real, the concept of reality as simulation (or simulation as reality) still presupposes another reality somewhere that is or was more "real" than what exists here and now.

These Platonic echoes reverberate throughout theatre's history, from Chris Burden's bloodied body pieces back to the *Quem Quaeritis,* beyond Palestine and its Roman law, beyond the "tomb of Jesus, where he lay," to the Phobic/Deimic split that articulates the self that is thought in terror. This tyranny not only appears throughout the history of performance[9] as such, it also occurs, as I have already mentioned, in the recent notion of "theoretical terror" that is often applied to the "performative" writings of Baudrillard and others whose theories seem to end or exclude the processes of discourse itself through various kinds of *discursive* power plays.

This "theoretical terror," as Jean-Francois Lyotard writes, denotes "the efficiency gained by eliminating, or threatening to eliminate, a player from the language game."[10] Yet in the historical context of the productions of terrorism, we can see that "theoretical terror" is yet one more attempt to wield power through the performative, in order to gain access to the power of terror's invocation *as* performance. But the use of this term—terrorism—in this context bespeaks a misperception both of performance and of terrorism, each of which insists, as I have already said, on the perceived historical presence of a real, wounded body (albeit absent or concealed) as the focal point of terrorizing discourses and disciplines. Though certain kinds of theory may be violent *as* theory, to equate *theory* with shrapnel in the belly is to forget the real pain of the bodies upon which the theatrical performances of culture—whether as "art" or as political violence—are founded.

Indeed, what distinguishes terrorism as a mode of power in the theatre (as opposed to its modality "in the world") is that it is unequivocally violent, that its brutality is referred to a real body, and finally that, paradoxically, the actuality of its violence is always signified, always displaced or concealed. Terror's many translations into terrorism in the theatre represent the endless procession of masks, behind which and through which the simultaneous concealment and spectacular display of power are utilized as a means of control in the theatrical productions of violence. Although in his numerous historical studies Michel Foucault is careful to point out the essentially neutral quality of power, I would suggest that in the theatre, the terror of appearances, translated again and again into the appearance or threat of terrorism, demonstrates the precise historical movement of power *as* violence, pain, and extortion.

This violence is concealed *because* it exists as theatre, as representation, even when it *is* real. This is theatre's purpose, to seemingly conceal its violence as "mere" representation, while referring its effects elsewhere, into culture. This representational power play is, finally, unequivocal: the force of the theatrical ontology shows itself again and again in its power to transform everything, even "reality," into itself, into "mere appearance." In fact, while it is true that theatre in the West historically has gone to great lengths to conceal the practice of real violence on stage, this concealment has never had a purely aesthetic or ethical basis. Theatre has by and large resisted or covered over actual violence, simply because real violence in performance, as Girard shows us, is not as efficient as its mimetic representations: real violence in performance, then, is not transgressive but merely inefficient.

The representations of violence that outline the history of theatre also underline and clarify theatre's intentions and complicities not just with power, but also with the historical enormities of power exercised by the state, which, like the theatre, often chooses to hide its violence "offstage" in interrogation cells and empty warehouses, simply because the threat of violence as disappearance terrorizes large groups of people more effectively. Disappearance is "seen" by more people through time than is a single act of violence. The remembrance of violence is, in other words, very often more proficiently invoked by its spectacular absence.

The complaint, then, of theorists like Baudrillard—that theatre's impact, the impact of real violence, has disappeared—ignores the obvious. Theatre always seems to leave real violence behind because this is precisely theatre's function—to conceal violence even when (or especially when) it is seemingly exposing it in the violent spectacle. Theatre, as I said earlier, has always been the precise ontologic location in which terror and its violence *becomes thought* and ejaculates its reforming isms more and more deeply into the interpersonal lives of all of us.[11]

We live today in these oscillations. While at some perverse extreme we still seem to be fascinated by the violence of performance, we have also come to live in terror, as every moment of "real life" seems to hold within itself the absolute threat of catastrophe in the promise of terror's spectacular return—as either crime, domestic violence, natural disaster, environmental cataclysm, incurable disease, or terrorist act. At the same time, the great arc of disintegration that we already see beginning in the plays of Euripides—and which continues today in the incessant repetitions of violence in the video image—seems to describe an emptying out of violence, an attenuation that appears to make violence both absolutely ubiquitous and completely nonexistent, as the power of culture becomes solidified at the cost of the individual's seeming disappearance.

At some extreme of performance the tension becomes unbearable, and individual artists try to resist the violent commodification and objectification of the body in the "real world" by resubjecting their own bodies to self-inflicted violence in the performative space. But, as we have already seen, even this effort is doomed to failure in the representative tyranny of theatre.

Ultimately, as real violence becomes objectified in various representative forms, we desire it more and more because we see in its remote repugnance the externalization of what we most deeply fear. We desire this Phobic exteriorization because, like Webster's Ferdinand, the more we see the violence "out there," the more it distracts our terrorized thought from itself, from what is "in here": Deimic nothingness. We desire, in a sense, a repression or *forclusion*. But "in here," in thought, is precisely where this terror is born *as* thought and *as* perception. "In here" is where theatre needs to turn its dysarticulating eye.

The terror of nothingness, of *thought,* in the theatre is a "ghosted" terror. It is a terror that is real, but only becomes perceptible, paradoxically, in disappearance, in the fading residue of a presence in the returning memory, in those traces that play over the suspect appearance of the body.[12] This terror exists, in other words, both as the perception of disappearance, and the disappearance of perception. We can only hope to wrest from this tyrannical, aphanic, specular double bind a space of possibility, a "line of escape." We close in, finally, on this critical difference: in the first place, we see the possibility of an *investigation of terror* as a socializing force, an investigation that would allow the reflection of terror to show itself *as* the unpresentable in all of its potential violence. In the second place, we see an *implementation of terror* as a concealed political force applied to the body.

The appearance of *real* theatre, the Deimic theatre of thought, is the return of a terror that resists spectacle, especially the spectacle of disappearance itself, and tries (impossibly) to understand the seeming substance of terror. The appearance of terror's double in the Phobic theatre is, on the other hand, the return of a terror that demands the spectacle, that uses the spectacle to transform its mask, the mask of the terrorizing Enemy who shapes us to his own image.

We must not underestimate the pervasive power of the Phobic theatre in history. The invocation and re-invocation of "pity and fear" or "pity and terror," again and again throughout theatre's historical preoccupation with tragedy,[13] enunciates at least a subliminal understanding of the interrelation between the violence of terror and tragedy's function in stabilizing social disharmony. In fact, almost without exception, when pity and terror are invoked as either the cause or the effect of tragedy, the final result is one or another kind of "moral instruction." Even when the purgations of terror are explained in terms of the pleasure they produce, the final result of that pleasure more often than not seems to be something like stasis, stability, or harmony (Harmonium, sister of the terrors), a "harmony" that functions as a cloaking of violence.

Theatre and performance become the victims of this masking when they lose sight of the difference between the representation of terror, and terrorism as representation. This difference in theatre is critical, and is one that, in the shadow of Artaud, has been misunderstood. By replacing representations of violence with real violence, we have not, and cannot, escape representation itself. The larger danger is that we forget, as Artaud never could, the *power* of theatre to determine cultural reality and truth. We forget that theatre is the primary condition of life, that life itself is "always already" subsumed by the theatrical (inasmuch as human life is consciousness and perception), that theatre is always able to transmute what is actual, what is real, what is *life,* back into itself, back into "mere" representation.

Thus any theatre that appears, that is staged, is "Phobic"—is objectified or enacted thought. Even Artaud understood the impossibility of presenting *life* on the stage. Knowing the inevitability of this theatre's failure, the question that should concern us here is the Phobic theatre's relationship to its Deimic origin in thought. To what degree does the appearance of objectified violence repress thought and historical understanding? To what degree does this or that performance mask its relation to the violence of culture? The problem, ultimately, is not whether theatre is Phobic or not, but to what degree does any given performance turn its gaze upon its own thought, its own perception, its own complicities; to what degree does this or that theatre repress the connections between its Deimic origins and the theatre of state. As Brecht says in the closing words of the *Short Organum:*

> Our representations must take second place to what is represented, men's life together in society; and the pleasure felt in their perfection must be converted into the higher pleasure felt when the rules emerging from this life in society are treated as imperfect and provisional. In this way the theatre leaves its spectators productively disposed even after the spectacle is over. Let us hope that their theatre may allow them to enjoy as entertainment that terrible and neverending labour which should ensure their maintenance, together with the terror of their unceasing transformation. Let them here produce their own lives in the simplest way; for the simplest way of living is in art.[14]

Thus for all of theatre's complicities in the processes of cultural domination, it is perhaps theatre itself that can still serve us best as the means by which that violence is remembered and resisted within the interval between terror's thought and its appropriation. It is, in fact, precisely this interval, this emergent *difference,* that might suggest an aesthetics of performance in the face of terror's history. This difference appears, for example, in the interval between terror's elucidation in the theatre, wherein it can operate as a resistance to cultural violence, and its appropriation by culture as an "object lesson" in discipline. It also appears in the interval between a given performance's operation as a repressive mechanism, and its resistance to repression in the *elucidation* of its repressive technique; it appears in the difference implied between self and Other, or the Other's inverse, performative incarnation, the Enemy; it appears in the gap between the terror and terrorism, between the real and its sign. But it is crucial to remember in this era of sign slippage and deconstruction that the difference is not only liberating, it is also enslaving: "We are not free," writes Artaud, "and the sky can still fall on our heads. And the theatre has been created to teach us that first of all."[15] Floundering in the differential breach, we may not be free, but we must somehow try to maintain the distinctions. For when difference collapses, life will indeed become simulation, and the possibility of theatre—even *as* possibility—will cease, and the sky will indeed crash upon our heads.

NOTES

1. Introduction

1. These theoretical musings, which serve as an introduction to the historical study that follows, are only very loosely structured on the *Poetics,* and should not be taken as an explication of the *Poetics.* The breakdown into tragedy's elements is a way of punctuating what might otherwise be a more taxing theoretical discussion. Nevertheless, this discussion finds its real point of departure in the Aristotelian theory of tragedy. The critical suppositions that are developed throughout the work that follows also show the rather arbitrary nature of such structural and formal features as "plot," "character," etc. The empirical existence of these features is called into question by the very theory that is seemingly organized by them.

2. "Terrorism and the Media: A Discussion," *Harper's* (October 1984): 47.

3. Ibid., 50.

4. Since the first drafts of this book were completed, a fascinating and germane work has appeared—*The "Terrorism" Industry,* by Edward Herman and Gerry O'Sullivan (New York: Pantheon, 1989). This book specifically argues that the image and reality of "the terrorist" and "terrorism" are products of American political and economic influence in and on the media. This influence comes out of the American need and desire for the Other of the terrorist, who, according to the authors, exists only as a kind of mediated artifact or effect of American foreign policy.

5. The hubris implied in this description is duly noted. In moving through the various periods of theatre history, I will at many points betray in my omissions the fact that I am neither a period specialist, nor a "theatre historian" in the old sense. The work that follows is neither exhaustive of the various periods, nor is it, really,

an attempt to write a "theatre history." It is, instead, a kind of conceptual history of theatre—an attempt to address and engage theatre practice in the modern period.

6. The name "Panic," as I will show later, is the name assigned to the sibling Terror who represents the "outward show of fear." The name also suggests the later association between Pan, the god of panic and rout, and his absorption into the image of Dionysus, god of wild spaces, god of theatre, god of terror-as-madness.

7. Seneca, *Medea,* trans. Frederick Ahl (Ithaca: Cornell UP, 1986) lines 879–86.

8. I should state at the outset the clearly English bias of this study. Because of the broad historical nature of my inquiry, I have had to limit myself, at least in the middle chapters, to a single tradition, although in my reading of other plays, and in the comments I have received on the present work, it is clear that the issues I am developing could be applied to any number of other European works (and, I suspect, to works outside the Euro-American tradition—the ghosts and demons of Kabuki and Noh drama come to mind). Other European works to which this work applies include the following: in Spain, certainly the plays of Calderon; in France the emotional and instructive works of Marivaux, perhaps, but also the claustrophobic plays of Pierre Corneille and Racine, or even the crude terrors of the *Grand Guignol* later on; in Germany, the plays of Gryphius and Lohenstein as Walter Benjamin presents them to us in *The Origin of German Tragic Drama,* trans. John Osborne (London: Verso, 1985), and, at a later date, the work of Heinrich von Kleist (see Kleist's *Penthesilia,* and *The Prince of Homburg,* and also *Über das Marionettentheater* and the work appearing in *Phobus*). And finally, one of the prophets of modern terror and absurdism, Anton Chekov.

These connections notwithstanding, I have decided to address the Continental tradition for the most part only in the latter chapters on the romantic and modern theatre, because at this point, it seems to me, the historical and geographical disjunctures are somewhat less problematical.

9. Michel Foucault, *Madness and Civilization,* trans. Richard Howard (New York: Random, 1965) 202.

10. See chapter two and following for Stephen Greenblatt's work, as well as the work of Joel Fineman, Jonathan Dollimore, Terry Eagleton, Michael McKeon, Michael Neill, Robert Markley, and Nina Auerbach, among others.

11. *Political Shakespeare: New Essays in Cultural Materialism,* ed. Jonathan Dollimore and Alan Sinfield (Ithaca: Cornell UP, 1985) 15.

12. Herbert Blau, *Take up the Bodies: Theater at the Vanishing Point* (Urbana: U of Illinois P, 1982) 163.

13. The reader should note that I am not necessarily using the Marxist terms in any strict sense—indeed, I will often employ the term "dialecticism" where a few years ago I might have spoken of "deconstruction." Inasmuch as deconstruction has shown us the merely provisional nature of binarisms, it seems somehow safe to use the term dialectics again. Moreover, as I hope to show throughout this work, theatrical perception represents above all else the impossibility of using *any* term in a stable sense—thus even the term "deconstruction" becomes problematic in the theatre, as the "merely provisional" reverts at once before the eye into its opposite, the monolithic. Accordingly, I hope the reader forgives the rather imprecise use of these and other terms.

14. Hartvig Frisch, *Might and Right in Antiquity,* trans. C. C. Martindale (New York: Arno, 1976) 86. Although Phobos and Deimos appear earlier in Homer's *Iliad,* their filiation with Ares is not as clearly stated there as it is in Hesiod. Moreover, the form that the brothers take in Homer is uncertain and variable: at one point Phobos and Deimos are described as steeds of Ares, but at another point Phobos is directly referred to as the son of Ares. Most interestingly for the present study, in a passage that closely resembles the quote below from *The Shield of Herakles,* Richmond Latti-

more, who has also provided the translations of Hesiod given here, describes Phobos and Deimos as inscriptions. Hesiod, on the other hand, especially in *The Shield of Herakles,* confronts us with an image of the face of Phobos, a mask that represents a terror that is separate from but essential to the hidden, "unspoken," or disavowed, Deimos. The relationship in Hesiod strikes me as more metaphoric, spatial, synchronic; in a word, as more theatrical than the relationship described in Homer.

15. Kenneth Burke, *Attitudes toward History* (Berkeley: U of California P, 1984) 80–83.

16. Hesiod, *The Works and Days, Theogony, The Shield of Herakles,* trans. Richmond Lattimore (Ann Arbor: U of Michigan P, 1959). Line numbers appear in text.

17. I am using the word "thought" throughout in Artaud's sense. This thought is not "thought-image," but is the vital process of perception itself before perception is circumscribed in language.

18. Liddel and Scott's *Greek-English Lexicon* defines *Deimos* as fear or terror which is close in meaning to the Latin *timor,* fear or dread. *Phobos* is defined as fear, terror, or dismay, but is translated in Homer as flight, or "the outward show of fear."

19. I would like, at least for the moment, to bracket the distinction between metaphor and metonymy as they have been developed through Jakobsen and Lacan in relation to psychic pathologies. My own use of these terms will differ markedly at times from their current usage in psychoanalysis and linguistics, particularly in my conviction that metaphor represents something much more radically indeterminate than metonymy, and my further conviction that synecdoche is conceptually aligned with metonymy and not, as some say, with metaphor. See Anthony Wilden's *System and Structure: Essays in Communication and Exchange* 2nd ed. (London; New York: Tavistock, 1980).

20. For a full discussion of this particular relationship between production and desire, see Gilles Deleuze and Felix Guattari, *Anti-Oedipus: Capitalism and Schizophrenia,* trans. Robert Hurely, Mark Seem, and Helen R. Lane (Minneapolis: U of Minnesota P, 1983), especially section four. The final quote is from Aeschylus' *Oresteia: Agamemnon, The Libation Bearers, The Eumenides,* trans. Richmond Lattimore (Chicago: U of Chicago P, 1953) line 32.

21. Thomas Kyd, *The Spanish Tragedy,* ed. Andrew S. Cairncross (Regents' Renaissance Drama Series) (Lincoln: U of Nebraska P, 1967) 2.4.34–35. Subsequent citations in text.

22. *Forclusion,* sometimes translated as foreclosure, is cognate with the Freudian term *repudiation (Verwerfung,* in Freud's text). But while Freud uses *repudiation* to describe the mechanisms of both neurosis and psychosis, the term becomes problematic. I have chosen for this reason to use the Lacanian term *forclusion,* which is used by Lacan only to describe the mechanism of psychosis that entirely rejects the Symbolic order, the order of law, the "Name-Of-The-Father." As a result of this refusal, stimuli that are experienced cannot be "placed," are subsequently cast out into the Real, and reappear *as* real and terrifying to the individual who has refused them entry into Symbolic or Imaginary thought, but are "not there" to those who might be looking on. They appear to others as hallucinations, in other words.

Although I harbor many reservations about Lacan's work, I have found much that is extremely useful, especially when discussing the theatre at a theoretical level. For that reason, the reader should be aware of the many specifically Lacanian terms being employed—*aphanisis,* the Other, the Imaginary, the Real, the Symbolic and so forth—even though they may sometimes not be employed specifically as Lacan intended. I have relied heavily on Anthony Wilden's translation and explication of Lacan. Finally, I have applied the idea of Lacan to the political and social realm in ways that have been strongly influenced by Fredric Jameson's *The Political Unconscious: Narrative as a Socially Symbolic Act* (Ithaca: Cornell U, 1981).

23. In a recent book, *Nomadology: The War Machine,* trans. Brian Massumi (New York: Semiotext(e), 1986), Gilles Deleuze and Felix Guattari point out the uniqueness of metallurgy among the arts, commenting on the reformable, plastic qualities of metal as it is shaped, melted, and reshaped into weaponry. I am also reminded of that ancient technique of metal casting referred to as "the lost wax technique," in which the wax mold is destroyed as the molten metal is poured into it. The traces of the original mold are visible only as a negative space in the finished object.

24. Anthony Wilden, "Lacan and the Discourse of the Other," in *Speech and Language in Psychoanalysis* by Jacques Lacan, trans. Anthony Wilden (Baltimore: Johns Hopkins UP, 1968) 98.

25. Although, as we will see, a text like Christopher Marlowe's *Edward II* might serve as a paradigm or metaphor for some of the ideas already presented, the text must not, of course, be confused with "reality": the Real in the play, for instance, must be read as the Real in relation to the play as it is performed, whatever that may be. Needless to say, *forclusion* is, by nature, unrepresentable, and yet it appears again and again in the theatre as representation. This is a very complicated theoretical issue, which I hope to clarify more fully in the course of this inquiry.

26. Antonin Artaud, *The Theatre and Its Double,* trans. Mary Caroline Richards (New York: Grove, 1958) 92.

27. See chapter two following.

28. Christopher Marlowe, *Edward II,* ed. H. B. Charlton and R. D. Waller (New York: Gordian, 1966) 5.5.15–19. Subsequent citations in text.

29. From Holinshed's *Chronicles of England,* as quoted in H. B. Charlton and R. D. Waller's edition of Christopher Marlowe's *Edward II* (New York: Gordian, 1966) 194n.

30. See the extremely provocative article by Robin Wagner-Pacifici in *Journal* Spring (1987): 20–29, entitled "The Text of Transgression: The City of Philadelphia Versus Move," in which she suggests that part of the decision to murder the MOVE community is reflected in the dropping of the quotation marks around specific descriptive terms applied to the community, a *forclusion* that transforms a "terrorist" into a terrorist. The punctuation, when it first appears, quite literally marks a *béance* in the text—the place in the text that was "rent" or opened up to allow the insertion of the provocative and empty phrase—"terrorist." This very word, as I have already suggested, in turn "covers" the anxious and indeterminate moment of political confrontation and violence, which is then justified or explained—as it is in Holinshed's *Chronicles*—by dropping the punctuation. In the case of MOVE, we might imagine that same punctuation returning in the Real as the bullets and bombs rained upon the community in order to "contain" and neutralize it.

31. Charlton and Waller, 195n.

32. Similarly, we might make a distinction between the *a*nontologic theatre and ontological theatre. Inasmuch as theatre is a space of transformation, it is "anti-ontological"; on the other hand, the investigation of theatre's anontology is itself ontological, and thus to avoid confusion I will use the term *ontology* throughout.

33. Unfortunately, one cannot easily align these two types politically: while some seemingly "leftist" plays indulge in a kind of reactionary didacticism, other inadvertently reactionary plays seem oddly avant-garde in appearance and form. I will look at some examples of each type through the course of this study, and show how difficult it really is to determine the "subversive" or revolutionary character of any play.

34. Wilden, *System and Structure* 108–109.

35. An interesting example of this affiliation carried into performance appears in the relationship between the characters Verhovenski and Stavrogin in Dusan Jovanovic's production of Dostoyevsky's *The Possessed,* performed in 1985–86.

36. While I would take exception to this last observation—even when the law is benevolent and is "doing good" it is violent—I think Wilden makes a valid and valuable point: when we discuss the "violence" of language or authority, especially in literary theory, we must speak in terms of *degrees* of violence in the Symbolic order. In terms of the theory and practice of law, the question always remains: to what degree is the implementation of law, especially criminal law, purely specular, purely imaginary? The current debates on the inherently theatrical practice of capital punishment, for example, throw an interesting light on this question. At any rate, the relationship between the theory and the practice of law is not unlike the relationship between drama and theatre (see below).

37. Antonin Artaud, in "Fragments of a Diary from Hell," *Antonin Artaud: Selected Writings,* ed. Susan Sontag, trans. Helen Weaver (New York: Farrar, 1976) 95:

> No precise information can ever be given by this soul that is choking; for the torment that is killing it, flaying it fibre by fibre, is occurring below the level of thought, below the level that language can reach.

38. Blau, *Take up the Bodies* 133.

39. See Burke, *Attitudes toward History* 38. See also my discussion of this development in chapter two, below.

40. This is in fact the phrase that Lacan uses at one point to describe repression.

41. Friedrich Nietzsche, *The Birth of Tragedy,* trans. Walter Kaufmann (New York: Random, 1967) 68.

42. Jacques Lacan, *Speech and Language in Psychoanalysis,* trans. Anthony Wilden (Baltimore: John Hopkins, 1968), 98.

43. Benjamin, *The Origin of German Tragic Drama.*

44. Nietzsche, *The Birth of Tragedy* 45–66.

45. Herbert Blau, "Universals of Performance," *SubStance* 37/38 (1983): 150.

46. Although one might take issue with my rather broad use of terrorism—the objectification and implementation of terror's threat for ideological ends—I would, for the present moment, insist on this definition. One point of the present study is to show how terror and its isms have always been part of the theatrical consciousness and its history, how terrorism has always been a product of theatre, how theatre has always been the space of ideological coercion framed by reference to real terror. So while some have argued that terrorism is really a modern phenomenon (and I would, at one level, agree), there is another sense in which modern or modernist terrorism is but one more manifestation of theatre's terror in history. I would, as a result of this disagreement, suggest that we think of terrorisms (plural) as different forms of the coercion that has its own, unique, modern form. By the same token, I would insist on the differences between the various kinds of terrorisms: between right- and left-wing terrorisms, between terrorism from above and terrorism from below, between modernist and other kinds of terrorism. If there is a single threat connecting these various terrorisms, it is the continuous deployment of the thread of death and pain, a threat that takes different forms in different ages.

47. While I will touch upon these various axes of terrorism, the point of this study is not to outline in any explicit way a history of gender, race, or class, simply because I do not want to limit the discussion of terror's modes to any one system of coercion. My purpose is, rather, to look at theatre as the focus of history's attempts to create any number of ideological coercions (of which gender may, arguably, be the most powerful), and to look at theatre's terror as a model of empiricism that generates the *myth* of empiricism, an empiricism that is the ground for the ideologies of class, race, and gender. It would be contradictory in this sense to try to provide any kind of empirical (i.e. social, economic, scientific) evidence for my arguments when I am

suggesting that it is theatre itself that generates the bias of empiricism and supports *it*.

48. René Girard, *Violence and the Sacred,* trans. Patrick Gregory (Baltimore: John Hopkins UP, 1977). Here I should clarify some points: while I find many of Girard's perceptions on the mechanisms of violence and representation useful and enlightening, I am in no way citing him as a final authority on matters of expulsion and mimesis. I especially disagree with his conclusions, in which he seems to see the threat of anarchic violence as a justification for not only law, but religion as well. I find this deeply disturbing, especially in light of the religious Right's current love affair with government and law, and its fascination with foreign and domestic violence. I should also point out that Girard does not use the term "Other" to describe the figure of identification and opposition that he calls a Double, and indeed the Double is *not* the same as the Lacanian Other; however I see a great deal of overlap between the two concepts, inasmuch as they both come to represent the locus and mechanism of law and social stasis, and inasmuch as they represent similar generative mechanisms by which desire is produced within the individual in society. I hope the reader will forgive this rather terse apology for a very complicated relation.

49. See also Alexander Kojeve's analysis of Hegel's master/slave relation in *Introduction to the Reading of Hegel,* trans. James H. Nichols Jr. (Ithaca: Cornell UP, 1969).

50. I have chosen this particular spelling in order to distinguish between *katharsis* in the theatre, a sense that I will develop at length below, and the more usual and indistinct uses of the term catharsis.

51. G. M. A. Grube, in a note on his translation of Aristotle's *On Poetry and Style* (New York: Liberal Arts, 1958), says this:

> After some hesitation, I have translated phobos by "fear" rather than by "terror." It is true that the original Homeric meaning was panic or rout, and that *deos* is the milder word, but by the fourth century phobos was by far the most common word to indicate every kind of fear, while our own word "terror" seems to indicate a very violent, rather sudden, and often short-lived emotion. (12)

Conversely, I have chosen to follow Milton's translation of phobos, which is terror, because the precise point I wish to make is that it is terror that generates the necessity of performance, not merely heightened fear. Beyond this, I wish to show terrorism's correlation with and development from an Aristotelian/Hesiodic phobos lying somewhere within the genealogical strata of performance history.

52. For example, in a small book entitled *Inspiration and Katharsis* (Stockholm: Almqvist, 1966), the author, Teddy Brunius, outlines the last three points of his seven-point "solution" of the definition of *katharsis* in these terms:

> 5. This study will give a convincing interpretation of where Aristotle's *katharsis* is to be found in the use of a tragedy, and the solution says that if there is a *katharsis* it is to be found in every link of the communication of the tragedy— except in the text. 6. The meaning of *katharsis* will be explained in connection with a source material of Asclepian therapeutical practice. 7. According to the linguistic hypotheses of Richards, Sapir, Whorf, an exact word-to-word translation of *katharsis* cannot possibly be made because of the change in the cultural situation from Aristotle's time to ours.

What is interesting here is the way that the author attempts to de-objectify *katharsis* by precluding it from the text itself.

Gerald Else, another scholar in this area, in true New Critical style had attempted to place *katharsis* "in the text" and nowhere else. See Else's note on pages 97–99 in his translation of Aristotle's *Poetics* (Ann Arbor: U of Michigan P, 1970). However, Brunius sees the difficulty in this, because the drama "is a matter of action, of reading aloud, not of a silent text." Thus, he says, *katharsis* is to be located in the audience. Apart from the theoretical difficulties endemic to such concepts as "the audience," this "solution" does nothing to solve the problem: the author himself says that Aristotle "did not give any particular location of the particular state of mind" called *katharsis*. Both Else and Brunius insist on identifying *katharsis* as an emotion, or "state of mind," or textual fact, or something that can and must be located somewhere. And yet, by the author's own characterization cited above, Aristotle conceived of *katharsis* not as a thing to be located, but as an essential lack characterized by dislocation. Brunius finally tries to dislocate the problem itself by references to philology (what is the origin of the term?) and finally, rather lamely, by reference to the Sapir-Whorf hypothesis. See also the chapter on *katharsis* in *The Politics of Aristotle,* ed. and trans. Gregory Vlastos (New York: Arno, 1976).

53. Aeschylus, *The Oresteia: The Libation Bearers,* trans. Richmond Lattimore (Chicago: U of Chicago P, 1953) line 968.

54. Aristotle, *Rhetoric,* vol. 2, *The Complete Works of Aristotle,* ed. Jonathan Barnes (Bollington Series 71) (Princeton UP, 1984) 2.5.1382 a 21, my emphasis.

55. This is the sense of Kant's Sublime, which becomes crucial in the theatre theory and praxis in the nineteenth century.

56. Aeschylus, *The Oresteia: Agamemnon,* trans. Richmond Lattimore (Chicago: U of Chicago P, 1953) lines 848–50.

57. In addition to Friedrich Nietzsche's *On the Genealogy of Morals,* trans. Walter Kaufmann (New York: Random, 1967), see especially Michel Foucault's *Discipline and Punish: The Birth of the Prison,* trans. Alan Sheridan (New York: Random, 1979) and *Anti-Oedipus,* by Deleuze and Guattari.

58. Sigmund Freud, "The Interpretation of Dreams," trans. James Strachey (New York: Avon, 1965) 293–94.

59. Deleuze and Guattari, *Anti-Oedipus* 213.

60. Guy Debord, *Society of the Spectacle* (Detroit: Black and Red, 1977, 1983) sections 214 and 215. Debord's book has no pagination, so all further references will be by section number.

61. Wilden, "Lacan and the Discourse of the Other," in *Speech and Language in Psychoanalysis* 150–53.

62. "If something is to stay in the memory it must be burned in: only that which never ceases to *hurt* stays in the memory" (Nietzsche, *Genealogy* 61).

63. "History is what hurts," says Jameson. *Phobos* "is a species of pain," says Aristotle in *The Rhetoric,* a species of pain that "awaits us" in the future, in *history.* Completing the argument, perhaps, history becomes terror.

64. One of the most valuable experiences one can have with students in performance classes is the initial experience of the breakdown of theatre, the moment when the frightening spectre of "real life" seems to intrude into the improv or exercise. This is the moment when theatre seems to become "real," and the real seems to dissolve itself into "mere" theatre. The breakdown of thought and perception, and the danger that emerges in these moments, are among the most valuable pedagogic experiences my students have had.

65. This is what I mean by terrorism in the theatre or "theatres of terrorism." I would like to distinguish this usage from the more popular idea of terrorism *as* theatre, which, in the age of mediation, it certainly is not. When I speak of terrorism in the theatre, I mean the specular image of a practice that is really occurring somewhere, that has real bodies as the object of its violence, and which represents an actual threat of non-being.

66. See André Breton, *Manifestoes of Surrealism,* trans. Richard Seaver and Helen

R. Lane (Ann Arbor: U of Michigan P, 1972) 125. Breton's suggestion (apparently inspired by his friend Vaché) that "the simplest Surrealist act consists of dashing into the street, pistol in hand, and firing blindly, as fast as you can pull the trigger, into the crowd" was meant to awaken the spectator to his own "debasement" and to the exhilarating danger—and beauty—of performance menacing art.

67. Jacques Derrida, "Freud and the Scene of Writing," in *Writing and Difference*, trans. Alan Bass (Chicago: U of Chicago P, 1978) 202:

> It is because breaching breaks open that Freud, in the *Project*, accords a privilege to pain. In a certain sense, there is no breaching without a beginning of pain, and "pain leaves behind it particularly rich breaches."

2. Trial and Terror

1. Seneca, *Medea*, lines 514–16. Subsequent citations in the text indicate line numbers, but because of the somewhat arbitrary line breaks in Ahl's translation, these numbers are only approximate.

2. Michel Foucault speaks to the theatricality of correction in his book *Discipline and Punish: The Birth of the Prison*. It is interesting to note the ways that theatre reflects the methods of correction, and deflects them back into society (I am reminded especially of theatre practice in recent decades, with its emphasis on "actor training," and its insistence on discipline that is both regimented and general). This relationship between reflection and deflection will become a little clearer, I hope, when I discuss plays from the Restoration period of the English stage.

3. Burke, *Attitudes toward History* 38; Frisch, *Might and Right in Antiquity* 81–139.

4. Nietzsche, *The Birth of Tragedy* 82.

5. Benjamin, *The Origin of German Tragic Drama* 109–10.

6. But see *The Bacchae*, a play that seems somehow marginal, haunted by the impasses of representation in the doubling of images that occur throughout that play.

7. Deleuze and Guattari, *Anti-Oedipus* 212–13; Blau, *Take up the Bodies* 70.

8. Deleuze and Guattari, *Anti-Oedipus* 212.

9. Once again, I am using the work of Jacques Lacan for the theatrical underpinnings linking together language (representation), law, and *mise en scène*. For Lacan, the location of language/law was in the Other, the place of the Symbolic order. See also my note on Lacan and the Other in chapter one.

10. One reads time and again of the superiority of the Greek drama because of its "balance," its "decorum." But this is an obvious bias generated by the same submission to the laws of propriety and "good taste" that characterize Greek drama, and determine the limits of its vision. This bias is so widely accepted that some commentators go so far as to claim that Renaissance playwrights used Seneca instead of Euripides or Sophocles because they did not have good Greek translations. I would suggest that Renaissance playwrights used Seneca because of the sheer power and grandiose performability of his work. These plays are not "rhetorical chamber pieces," they are theatre, the kind of plays that remind one of Artaud in their physical and ontological excess. For an excellent reassessment and historical placing of Seneca's drama see the introduction to Frederick Ahl's recent translation of *Medea*, pages 9–32.

11. Euripides, *Medea* in *Euripides I*, trans. Rex Warner, ed. David Grene and Richmond Lattimore (Chicago: U of Chicago P, 1955) 130–31. Subsequent citations in text are by line number.

12. See Benjamin, *The Origin of German Tragic Drama*.

13. Euripides, like Hesiod earlier, becomes quite ambivalent about this pessimism later on, when like Nietzsche two millennia later, he has to deal with the Dionysian

reality of the theatre—the experience of the Bacchic frenzy of performance—and still admit to the murderous implications behind that phenomenon.

14. Walter Benjamin, "Critique of Violence," in *Reflections*, trans. Edmund Jephcott, ed. Peter Demetz (New York: Schocken, 1986) 297. I might remark here on the distinction between divine violence and religious violence with reference to William Blake, who allied religion with science over and against divine inspiration and imagination. I am not certain this is Benjamin's distinction, but it is thought-provoking in the present context—mythic violence as the violence of law, and divine violence, the violence of terror.

15. Nietzsche, *The Birth of Tragedy* 82, 86.

16. Ibid., 60.

17. *The Origin of German Tragic Drama* 109.

18. Again, Walter Benjamin in *The Origin of German Tragic Drama:*

> The silence of the hero . . . neither looks for nor finds any justification, and therefore throws suspicion back onto his persecutors. For its meaning is inverted: what appears before the public is not the guilt of the accused but the evidence of speechless suffering, and the tragedy which appeared to be devoted to the judgment of the hero is transformed into a hearing about the Olympians in which the latter appears as witness and, against the will of the gods, displays the honor of the demi-god. (109)

19. Certainly "the family" doesn't yet exist in the sense that we come to understand it in the nineteenth century. The family in classical drama exists *as* concealment, as the place within which violence is hidden from view. It is not until the nineteenth century that this family violence is "published," first through sentimental drama, then in the dramas of such playwrights as Ibsen.

20. Blau, *Take up the Bodies* 272.

21. This is the argument of Augusto Boal in *Theatre of the Oppressed*, trans. Charles A. Leal McBride and Maria-Odilia Leal McBride (New York: Theatre Communications Groups, 1985). Although I think Boal's definition of tragedy is a little too restricted, and thus a bit naive, the argument put forth in his book is quite interesting. The influences of Brecht on his writing are particularly evident.

22. Walter Benjamin, in the now well-known ending to his essay "The Work of Art in the Age of Mechanical Reproduction," says that fascism appears when politics is aestheticized, communism when aesthetics is politicized. While this may seem too simplistic to describe the complexities of today's aesthetics/politics relationship, it nonetheless reminds us of fascism's need to display its centralized power in monumental, theatricalized, political events. Benjamin was no doubt influenced by the magnificently staged propaganda events of the Third Reich. See the above essay in *Illuminations*, ed. Hannah Arendt, trans. Harry Zohn (New York: Schocken, 1969) 217–51.

23. One need only think of such phenomena as snuff films, body art, or even the popularity of videotapes that show footage of "real" executions, to see this tendency alive in our own culture.

24. Jean-Francois Lyotard, *The Postmodern Condition: A Report on Knowledge*, trans. Geof Bennington and Brian Massumi (Minneapolis: U of Minnesota P, 1984).

25. "Therefore, I propose a theater in which violent physical images pound and hypnotize the sensibility of the spectator, who is caught in the theatre as if in a whirlwind of higher forces": Antonin Artaud in *The Theater and Its Double*, in *Antonin Artaud: Selected Writings*, ed. Susan Sontag, trans. Helen Weaver (New York: Farrar, 1976) 259. There is more of the mad lucidity of Artaud in Seneca's work than in anything written by Euripides. This is not to hold up Seneca as the preferred play-

wright, or to proclaim his work "better" than Euripides', but merely to redirect attention to Seneca's work in light of recent literary theory, and the work of such modernists as Artaud.

26. Seneca, *Oedipus,* trans. E. F. Watling (Baltimore: Penguin 1966) 1055–63.

27. Hannah Arendt, *On Violence* (New York: Harcourt, 1970) 56, 42.

28. Ibid., 55.

29. Ibid., 53.

3. Trope to Tragedy

1. In Derridean theory, the term *sous rature* ("under erasure") is used to indicate a word (like the word "being," for example) that has a non-existent referent and so "should be" expunged, but cannot be because it is "always already" part of the lexicon. The word is thus both meaningless and meaningful, "there" and "not there;" it is under erasure, expunged, but still visible beneath the cancellation.

2. Although I will discuss them more specifically in the final chapters of this book, I am thinking here primarily of those performance artists who use the substance of the body as a performative medium, and who literally inscribe its surface through the force of a historical necessity: Chris Burden, Vito Acconci, Linda Montano, Stelarc, and others.

3. Eventually, during the later Middle Ages, theatre could not *be* thought, or could *only* be thought. See, for example, the plays of the tenth-century nun Hrosvitha (*Dulcitius* and *Paphnutius* are two of the better-known examples), which were modelled on Terence, but were apparently "not written to be performed as theatre."

4. Johan Huizinga, *The Waning of the Middle Ages* (New York: Doubleday, 1954) 24.

5. "Pilate wrote out a notice and had it fixed to the cross; it ran: 'Jesus the Nazarene, King of the Jews.' This notice was read by many of the Jews, because the place where Jesus was crucified was not far from the city, and the writing was in Hebrew, Latin, and Greek. So the Jewish chief priests said to Pilate, 'You should not write "King of the Jews," but this man said: "I am King of the Jews." ' Pilate answered, 'What I have written, I have written.' " (Jn 19:19–22). Once again, the truth of seeming is concealed by the exclusion—"You should not write . . ."

6. Girard, *Violence and the Sacred* 148; emphasis original.

7. We should perhaps recall the moment of the wordless elevation of the body/bread following those terrible words, "Take and eat, this is my body . . ."

8. See Girard, *Violence and the Sacred* 7. In the case of the medieval Mass, the distinction between the aesthetic and the ethical was obscured in the production of "liturgical drama."

9. All quotations are from one of the earliest extant versions of the Easter trope, "Item De Resurrectione Domini," dated about 950, from the monastery of St. Gall, translated and quoted in *Medieval Drama,* ed. David Bevington (Boston: Houghton, 1975) 26.

10. See "Plato's Pharmacy," in Jacques Derrida's *Dissemination,* trans. Barbara Johnson (Chicago: U of Chicago P, 1981). Derrida discusses Plato's use of the related terms *pharmakeia, pharmakon, pharmakeus,* and notes the absence of the term *pharmakos,* an absence that Derrida links to the double meaning of *pharmakon* (poison and remedy), a word whose darker sense is concealed and expelled in the ideological tactic of translating the same term in various ways. Thus the perversion, the darker ideologic reality of philosophical meaning, is, like the *pharmakos,* banished from the *polis.*

11. In fact, in the mythology surrounding Christ in the early Church the miracles—of which the Resurrection was considered the greatest—were called "signs."

12. In Argentina, where political disappearances were, until fairly recently, every-day occurrences of state terrorism, the empty tomb of Eva Peron became the symbol of ecstatic hope for the families of the Disappeared.

13. Girard, *Violence and the Sacred* 151.

14. Derrida, *Dissemination* 128.

15. Bevington, *Medieval Drama* 5.

16. Huizinga, *The Waning of the Middle Ages* 107–109.

17. Michel Foucault has written extensively on this theme, especially in his book *Discipline and Punish: The Birth of the Prison,* in which he amplifies and historically situates Nietzsche's views of culture, order, and law explicated in *On the Genealogy of Morals.*

18. See Anthony Wilden, *System and Structure* 92:

> The birth of modern individualism is the story of the birth of the myth of autonomous desire. The question of the desire of the Other . . . cannot become a social question until the Other ceases to be God.

A complementary trajectory is described by Erich Auerbach in his classic study *Mimesis,* trans. Willard R. Trask (Princeton: Princeton UP, 1968), in which he demonstrates, among other things, how the autonomy of mimetic desire has been approached in the tradition of Western literature at two distinct historical points: in the Gospel stories, and in the rise of modern realism, which he locates in the early eighteenth century.

19. I have written more extensively on this topic in an article entitled "Disappearance as History: The Stages of Terror," published in the March 1987 issue of *Theatre Journal.* This article began to explore some of the ideas that are more fully explicated in the present study.

20. What will, I hope, become clearer in the course of this study is that this silence—at times the inscribed repression of language and history, at other times the inarticulation of history (a *béance,* discovered in the verbal flowage of Seneca)—recurs over and again in theatre in varying forms.

21. This *béance,* we might add, exists in the consciousness of theatre itself, demonstrated by theatre's inability to adequately discuss this lack in terms of its own self-understanding.

22. This and all following quotes, are from the various versions of the *Quem Quaeritis* trope as documented in Bevington's *Medieval Drama,* 21–49.

23. George Bataille: "The triumphal song of the Christians glorifies God because he has entered into the bloody game of social war, and because he has 'hurled the powerful from the heights of their grandeur and has exalted the miserably poor.' Their myths associate social ignominy and the cadaverous degradation of the torture victim with divine splendor" ("The Notion of Expenditure" in *Visions of Excess,* trans. Alan Stoekl et al. [Minneapolis: U of Minnesota P, 1985] 127).

24. "From the very first, it appears that sacred things are constituted by an operation of loss: in particular, the success of Christianity must be explained by the value of the theme of the Son of God's ignominious crucifixion, which carries human dread to a representation of loss and limitless degradation" (Bataille, "The Notion of Expenditure" 119).

25. The distinction between seeing violence and reading it is one that I first saw delineated in Klaus Theweleit's *Male Fantasies,* 2 volumes, trans. Stephen Conway (Minneapolis: U of Minnesota P, 1987).

26. Perhaps I am stating too strongly the linear movement of these concepts in Aristotle's formula, especially the final moment of catastrophe. It seems unclear whether Aristotle understood these dramatic moments to occur in the strict synchronic sense

that I have described here. There is, nonetheless, a clear reorientation of catastrophe as an unspoken origin in much of the Western drama that follows from the medieval period.

27. For an alternative reading see Maurice Blanchot's *The Writing of the Disaster*, trans. Ann Smock (Lincoln: U of Nebraska P, 1986), in which he points out that the catastrophe, or rather the concept of the catastrophe, is "always already there," shadowing and ghosting history with the continuous threat of disappearance into chaos and destruction. Moreover, Blanchot's definition of the disaster as "that which does not have the ultimate for a limit: it bears the ultimate away in the disaster," is very much akin to what we have already said about terror: that it is unrepresentable, that it seeks the destruction of history in a sublime act of absolute and unspeakable violence that "does not have the ultimate for a limit."

28. More properly, the history of the transposition of terror into terrorism, the operational conversion of an inexpressible *memory of pain* into the *instrumentality of pain*, and thus into the excruciating appearance of an absolute ontopolitical power.

29. *The Croxton Play of the Sacrament* in *Medieval Drama*, ed. David Bevington, pages 207–208, lines 754–88. All subsequent references are to line numbers. Subsequent line numbers will appear in the text.

30. This is indicated by Elizabeth I's balancing act in trying to maintain a secularized state religion, while allowing for a modicum of religious tolerance; the economic forces at play demanded this kind of compromise.

31. Benjamin, *The Origin of German Tragic Drama* 176.

32. Bevington, *Medieval Drama* 939.

33. Benjamin, *The Origin of German Tragic Drama* 178.

34. Thomas Preston, *Cambyses, King of Persia* in *Drama of the English Renaissance I: The Tudor Period*, ed. Russell A. Fraser and Norman C. Rabkin (New York: Macmillan, 1976). Subsequent citations in text refer to line numbers.

35. For a more thorough background to the theories of power in the Renaissance see Stephen Greenblatt's *Renaissance Self-Fashioning: From More to Shakespeare* (Chicago: U of Chicago P, 1980), and "Invisible Bullets: Renaissance Authority and Its Subversion, *Henry IV* and *Henry V*," by the same author in *Political Shakespeare: New Essays in Cultural Materialism*, ed. Jonathan Dollimore and Alan Sinfield (Ithaca: Cornell UP, 1985). See also in the same volume the "Introduction," and "Transgression and Surveillance in *Measure for Measure*" by Jonathan Dollimore. Other helpful works include *Representing the Renaissance*, ed. Stephen Greenblatt (Berkeley: U of California P, 1988); Terry Eagleton, *William Shakespeare* (New York: Blackwell, 1986); and Stephen Orgel, *The Illusion of Power: Political Theatre in the English Renaissance* (Berkeley: U of California P, 1975). See chapter four for critical references to the period of the Restoration and beyond.

36. This is Foucault's view in *The Order of Things: An Archeology of the Human Sciences* (New York: Random, 1973).

37. Thomas Kyd, *The Spanish Tragedy* 2.2.26–32. Subsequent citations in text.

38. Blau, *Take up the Bodies* 156.

39. See chapter six, "Terminal Stages," in which we see the reappearance of the letter/body correspondence in the late work of Antonin Artaud.

40. Blau, *Take up the Bodies* 164.

41. See chapter four ("Nothing") in Terry Eagleton's *William Shakespeare*, and chapter six ("The Improvisation of Power") in Greenblatt's *Renaissance Self-Fashioning* for somewhat different but related views of *Othello*.

42. William Shakespeare, *Othello*, ed. M. R. Ridley (London: Methuen, 1965) 2.3.342–47. Subsequent citations in text.

43. See *Renaissance Self-Fashioning*: "Iago knows that an identity that has been fashioned as a story can be unfashioned, refashioned, inscribed anew in a different

narrative: it is the fate of stories to be consumed or, as we say more politely, interpreted" (238). My point of departure with Greenblatt is precisely his emphasis on narration as the "source" of the theatrical lie and the source of theatrical "self-fashioning." His comment that "the conditions of theatrical identity" and "existence" are produced by "the playwright's [who, exactly, is that?] language and the actor's performance" (245) seems oddly naive, especially when we think of theatre and performance in the modern and postmodern period, in which the very eradication of "theatrical identity" is the end and purpose of certain kinds of performance.

Conversely, I would place the process more distinctly in the imaginative, specular moment of the theatrical itself. Indeed, Greenblatt's reference to Lacan (244) underscores the sense in which self-construction might be seen to erupt in the "pre-Symbolic" specular dis/course of the mirror stage.

44. As always, "death" is to be understood in its Freudian sense as a construct, as the inverse of the constructed Eros.

45. As Joel Fineman writes in *Shakespeare's Perjured Eye* (Berkeley: U of California P, 1986) 184:

> In the tragedies, in quite a different fashion and to quite a different dramatic effect, this staged relation of vision to language grows increasingly more complicated. In the tragedies the difference between language and vision grows both more powerful and less reconcilable, and this is responsible both for the more individuated texture of Shakespeare's tragic heroes and for specific narrative developments, as when Othello demands 'ocular proof' (3.3.360) for that which 'it is impossible you should see' (3.3.402) and receives instead what 'speaks against her with the other proofs' (3.3.441).

46. Roland Barthes, *Image/Music/Text,* trans. Stephen Heath (New York: Hill, 1977) 208.

47. We might take a cue from chaos theory here and suggest that the myriad small differences and indeterminacies inherent in the economic systems of perception and specularity quickly overwhelm the abilities of those systems to make accurate predictions about the world. Chaos theory seems to inform a play like *Othello,* whose myriad indeterminacies of perception, truth, and exchange add up to an absolutely false vision of reality.

48. The possible kinds of "supporting evidence" are nearly limitless: from the appearance in theatre of an economic theory of wealth-as-production in Thomas Otway's *Venice Preserved,* a theory that only appears *as* theory some one hundred years later in Adam Smith's *The Wealth of Nations,* to the planning of theatres themselves modelled on the triangulations of the panoptical number/grid system in the mid-nineteenth century—a triangulation set up very nicely in Restoration comedy. The problem in any of the possible examples is that theatre produces the model of control before it appears in culture. Theatre's prolepsis thus makes it difficult to support the *later* appearance of these methods of control as supporting proof of my argument. The only possible responses are that theatre is the generating principle of culture's violence, or that I am seeing what is not there, and am thus reenacting *Othello* as performance theory.

49. I have kept the text's variable spellings of Desdemona's name as a kind of testimony to the deeply unknowable nature of her character, a character that is constructed through the male "gaze."

50. See note 52, below. As I will explain later, I am not prepared to claim that this objectifying gaze is essentially male. Although the sheer ubiquity and powerlessness of women in any given society casts them as the most convenient Other to fill the role (or hole?) as Enemy, an Enemy created through dread perception, we can see

how the problems of gender emerge from the seeing, and thus are in a sense posterior to a more fundamental problematic of terror engendering power. Thus when female characters utilize the gaze to their own ends, it is not just a matter of appropriating the male gaze, but is, rather, indicative of a more fundamental problem of seeing power.

51. John Webster, *The Duchess of Malfi, The Selected Plays of John Webster,* ed. Jonathan Dollimore and Alan Sinfield (Plays by Renaissance and Restoration Dramatists) (New York: Cambridge UP, 1983) 4.2.269–70. All other citations from the play will appear in the text.

52. For a slightly different but complementary approach to this "phobic/fetish object," see Laura Mulvey's essay "Visual Pleasure and Narrative Cinema," in *Narrative, Apparatus, Ideology,* ed. Philip Rosen (New York: Columbia UP, 1986), which explores the two different axes (phobic/fetish) along which the female body is created in the cinema. Although Mulvey is correct, I think, in her elucidation of this mechanism, she does not adequately problematize a very complex production, because the desire implicit in the creation of the concept of the "male gaze" is itself inadequately theorized. Following my own argument in this chapter, for example, how do we explain the male gaze in its relation to the crucified and tortured male body? We might have recourse to some theory of sadomasochism, by which we might see the phobia/fetish of the woman's body emerging from some basic phobia of death, pain, and bereavement in the male body; but this, it seems to me, deeply complicates and problematizes the entire concept of the "male gaze." Thus although the "gaze of power" is almost always a male gaze, I am reluctant to assign its efficacy wholly to the province of gender because this does not seem adequate to the complexity of the phobic/fetish object as it appears through history.

Indeed, at the level of terror, I would suggest that the fetish object and the phobic object tend to collapse into one another, inasmuch as each is the representation of a potentially lethal and unimaged desire that exists only as a lack. In each case the object that "stands in" for the unspoken desire covers over an absence, and represents the desire for there to be something where there is nothing (the *Quem Quaeritis*). The realization that there really is nothing where there seems to be something, or that there really is nothing where there *should* be something, is the realization of terror. For a more extended discussion of the perceptions of nothingness in relation to neurosis and schizophrenia, see Anthony Wilden's translation of Lacan's *Speech and Language in Psychoanalysis* 187–88, 131.

53. This, it seems to me, is one of the more important and problematic subtexts of the New Historicism. While many of these critics illuminate the sense in which power, situated center stage, reflects the essential theatricality of power in culture, they also forget the ways in which theatre deflects the eye from power as it exists in the world, even as it tries to point to and demystify that power as theatre (in his defense, Greenblatt points to this conundrum in Marlowe's work). Unfortunately, much New Historicist criticism exhibits a too ready belief in the myth of theatrical "subversion," or similarly, a too easy acceptance of the impossibility of subversion. Criticism, in other words, submits itself to the repressive power of a theatre that always subverts the subversion. See chapter six and following.

54. Benjamin: "In the ruin, history has physically merged into the setting." *Origin of German Tragic Drama* 177–78.

55. Derrida, *Dissemination* 128.

56. I am reminded, as I read this play, of the figure of Elizabeth Carey, (apparently) the first woman playwright to appear in the English tradition, and the ways in which her identity and work have been similarly excluded and redefined according to specific canons of taste. There is something of the Duchess in Carey's "presence/absence" in theatre history, as anyone who has tried to find her work can attest—she

is often cataloged under different and mutually exclusive last names (Carew, Carey, Falkland).

57. Bataille, "The Notion of Expenditure" 127.

58. I am speaking, as I said, exclusively of the English stage. And yet although the Interregnum and its censorship was a non-event on the Continent, the "closing of the theatres," as has often been pointed out, has become an emblematic political response to social unrest: the American Congress tried a similar tactic during the Revolutionary period in the colonies.

4. Gesturing through the Flames

1. Martin Jay, *The Dialectical Imagination: A History of the Frankfurt School and the Institute for Social Research 1923–1950* (New York: Little, 1973) 86.

2. See for example the introduction, written by Michel Foucault, to Deleuze and Guattari's *Anti-Oedipus* xviii.

3. Karl Marx, in *Capital I*, marks the beginning of the capitalist era in England in (roughly) the sixteenth century, when the epoch of "primitive accumulation" associated with feudalism begins to give way to the more complex systems of exchange, surplus value, and money that characterize the emergence of "real" capitalism. This "bourgeois revolution" is effected, Marx suggests, in countless skirmishes, and finally "comes on the stage, that is, on the market . . . in the shape of money that by a definite process has to be transformed into capital." Karl Marx, *Selected Writings*, ed. David McLellan (Oxford: Oxford UP, 1977) 445.

4. In the Marxist theory of the commodity fetish, people become objectified and alienated in the processes of production, while commodities take on the signs of human desire. The self (or the *appearance* of the self—an effect of alienation on the worker) and its commodity extension both become mystified and alienated in each other, as commodities begin to represent *in themselves* the character of human relations. Meanwhile, the people who produce those objects become marginalized in a society of increasing fragmentations and alienation.

5. This "doubled" economics is, of course, an oversimplification. The "self" in fact represents something more like the chiasmus of many intersecting energy economies. The isolation of two of these—mind and society—really represents an Imaginary opposition of forces that "covers up" a complex of forces.

6. Indeed, the work of Michael Neill and Michael McKeon, especially their essays on ideology and sexuality that appeared in *The Eighteenth Century: Theory and Interpretation* (Spring, 1983), reflects this concern with a sexuality and ideology that forms in the very fragmentation of the period itself. In very different ways both Neill and McKeon see an emergent dialectics forming in this fragmentation, a dialectics that is the generating principle of gender and the bourgeois class in the seventeenth and eighteenth centuries. While I generally agree with both Neill's and McKeon's approaches, I would submit that this fragmentation as a principle of change is empty of necessary force unless one sees the terrorizing implications of such a social atomization as a particular function of power in/as theatre.

7. One need only think of *fashion* as one context in which this circulation occurs: in the marketplace of sign as fashion, it is clear that neither idea nor materiality can be posited as an a priori state of production.

8. A recently published book by Robert Markley, *Two Edg'd Weapons: Style and Ideology in the Comedies of Etherege, Wycherley and Congreve* (Oxford: Clarendon, 1988), takes this sign economy as its point of departure from the other studies on Restoration ideology.

9. Michael McKeon, "Marxist Criticsm and *Marriage à la Mode,*" *The Eighteenth Century* 24.2 (1983): 141–62.

10. Although I am not, unfortunately, equipped to argue the absolute uniqueness of Otway's play in this period, I know of no other plays in earlier periods that demonstrate a similar predisposition to exchange and distribution. Certainly the closest we come in Jacobean theatre is the ubiquity of violence *as* violence—the plenitude of dead bodies and forms of mayhem in which violence exhausts itself (as it does not in Otway's play) as death.

11. I include the "minor figure" of Aphra Behn because her plays, more than any others in this period, reflect a concern with real-life economics—the financial plight of women in Restoration society, a plight that directly coincides with the plight of women as sexual objectives.

This admiration for her position in Restoration drama also accounts for my decision to exlude Behn's work from analysis. Aphra Behn was certainly a brilliant and courageous rebel against many of the social tyrannies around her, and others have written about her with insight (see, for example, Jean A. Coakley's introduction to Aphra Behn's *A Lucky Chance* [New York: Garland, 1987]). I see no point, however, in discussing the ways in which her work is finally neutralized by the very theatre she hoped would operate as a platform for her concerns. Behn's work is far more meaningful and powerful as a testament of emerging resistance, and should, from the critical standpoint of the present study, remain as such.

12. "The mouth of the anorexic wavers between several functions: its possessor is uncertain as to whether it is an eating-machine, an anal machine, a talking-machine, or a breathing-machine (asthma attacks)" (Deleuze and Guattari, *Anti-Oedipus* 1). I might add that Otway's text wavers as well: the attempt to (d)evaluate the body, and to allow its passage into the systems of exchange, is a flawed attempt, but one that shows more clearly than most the processes at work on the body "beneath the gaze."

13. The translation of the individual experience of terror, which must always remain wordless, into terrorism, which is pure *information,* is the crux of the argument here—the process of economic deployment that brings the unrepresentable into representation so it may be utilized as a means of control.

14. Thomas Otway, *Venice Preserved or a Plot Discovered* in *British Dramatists from Dryden to Sheridan,* ed. George H. Nettleton and Arthur E. Case (Carbondale: Southern Illinois UP, 1969) 1.1.122–28. Additional citations will appear in the text.

15. Thus in the epilogue to Rudolph Bell's *Holy Anorexia* (Chicago: U of Chicago P, 1985), written by William N. Davis:

In anorexia nervosa [feminist theorist Susie] Orbach finds the expression of every woman's plight. The disorder poignantly and graphically depicts the self-starved female who is unable to feed or nurture herself, who must reject her own needs and desires, and who is too frightened and uncertain to find a means for authentic self-assertion. (186)

This could easily be an excerpt from a character study on Belvidera, or more cryptically, a statement of the ethos of the period of the Restoration itself, that "frightened and uncertain" time, which eventually tried so desperately to find its means of "authentic self-assertion" through the implicitly impotent rage of male "wit" and manners.

16. "The various forms of expenditure . . . constitute a group characterized by the fact that in each case the accent is placed on a *loss* that must be as great as possible in order for that activity to take on its true meaning." Bataille, "The Notion of Expenditure" 118.

17. Ibid., 117. The fact that terrorism and its economic vision "conform to well-

defined needs" in society at large is implicit here. When unimaged terror enters the systems of representation and becomes terrorism, it serves the needs of society at the expense of the person.

18. Ibid., 120; Artaud, *Theatre and Its Double* 24.

19. This is one of the themes of Walter Benjamin's "The Work of Art in the Age of Mechanical Reproduction," *Illuminations,* trans. Harry Zohn (New York: Schocken, 1969) 217–51.

20. Much of what follows is somewhat over-simplified and lacking in detail: for a more complete sense of the complexities of Restoration politics, ideology, and theatre see Robert D. Hume's *The Development of English Drama in the Late Seventeenth Century* (Oxford: Clarendon, 1976), and for a more recent analysis, Robert Markley's *Two Edg'd Weapons: Style and Ideology in the Comedies of Etherege, Wycherley and Congreve.*

21. This production was achieved not merely pedagogically, as some critics have maintained (i.e., that the culture of seventeenth-century England learned how one was to behave through the example of the mannered gentleman—a figure tht emerges later in the period), but rather through the very real threat of humiliation and even abuse. One must remember that the "lesson" of good gentlemanly and ladylike behavior was always accompanied by images of violence and abuse for those (usually women) who did not measure up: thus Restoration comedy functioned something like a "mirror for Magistrates," what we might now call a "mirror for Gentlemen and Ladies."

22. See Nancy Armstrong's *Desire and Domestic Fiction* (New York: Oxford UP, 1987), for an interesting study of the ways in which this trend develops into the domestic "contract" of the nineteenth-century novel. While I generally agree with Armstrong's insights, I would place Armstrong's site of "contractual law" on the Restoration stage, some one hundred years before she begins to analyze it as a novelistic paradigm.

23. As Jonathan Dollimore writes in *Political Shakespeare:*

> An analysis by the new historicism of power in early modern England [has been shown] as itself deeply theatrical—and therefore of the theatre as the prime location for the representation and legitimation of power. (3)

My own digression from this body of work should by now be clear: I am insisting at every point on theatre's *priority* as a cultural phenomenon, and I insist as well on its utilization of coercive violence as ideology—on theatre's formation and use of terrorism, in other words—as the specific means to this legitimation of power.

24. I refer the reader once again to Markely and to Hume for a more detailed look at the problematic of form and genre on the Restoration stage.

25. This is Joseph Roach's insight in *The Player's Passion* (Newark: U of Delaware P, 1985), a brilliant study that nonetheless lacks the central import of *fear and coercion* in the production of social/theatrical deportment from seventeenth-century "manners" to the various tyrannies of twentieth-century performance.

26. George Etherege, *The Man of Mode or Sir Fopling Flutter, The Plays of Sir George Etherege,* ed. Michael Cordner (Plays by Renaissance and Restoration Dramatists) (Cambridge: Cambridge UP, 1982).

27. Some recent work by well-known performance artists examines the nature of torture and its sometimes subtle effects on the body. The endurance works of Abramovic/Ulay, for instance, demonstrate among other things the intense pain of sameness and the minuscule changes that appear within that sameness as a result of fatigue, hunger, and deprivation.

28. Sigmund Freud, *Jokes and Their Relation to the Unconscious,* in *The Standard*

Edition of the Complete Psychological Works of Sigmund Freud, ed. and trans. James Strachey (New York: Norton, 1960).

29. See, for example, Greenblatt's *Renaissance Self-Fashioning.*

30. Markley develops this point of view through reference to Bakhtin, who, Markely writes, "anticipates Lacan" in placing the unconscious within the social field of language. But it seems to me that Bakhtin's theory inadequately confronts the sense in which this field of speech operates according to a principle of violent repression both within and without the individual. The individual, in fact, guards these repressions more carefully than any dictator might, and indeed recreates the terrorizing dictator with every single speech act. Bakhtin's theory, in short, underestimates the pathological nature of desire in the field of dialogic speech; he, like many current theorists, seems to confuse the "slippages" of dialogism with liberation. This confusion, as I will discuss in later chapters, is dangerously naive.

31. William Congreve, *The Way of the World, The Comedies of William Congreve,* ed. Anthony G. Henderson (Plays by Renaissance and Restoration Dramatists) (Cambridge: Cambridge UP, 1982).

32. Marriage certainly exists as a contract before this period, but in Restoration comedy, the contractual agreements made between men and women are based more on the social position and behaviors of each than on love or property. This, it seems to me, is unique in the history of Western drama, and is a result of the society of manners. I would direct the reader's attention once again to Nancy Armstrong's study, which discusses the notion of sexual contract (largely) in the nineteenth-century novel.

33. Foucault, *Discipline and Punish* 171.

34. Bertolt Brecht, *Brecht on Theatre,* trans. and ed. John Willet (New York: Hill, 1964) 43.

35. Ibid., 32.

5. The Body's Revision in the Theatre of Mind

1. Displacing truth (history?) "within" also suggests the Lacanian postulate of the Unconscious—that what is displaced within (repressed), creates the very "space" of the Unconscious. In other words, the Unconscious does not exist before repression, and only exists after repression as the shared, social structurations of an unutterable language.

2. The reversal and redundancy is intentional: while we usually think of psychology as that which elucidates a certain topography of mind, I am suggesting the romantic ideology of the imagination as a category that facilitated the formation of psychological theory. Thus, quite literally, these plays describe topographies (the Indian Caucasus, the terrain surrounding Manfred's castle) that describe an emergent psychology.

3. This is naturally more complicated than I have just stated it: what the Restoration exteriorized, romanticism "re-interiorized." The body thus appears in the Restoration as a metaphor of the mind or passions, while in romanticism the mind is rearticulated as another kind of body surface. This oscillation is best understood dialectically—that is, as "interior" and "exterior" mutually constructing one another in another permutation of the Phobos/Deimos paradigm. For an interesting insight into the mind reconstructed as body, see J.-B Pontalis's *Frontiers in Psychoanalysis: Between the Dream and Psychic Pain,* trans. Catherine Cullen and Philip Cullen (London: Hogarth, 1981), chapter twelve.

4. Romanticism was, of course, not the first artistic movement to theorize the imagination as a force of creative thought and practice. From the medieval period through the Renaissance and neoclassicism, the imagination was perceived as the in-

ventive faculty of perception, which was in some critical sense opposed to reason and/or faith. But the focus was never on imagination as a process or power capable in its own right of transforming the spiritual or material world; the imagination was a faculty that was prone to *misprision* and that usually wanted correction, either by faith or by reason, depending upon the particular privileges of the age. See, for example, the various definitions of imagination given in such standard literary reference books as *A Handbook to Literature* by C. Hugh Holman (Indianapolis: Bobbs, 1972).

Romanticism took the theory of imagination beyond this, however. Now imagination's perceptive powers were not only a means of seeing what was before the (mind's) eye, but were also able to disarticulate and recreate, deconstruct and reconstruct reality and the world through sheer creative force. The generation of the romantic imagination was, in short, the establishment of a new space of *mythic/ideologic production* effected through the agency of a Kantian Sublime that was posited against the seeming repression of an effete neoclassical age. For a full explication of this ideological move and its meaning and implication, see Jerome J. McGann, *The Romantic Ideology* (Chicago: U of Chicago P, 1983).

5. For a look at this development in the novel, see Nancy Armstrong's *Desire and Domestic Fiction.*

6. I do not wish to conflate "mind" and romantic "imagination." They are not the same, and should not be confused. However, I do think that the creation of the imagination in romanticism allowed for the development of the psychic axis of "mind." The development, later in the century, of techniques by which the *landscape* of mind could be traversed (psychology) attests, I think, to the productive relationship between mind and imagination. I should also add that the romantic sensibility would have been horrified at the dissection of mind, and the separation of mind/body, that are suggested by much of psychoanalysis. Nonetheless, the reinscription of the body into mind as imagination set the stage for this very process to occur.

7. William Wordsworth, *The Borderers, Nineteenth-Century English Verse Drama,* ed. Gerald B. Kauver and Gerald C. Sorenson (Madison: Fairleigh Dickinson UP, 1973) 3.1.28–36.

8. Percy Bysshe Shelley, *The Cenci, Nineteenth-Century English Verse Drama,* ed. Gerald B. Kauver and Gerald C. Sorenson (Madison: Fairleigh Dickinson UP, 1973) 2.2.108–13. All subsequent citations will be found in the text.

9. Michel Foucault, when speaking of the rise of the mental institution during this period on the Continent, is very careful to distinguish the psychological from the psychoanalytic: "It is not psychology that is involved in psychoanalysis: but precisely an experience of unreason that it has been psychology's meaning, in the modern world, to mask" (*Madness and Civilization* 198).

10. See *A Mental Theatre: Poetic Drama and Consciousness in the Romantic Age* (University Park: The Pennsylvania State UP, 1988) by Alan Richardson, or Stuart Curran's classic *Shelley's Cenci: Scorpions Ringed with Fire* (Princeton: Princeton UP, 1970) for example, or even the introduction to *The Cenci* in *Nineteenth-Century English Verse Drama* by Gerald B. Kauver and Gerald C. Sorenson, 128–29. But notice also the chapter in Jerome McGann's *The Romantic Ideology* entitled "The Mental Theatre of Romantic Poems," a chapter almost devoid of theatrical references or content.

More recently, a book by Evlyn Gould, *Virtual Theater: From Diderot to Mallarme* (Baltimore: John Hopkins UP, 1989), takes the "mental theatre" in the direction of a "virtual" or conceptual space, but still implicitly maintains distinctions between "real" and mental theatres that are not adequately investigated.

Finally, see Nina Auerbach's excellent study of Victorian theatrical sensibility, *Private Theatricals: The Lives of the Victorians* (Cambridge: Harvard UP, 1990), in which she discusses the deep terrors both brought on and masked by theater and theatricality. Auerbach's insights, however, are still bound up with a conception of a theatre that is absorbed or imitated by consciousness, and not by a theatricality generated *by* consciousness. Theatre thus remains, as it does in Freud, a model upon which thought constructs itself. I am suggesting however that thought itself is theatrical at its inception.

11. Deleuze and Guattari, *Anti-Oedipus* 305.

12. Immanuel Kant, *The Critique of Pure Reason, The Critique of Practical Reason and Other Treatises, The Critique of Judgement*. All quotes and paraphrases are from Kant's *Critique of Judgement*, translated by James Creed Meredith (Chicago: Encyclopedia Britannica, 1952).

13. Thus Percy Shelley in *A Defense of Poetry, English Romantic Writers*, ed. David Perkins (New York: Harcourt, 1967) 1085: "Poetry is indeed something divine. It is at once the center and circumference of knowledge" (1084). Subsequent page numbers will appear in the text.

14. For an interesting analysis of Kant's thought, see one of the "philosophers of slippage," Gilles Deleuze's work on Kant, *Kant's Critical Philosophy*, trans. Hugh Tomlinson and Barbara Habberjam (Minneapolis: U of Minnesota P, 1984).

15. Shelley, *A Defense of Poetry* 1085.

16. Foucault, *Madness and Civilization* 158.

17. Jerome McGann is the central influence in this line of thought, but it seems to me his work does not adequately account for the role of the Sublime in romantic ideology, and it is the Sublime that determines the very "limn" of mind that edges into the particular terror of romanticism. In shortchanging the role of terror and its isms, McGann's book misses the very mechanism that enforces ideology in the theatre. This "missing force" is also the theoretical shortcoming of some new historicist and historical materialist work, which, in reifying theories of power, forget the force of power as terror that lies in its (seeming) unspeakability. As I have already stated, in committing myself to this unspeakability, and refusing to theorize it away too quickly, I have opened myself to various charges of "essentialism." I have chosen to take this risk because of terror's relentless reality in the political world of today: the tortured, the disappeared, the marginalized really do seem to experience terror as ineffable—whether it is or is not, whether or not "ineffability" is merely the system keeping itself secret, I have chosen to respect this phenomenological description of the human experience of the monstrous. I have also become aware, through the writing of this book, of a personal sense of terror that will not be shared or signified, the "sacred" sense of terror that remains one's own.

18. Kenneth Burke, *A Grammar of Motives* (Berkeley: U of California P, 1969) 223.

19. Similarly, the apparent retreat into familial and sentimental dramas in the romantic theatre does not represent a *withdrawal* of theatre into more private spaces, but indicates instead the publication of the family—its forces, relations, and activities—as an artifact of culture created as performance. After the domestic and sentimental dramas of the late Restoration and early romanticism, the family would never again be a private institution. I would refer the reader to the sentimental dramas of the late Restoration theatre and early romanticism, which I will not discuss specifically.

20. I might point out that although these plays were rarely performed, it was not, contrary to literary bias, necessarily an inherent "untheatricality" that prevented them from appearing successfully on stage as effective drama, nor was it necessarily true that the conventions of the popular romantic stage could not accommodate the often expressionistic inertia of their poetry. Indeed, we should remember that Brecht himself felt that theatre could stage anything—and that this in fact was its danger. Today, after a generation in which numerous "rescored" and radically restructured dramatic texts have appeared in performance, we should not find it hard to imagine theatrically compelling versions of these plays being done, versions that would not necessarily do inordinate violence to the original texts.

I might suggest instead that these verse plays did not appear on stage because the theatricality of the romantic imagination, being a "space of production reduced to representation," could only exist in the "real" world as an absence or lack. In the context of the "political unconscious," then, romantic drama takes on the character of a *forclusion*.

My choice of these verse plays as preeminent examples of *theatre* might seem to require some justification in light of the long-standing criticism that would dismiss their performative qualities. Indeed, while the playwrights themselves on occasion chose to characterize their work as dramatic but not particularly theatrical, this characterization is often quite equivocal. Byron, for instance, claimed that *Manfred* was "impossible for the stage, *for which my intercourse with Drury Lane has given me the greatest contempt*" (emphasis added). I would suggest, in light of what I have said thus far, that the rejection of these plays as "poor theatre" needs careful reanalysis.

21. Foucault, *Madness and Civilization* 187–89 (emphasis mine).

22. These are not isolated examples: I could have treated such plays as *The Cenci*, or Coleridge's *Remorse*, or Wordsworth's *The Borderers* in similar fashion. The emphasis on the hidden crime, the invocation of large and almost surreal landscapes, the internalization of such emotions as grief, guilt, and remorse, tie all of these plays together as artifacts of the emergence of what I will later call "the fully ripened oedipal mind." This mind is *not* to be confused with a real "mind" or minds that exist somewhere as actual, or essential, "spaces of thought." What I am suggesting is that the entire romantic project gave birth to the spacial, topographical metaphor of mind as a category of thought itself.

23. Deleuze and Guattari, *Anti-Oedipus* 306:

> Every time that production, rather than being apprehended in its originality, in its reality, becomes *reduced (rabattue)* in this manner to representational space, it can no longer have value except by its own absence, and it appears as a lack within this space.

24. Foucault, *Madness and Civilization* 191.

25. This is an interesting development, if we think of hallucination in Lacan's terms. Indeed, the emergence of women in theatre in the nineteenth century bespeaks a "return in the real" of women's presence in the theatre. From this point on, we see more and more resistance on the part of women to their formulation by men on the stage. Although the resistance is still under the aegis of a "male" theatre, it is, from the work of Behn in the eighteenth century, beginning to formulate its own sense of power. See, for example the plays of Susanna Centlivre, Elizabeth Inchbald, Mercy Otis Warren, and Maude Gonne.

26. George Gordon, Lord Byron's *Manfred*, *Nineteenth-Century English Verse Drama*, ed. Gerald B. Kauver and Gerald C. Sorenson (Madison: Fairleigh Dickinson UP, 1973). All citations will appear in the text.

For a more comprehensive and complex look at the Byronic hero, Peter Thorslev's *The Byronic Hero* (Minneapolis: U of Minnesota P, 1962) is still very useful. Indeed, my own vision of the Byronic hero is, in many ways, an amplification of his.

27. The "colonization of consciousness" is a term used by Anthony Wilden in *System and Structure* to describe the process by which the contemporary mind has been restructured to insure its capitulation to the political processes of exploitation, both of the individual and of other cultures. A similar idea is expressed in the term Deleuze and Guattari use—"endocolonization"—to express the process by which the individual psyche is reprogrammed to desire its own exploitation. The continuous redeployment of terror in various kinds of terrorism is a critical aspect of this process.

28. Percy Bysshe Shelley, *Prometheus Unbound*, *English Romantic Writers*, ed. David Perkins (New York: Harcourt, 1967) 1.1.618–19. All subsequent citations to Shelley's play will appear in the text.

29. Deleuze and Guattari, *Anti-Oedipus* 219.

30. Foucault, *Madness and Civilization* 191.

31. Although the appearance of the great actor has its roots in the Restoration, it was in the romantic period that the actor rose in importance above the playwright.

32. Antonin Artaud, "Fragments of a Diary from Hell," 95.

33. Antonin Artaud, "Here Lies," *Antonin Artaud: Selected Writings,* ed. Susan Sontag, trans. Helen Weaver (New York: Farrar, 1976) 549.

34. Elaine Scarry, *The Body in Pain: The Making and Unmaking of the World* (New York: Oxford UP, 1985) 162.

35. Ibid., 161.

36. Rudolph Otto, in *The Idea of the Holy,* trans. John W. Harvey (New York: Oxford UP, 1923), argues that simple fear can be distinguished from holy dread or terror precisely because dread or terror has no discernible object or cause: it is a pure phenomenological perception of radical contingency. Similarly, Scarry herself recognizes the unique existence of this kind of fear and its lack of an object relation, but tends to dismiss the significance of "objectless fear" because, she feels, it is unusual in the world. I disagree. As I have shown throughout the present work, terror indeed "survives the ravin it has gorged" and continues its disciplining, reforming work at all levels of law and society because of its often concealed link to the Deimic, the terror that has no object.

37. "The functions of the poetical faculty are twofold: by one it creates new materials of knowledge and power and pleasure; by the other it engenders in the mind a desire to reproduce and arrange them according to a certain rhythm and order which may be called the beautiful and the good" (Shelley, *A Defense of Poetry* 1084).

38. Hence the role of poets as the "unacknowledged legislators of the world."

39. Foucault, *Discipline and Punish* 102–03 (emphasis mine).

40. This is Jerome McGann's thesis in *The Romantic Ideology,* a thesis that infuses much of the argumentation in this chapter.

41. Georg Buechner, *Danton's Death, George Buechner: The Complete Collected Works,* trans. Henry J. Schmidt (New York: Avon, 1977). Further citations are in the text.

42. See Walter Laquer and Yonah Alexander's *The Terrorism Reader* (New York: Penguin, 1987), for essays by these three revolutionary theorists. The selections in Laquer and Alexander's book are (especially in the case of Bakunin) not necessarily representative, however.

43. This is shown clearly in Foucault's history of the prison, which "inscribes" the landscape with the mark of concealed violence and pain. The prison is, in essence, the "hollow of its own mark," the *béance* of state power.

44. Foucault, *The Order of Things* 308.

45. Nechaev, quoted in Laquer and Alexander's *Terrorism Reader* 68.

46. If the theatre/terrorism link seems too ethereal to be real, one need only remember Herbert Blau's production of *Danton's Death* at the Lincoln Center, in which an entire theatre company was literally terrorized into non-existence as a result of the political controversy surrounding the production, a controversy initiated by its crucial and very germane commentary on the state terrorism of the period—the Vietnam war.

47. Jean Baudrillard, "Our Theater of Cruelty," *Semiotext(e),* 4 (1982) 108–109.

6. Terminal Stages

1. The term "molecularization" is peculiar to the work of Deleuze and Guattari, and indicates a progressive atomization of social relations.

Partly as a result of this molecularization, writing critically about modern theatre presents special difficulties, for no period has shown such a diversity of forms as modernism. Naturalism, realism, symbolism, avant garde theatre, absurdism, happenings, minimalism, performance art, the theatre of images: each represents an entire theatrical movement grounded in a single atomic nuance of theatre history.

In trying to discuss the general characteristics of modernist drama, then, what choices do we make? How can we hope to say anything coherent and cohesive about such an incohesive, incoherent period? We can only say what we have just said: that the fragmentation of forms is itself the identifying characteristic of modernist drama, a progressive disarticulation of dramatic styles and modes that signals a general molecularization of the genre itself, a collapse of genre that represents the political and cultural collapse within which it appears. On the other hand, in the work of someone like Robert Wilson or Heiner Muller, one can see the recuperation of the fragment or molecule as an emblem of a different sort of wholeness—an indication, perhaps, that the molecularization of the social is a mere strategy in the re-productions of postindustrial capitalism.

Whatever sketch one draws of the modernist/postmodernist period must be haunted by the sense of deficiency and fragmentation that is the defining principle of the age. It is for this reason that I have chosen to avoid a study of a "major figure" per se, and to concentrate instead on a critical principle, terror, as the thread that unifies the present chapter. This should in no way be understood as a rejection or diminution of any single modernist playwright that appears in this century, and that I fail to mention.

2. I will argue later for the preservation of the *dialectic* as opposed to the nomadic as the preferred model of political resistance. While nomadism proffers an attractive alternative to the impoverished dialectics of negation and *ressentiment,* power, both in and out of the theatre, seems still to operate according to the models of dialectical opposition. It seems to me, moreover, that the strategies of nomadic thought lend themselves to rather profound mystifications and reactionary appropriation. I will discuss this more at length later on.

3. See Jameson, *The Political Unconscious* 47–58.

4. It is perhaps too obvious: homelessness, racism, sexism, illegal wars in central America, the pathetic "war on drugs" that has supplanted the "war on poverty." These all contribute to the specular consolidation of power, the seeming integration of order emanating from Wall Street.

5. Henrik Ibsen, *Peer Gynt,* trans. Rolf Fjelde (New York: New American Library, 1964). All citations will appear in the text.

6. What is interesting in the development of Ibsen's work is the fact that some of the earlier "mythic" plays like *Peer Gynt* seem, in retrospect, closer in tone to a later modern theatre; Peer, for example, could be one of the progenitors of Jarry's King Ubu—brainless, boastful, and impotent—an alignment that also looks back to the beginnings of tragedy in Sophocles' *Oedipus Rex* or Aeschylus' *Agamemnon.*

7. Henrik Ibsen, *An Enemy of the People, Ghosts and Three Other Plays,* trans. Michael Meyer (New York: Anchor, 1966) 289.

8. For an alternative and decidedly more optimistic view of Ibsen's political effect, see for example Joan Templeton's article "The *Doll House* Backlash: Criticism, Feminism, and Ibsen," in the January 1989 *PMLA* (volume 104, number 1, pages 28–40).

9. See for instance *Dance of Death, Miss Julie, The Ghost Sonata, Comrades.*

10. *A Dream Play* and *To Damascus,* for example.

11. August Strindberg, *The Dance of Death, Part I, The Strindberg Reader,* trans. Arvid Paulson (New York: Phaedra, 1968). Citations will appear in the text.

12. August Strindberg, *The Father* in *Seven Plays by August Strindberg,* trans. Arvid Paulson (New York: Bantam, 1960). In text citation refers to page number.

13. August Strindberg, *The Pelican, Selected Plays,* trans. Evert Sprinchorn (Minneapolis: U of Minnesota P, 1986), Act 3. Further citations will appear in the text.

14. Antonin Artaud, "The Alchemical Theater," *The Theater and Its Double,* trans. Mary Caroline Richards (New York: Grove, 1958) 51.

15. Antonin Artaud, "Here Lies," *Antonin Artaud: Selected Writings* 550.

16. Antonin Artaud, "Situation of the Flesh," *Antonin Artaud: Selected Writings* 111.

17. Ibid., 110.

18. Stephen Barber, "A Foundry of the Figure: Antonin Artaud," *Artforum* 26.1 (1987): 88.

19. Ibid., 89.

20. Jacques Derrida, in "The Theatre of Cruelty and the Closure of Representation," *Writing and Difference,* trans. Alan Bass (Chicago: U of Chicago P, 1978), 233. Derrida also writes: "Theatricality must traverse and restore 'existence' and 'flesh' in each of their aspects. Thus, whatever can be said of the body can be said of the theatre" (ibid., 232).

21. Artaud, quoted in ibid., 233.

22. Ibid., 249.

23. Indeed, Michel Foucault's analysis of Artaud's madness is precisely that he was "not able" to produce works of art per se, or more precisely, that the "art" of Artaud was not recognized as such until after his death: for "madness is precisely *the absence of the work of art,* the reiterated presence of that absence, its central void experienced and measured in all its endless dimensions," *Madness and Civilization* 287.

24. Derrida, "The Theater of Cruelty and the Closure of Representation" 243–44.

25. Ibid., 245.

26. Derrida addresses the relationship of Beckett's negation to Nietzsche's affirmation in his essay "Structure, Sign, and Play in the Discourse of the Human Sciences," *Writing and Difference* 278–93.

27. Ibid., 243.

28. H. Porter Abbott, "Tyranny and Theatricality: The Example of Samuel Beckett," *Theatre Journal* 40.1 (1988): 82.

29. Samuel Beckett, *Not I, Ends and Odds* (New York: Grove, 1976).

30. Samuel Beckett, *Waiting for Godot* (New York: Grove, 1954) 18.

31. Samuel Beckett, *Catastrophe, Three Plays* (New York: Grove, 1984).

32. Again, Abbott writes:

> The aesthetic and the political are two faces of a single meaning in *Catastrophe,* and they merge in the insight that the political will that seeks to constrain human life to an imagined social order . . . is rooted with the aesthetic will that seeks to dominate human thought through formal representation. (87)

33. Jean Genet, *The Balcony,* trans. Bernard Frechtman (New York: Grove, 1966). Subsequent page numbers will appear in the text.

34. Brecht, *Brecht on Theatre* 43.

35. Ibid., 43.

36. See the introduction, written by the editors Ralph Mannheim and John Willet, in Bertolt Brecht's *Collected Plays, Volume 5* xii–xx.

37. "Adorno on Brecht," *Aesthetics and Politics,* trans. Francis McDonagh (New York: Verso, 1980) 190.

38. Ibid., 193, 189.

39. Adrienne Kennedy, *In One Act* (Minneapolis: U of Minnesota P, 1988). Caryl

Churchill, *Plays: One* (New York: Methuen, 1985); Maria Irene Fornes, *Fefu and Her Friends, Word Plays: New American Drama* (New York: Performing Arts Journal Publications, 1980).

40. Sue-Ellen Case, *Feminism and Theatre* (London: Macmillan, 1988).

41. As a corollary to my first mention of political terrorism in a footnote, I must now relegate plays *about* terrorism to footnote status. As valuable as these plays may be in delineating the *differences* in the types and motivations of various terrorist groups, the play about terrorism usually fails because it seeks to rationalize and formalize what, in its essence, defies form: that is, the unsignifiability of terror as it is truly experienced. Thus while providing valuable and even profound insights into the "problem of terrorism," the ability of plays, especially realistic plays, to deal adequately with the moment of terrorism remains limited. This explains, in part, the perceived dearth of plays that deal *directly* with the topic (see Walter Laquer's book *The Age of Terrorism,* especially the chapter "The Image of the Terrorist: Literature and the Cinema" (Boston: Little, 1987). Laquer, however, is speaking only of popular culture's movies. There have been a number of plays written about terrorism). It also explains the often-felt disappointment of having "missed something" in the explication of terror's motives. Finally, I am really speaking here of terrorism as it is experienced in the United States media. I am certain that the plays about terrorism in other countries (most notably in England, Germany, and Italy) can do much to explore the logistics of the phenomenon itself (see, for example, *Rat in the Skull,* by Ron Hutchinson, Sobol's *The Palestinians,* Tabori's *Stammheim,* and the works of Howard Brenton and Howard Barker). I remain skeptical, however, of those play productions that fail to understand terror's radical *otherness,* its essential appeal to arationality.

42. Jon Erickson, "The Objectification of the Subject in Performance Art," unpublished essay, 1986.

43. There is certainly disagreement over when "performance art" really makes its appearance. Some writers would locate its origins in the Dada performances in the early part of the century, others in the Happenings and Fluxus movements, still others in the more specifically "alienated" work of the artists just mentioned. This is of little concern to the present study; the inability to locate the phenomenon with any kind of precision only underscores its dispersion throughout theatre history.

44. Thomas McEvilley, "Art in the Dark," *Artforum* 21.1 (1983): 62–71.

45. Theodore Schank, "Mitchell's Death," *The Drama Review* 23.1 (1979): 46.

46. Ibid., 45.

47. Ibid., 47.

48. Recently, sociologists have expressed concern that young people—both male and female—not only have become accepting of real violence in the world, but have grown to crave it. Much of this craving is associated with the endless images of violence to which these young people are exposed—not merely fictionalized violence, but "actual" violence on the news, and now in such horrific artforms as the "Faces of Death" videos available in local stores. The numbing effects of "real" (mediated) violence seems to push desire outward in a craving for "the real thing," a disturbing development indeed.

49. I have been deeply influenced by the work of Herbert Blau for these various perceptions and analyses. Blau's work on terror and the theatricalization of culture, as well as his writings on the audience, have formed, sometimes unconsciously, many of the opinions expressed here.

50. R. D. Laing and D. G. Cooper. *Reason & Violence: A Decade of Sartre's Philosophy 1950–1960* (New York: Pantheon, 1971) 129–40.

51. Blau, *Take up the Bodies* 272.

52. Martin Jay, "The Politics of Terror," *Partisan Review* 38 (1971): 95.
53. Stephen Sloane, *Simulating Terrorism* (Norman: U of Oklahoma P, 1981).
54. Ibid., 19.

7. Conclusion

1. Theatre, it seems to me, is a broader and more richly textured category than writing, which is, ironically, more resolutely committed to its own presence in the inscription. Theatre, based as it is upon a perception of disappearance, suggests a more subtle sense of perception's ephemeral nature. Taking into account all we have learned about "the death of the author" and the indecidability of authorial intention, we are now able to discuss more fruitfully other recently "repressed" issues: the ways in which speaking in fact *differs* from writing, for example, or the ways in which subjective presence might denote something of more positive value than sham "authority" in performance and literature.

2. Debord, *Society of the Spectacle* sections 54, 63, 29, and 28. Debord's emphasis.

3. See, for example, the work of Deleuze and Guattari in this context.

4. However, as I have shown, the emergence of something like an alienated capitalist order of exchange does appear on the early Restoration stage, where it becomes immediately reified and broken off from the axis of the psychic. The psychic axis then becomes increasingly isolated, and develops in a quite different way in the nineteenth century as the psychologic and psychoanalytic modes of exchange.

5. Debord, *Society of the Spectacle* 10.

6. I am thinking specifically of the work of Jean Baudrillard, who has been characterized more than once as a "theoretical terrorist." In a larger sense, I am referring to all of those discourses that imply historical or philosophical closure as their product and end.

7. Baudrillard, "Our Theatre of Cruelty" 108–109.

8. Baudrillard describes terror's modern victim, who becomes both genius and product of terrorism's technique:

> [Terrorism's] blindness is the exact replica of the system's absolute lack of differentiation. For some time the system has no longer separated ends from means, tormentors from victims. In its deadly and indiscriminate taking of hostages, terrorism strikes at precisely the most characteristic product of the whole system: the anonymous and perfectly undifferentiated individual, the term substitutable for any other. Paradoxically, the innocents pay the crime of being nothing, of being lotless, of having been dispossessed of their name by an equally anonymous system whose purest incarnation they become. They are the end products of the social, of a now globalized abstract sociality. It is in this sense, in the sense in which they are precisely *anybody,* that they are the predestined victims of terrorism. ("Our Theatre of Cruelty" 108–109)

9. We might add art as well. The current scene, which embraces and *validates* Baudrillardian simulations, is now producing "smart" (i.e., "theoretical" or "conceptual") art, which in many cases epitomizes petty status quo concerns and bourgeois tastes: the stainless steel sculptures of Jeff Koons are indicative of this "old wave" of non-confrontational, easily multiplied and sanitized, "populist" art, a cynical art that smells suspiciously totalitarian in its appeal to clean form, monolithic presence and—antithetically to its claims of populism—"moneyed" means and tastes.

10. Jean-Francois Lyotard, *The Postmodern Condition: A Report on Knowledge,* trans. Geoff Bennington and Brian Massumi (Minneapolis: U of Minnesota P, 1984) 63.

11. See Bert O. States's *Great Reckonings in Little Rooms: On the Phenomenology of*

Theater (Berkeley: U of California P, 1985) for a particularly penetrating discussion of this "colonization of consciousness." Although States speaks with insight and clarity on what might have been an elusive and murky topic, he largely steers clear of the issue of violence in thought perception. This absence of a direct discussion of violence in theatrical perception is undercut, however, by metaphors and allusions that suggest a dimension of violence in perception that is perhaps not readily apparent, but that emerges in the theatrical moment. When discussing Aristotle's "co-reflexive terms, imitation and action," for example, States, quoting Webster, tells us that they come at us "like two chained bullets" (5). At another point, States suggests that anticonventions exist to pester or "wound" theatrical consciousness (12). Finally, however, States largely neglects the sense in which consciousness, with its theatre, is itself the wound that it pesters.

12. Herbert Blau writes: "In the dreaming body of the actor, the living image of the displaced person: self time memory consciousness desire. The theatre is always beginning over, that's the trouble. Where do we start?" (*Blooded Thought* [New York: *Performing Arts Journal*, 1982] 112).

13. See, for example, the discussions of "pity and fear" in such diverse critics as Averroes (Commentary on Aristotle's *Poetics*), Dryden (Preface to *Troilus and Cressida*), Lessing (*Hamburgische Dramaturgie*, last essay), Schiller *(Über die tragische Kunst),* Ludwig Lewisohn *(The Drama and the Stage),* Arthur MIller ("The Nature of Tragedy"), and Clifford Leech *(Shakespeare's Tragedies).* Each work is referred to in Marvin Carlson's excellent book, *Theories of the Theatre: A Historical and Critical Survey, from the Greeks to the Present* (Ithaca: Cornell UP, 1984).

14. Brecht, *Short Organum for the Theatre, Brecht on Theatre,* 205.

15. Artaud, *The Theatre and Its Double* 79.

BIBLIOGRAPHY

Abbott, H. Porter. "Tyranny and Theatricality: The Example of Samuel Beckett."
    Theatre Journal 40.1 (1988): 77–87.
Adorno, Theodore. "Commitment." *Aesthetics and Politics*. Ed. Ronald Taylor. Trans.
    Francis McDonagh. New York: Verso, 1980.
Aeschylus. *The Oresteia. Aeschylus I*. Trans. Richmond Lattimore. Chicago: U of
    Chicago P, 1953.
Alexander, Yonah, et al., eds. *Terrorism: Theory and Practice*. Boulder: Westview, 1979.
Allen, Beverely. "Terrorism Book Report." *Journal* Spring (1987): 8–14.
Althusser, Louis. *Lenin and Philosophy, and Other Essays*. Trans. Ben Brewster. New
    York: Monthly Review, 1971.
Amnesty International Report. London: Amnesty International, 1987.
Arendt, Hannah. *On Violence*. New York: Harcourt, 1970.
Aristotle. *On Poetry and Style*. Ed. and trans. G. M. A. Grube. New York: Liberal
    Arts, 1958.
———. *The Politics*. Ed. and trans. Gregory Vlastos. New York: Arno, 1976.
———. *Rhetoric. The Complete Works of Aristotle*. (vol. 2.) Ed. Jonathan Barnes. Bol-
    lingen Series 20. Princeton UP, 1984.
Armstrong, Nancy. *Desire and Domestic Fiction: A Political History of the Novel*. New
    York: Oxford UP, 1987.
Artaud, Antonin. "The Alchemical Theater." *The Theater and Its Double*. Trans. Mary
    Caroline Richards. New York: Grove, 1958.
———. "Fragments of a Diary from Hell." *Antonin Artaud: Selected Writings*. Ed.
    Susan Sontag. Trans. Helen Weaver. New York: Farrar, 1976.

———. "Here Lies." *Antonin Artaud: Selected Writings*. Ed. Susan Sontag. Trans. Helen Weaver. New York: Farrar, 1976.

———. "Situation of the Flesh." *Antonin Artaud: Selected Writings*. Ed. Susan Sontag. Trans. Helen Weaver. New York: Farrar, 1976.

———. *The Theatre and Its Double*. Trans. Mary Caroline Richards. New York: Grove, 1958.

Auerbach, Erich. *Mimesis: The Representation of Reality in Western Civilization*. Trans. Willard R. Trask. Princeton: Princeton UP, 1953.

Auerbach, Nina. *Private Theatricals: The Lives of the Victorians*. Cambridge: Harvard UP, 1990.

Aust, Stefan. *The Baader-Meinhof Group: The Inside Story of a Phenomenon*. Trans. Anthe Bell. London: Bodley Head, 1987.

Autonomia: Post Political Politics. Semiotext(e) 3.3 (1980).

Babcock, Gregory, and Robert Nickas, eds. *The Art of Performance: A Critical Anthology*. New York: Dutton, 1984.

Barber, Stephen. "A Foundry of the Figure: Antonin Artaud." *Artforum* 26.1 (1987): 88–95.

Barish, Jonas. *The Anti-Theatrical Prejudice*. Berkeley: U of California P, 1981.

Barthes, Roland. "Diderot, Brecht, Eisenstein." *Narrative, Apparatus, Ideology: A Film Theory Reader*. Ed. Philip Rosen. New York: Columbia UP, 1986.

———. *Image, Music, Text*. Trans. Stephen Heath. New York: Hill, 1977.

Bataille, George. "The Notion of Expenditure." *Visions of Excess: Selected Writings 1927–1939*. Trans. Alan Stoekl, et al. Minneapolis: U of Minnesota P, 1985.

Baudrillard, Jean. *For a Critique of the Political Economy of the Sign*. Trans. Charles Levin. St. Louis: Telos, 1981.

———. *The Mirror of Production*. Trans. Mark Poster. St. Louis: Telos, 1975.

———. "Our Theatre of Cruelty." *Semiotext(e)* 4 (1982): 108–109.

———. *Simulations*. Trans. Paul Foss, et al. Ed. Jim Fleming and Sylvere Lotringer. New York: Semiotext(e), 1983.

Beckett, Samuel. *Catastrophe. Three Plays*. New York: Grove, 1984.

———. *Not I. Ends and Odds*. New York: Grove, 1976.

———. *Waiting for Godot*. New York: Grove, 1954.

Behn, Aphra. *The Luckey Chance*. Ed. Stephen Orgel. New York: Garland, 1987.

Bell, Rudolph. *Holy Anorexia*. Chicago: U of Chicago P, 1985.

Benjamin, Walter. "Critique of Violence." *Reflections*. Trans. Edmund Jephcott. Ed. Peter Demetz. New York: Schocken, 1986.

———. *Illuminations*. Ed. Hannah Arendt. Trans. Harry Zohn. New York: Schocken, 1969.

———. *The Origin of German Tragic Drama*. Trans. John Osborne. London: Verso, 1985.

Bevington, David, ed. *Medieval Drama*. Boston: Houghton, 1975.

Blanchot, Maurice. *The Writing of the Disaster*. Trans. Ann Smock. Lincoln: U of Nebraska P, 1986.

Blau, Herbert. *Blooded Thought: Occasions of Theatre*. New York: Performing Arts Journal Publications, 1982.

———. *The Impossible Theater: A Manifesto*. New York: Macmillan, 1964.

———. *Take up the Bodies: Theater at the Vanishing Point*. Chicago: U of Illinois P, 1982.

Boal, Augusto. *Theatre of the Oppressed*. Trans. Charles A. Leal McBride and Maria-Odilia Leal McBride. New York: Theatre Communications Group, 1985.

Brecht, Bertolt. *Brecht on Theatre: The Development of an Aesthetic*. Trans. and ed. John Willett. New York: Hill, 1964.

————. *Collected Plays, Volume 1.* Ed. Ralph Mannheim and John Willett. New York: Random, 1972.

————. *Collected Plays, Volume 5.* Ed. Ralph Mannheim and John Willett. New York: Random, 1972.

Breton, André. *Manifestoes of Surrealism.* Trans. Richard Seaver and Helen R. Lane. Ann Arbor: U of Michigan P, 1972.

Breuer, Lee. *The Red Horse Animation. The Theatre of Images.* Ed. Bonnie Marranca. New York: Performing Arts Journal Publications, 1977.

Brockett, Oscar G. *History of the Theatre.* Boston: Allyn, 1974.

Brook, Peter. *The Empty Space.* New York: Atheneum, 1968.

Brunius, Teddy. *Inspiration and Katharsis: The Interpretation of Aristotle's The Poetics.* Stockholm: Almqvist, 1966.

Buechner, Georg. *Danton's Death. George Buechner: The Complete Collected Works.* Trans. Henry J. Schmidt. New York: Avon, 1977.

————. *Dantons Tod. Dichtungen.* Leipzig: Philipp, 1976.

Burke, Kenneth. *Attitudes toward History.* Berkeley: U of California P, 1984.

————. *A Grammar of Motives.* Berkeley: U of California P, 1969.

Burton, Anthony. *Revolutionary Violence: The Theories.* London: Cooper, 1977.

Butcher, S. H. *Aristotle's Theory of Poetry and Fine Art.* New York: Dover, 1951.

Carey, Lady Elizabeth. *The Tragedy of Mariam.* London: Oxford UP, 1914.

Carlson, Marvin. *Theories of the Theatre: A Historical and Critical Survey from the Greeks to the Present.* Ithaca: Cornell UP, 1984.

Case, Sue-Ellen. *Feminism and Theatre.* London: Macmillan, 1988.

Centlivre, Susanna. *The Dramatic Works.* New York: AMS, 1968.

Charlton, H. B., and R. D. Waller. Introduction. *Edward II.* By Christopher Marlowe. New York: Gordian, 1966.

Chomsky, Noam. "Libya in U.S. Demonology." *CovertAction Information Bulletin* 26 (1986): 15–24.

Churchill, Caryl. *Plays: One.* New York: Methuen, 1985.

Cixous, Helene. "The Laugh of the Medusa." *New French Feminisms.* Ed. Elaine Marks and Isabelle de Courtivron. New York: Schocken, 1981.

Clark, James W. *American Assassins.* Princeton: Princeton UP, 1982.

Clutterbuck, Richard L. *The Media and Political Violence.* London: Macmillan, 1981.

Congreve, William. *The Way of the World. The Comedies of William Congreve.* Ed. Graham Storey. Plays by Renaissance and Restoration Dramatists. Cambridge: Cambridge UP, 1982.

Croxton Play of the Sacrament. Drama of the English Renaissance I: The Tudor Period. Ed. Russell A. Fraser and Norman C. Rabkin. New York: Macmillan, 1976.

Curran, Stuart. *Shelley's Cenci: Scorpions Ringed with Fire.* Princeton: Princeton UP, 1970.

Dahl, Mary Karen. *Political Violence in Drama: Classical Models, Contemporary Variations.* Ann Arbor: UMI, 1987.

Debord, Guy. *Society of the Spectacle.* Detroit: Black and Red, 1977, 1983.

de Lauretis, Teresa. *Alice Doesn't: Feminism, Semiotics, Cinema.* Bloomington: Indiana UP, 1984.

Deleuze, Gilles. *Kant's Critical Philosophy: The Doctrine of the Faculties.* Trans. Hugh Tomlinson and Barbara Habberjam. Minneapolis: U of Minnesota P, 1984.

————. *Nietzsche and Philosophy.* Trans. Hugh Tomlinson. New York: Columbia UP, 1983.

Deleuze, Gilles, and Felix Guattari. *Anti-Oedipus: Capitalism and Schizophrenia.* Trans. Robert Hurely, Mark Seem, and Helen R. Lane. Minneapolis: U of Minnesota P, 1983.

———. *Nomadology: The War Machine*. Trans. Brian Massumi. New York: Semiotext(e), 1986.

de Man, Paul. *Blindness and Insight: Essays in the Rhetoric of Contemporary Criticism*. Minneapolis: U of Minnesota P, 1983.

Derrida, Jacques. *Dissemination*. Trans. Barbara Johnson. Chicago: U of Chicago P, 1981.

———. "Freud and the Scene of Writing." *Writing and Difference*. Trans. Alan Bass. Chicago: U of Chicago P, 1978.

———. *Of Grammatology*. Trans. Gayatri Chakravorty Spivak. Baltimore: Johns Hopkins UP, 1976.

———. "Structure, Sign, and Play in the Discourse of the Human Sciences." *Writing and Difference*. Trans. Alan Bass. Chicago: U of Chicago P, 1978.

———. "The Theatre of Cruelty and the Closure of Representation." *Writing and Difference*. Trans. Alan Bass. Chicago: U of Chicago P, 1978.

Doane, Mary Ann. "The Voice in the Cinema." *Narrative Apparatus, Ideology*. Ed. Philip Rosen. New York: Columbia UP, 1986.

Dollimore, Jonathan, and Alan Sinfield, eds. *Political Shakespeare: New Essays in Cultural Materialism*. Ithaca: Cornell UP, 1985.

Donohue, Joseph W. *Dramatic Character in the English Romantic Age*. Princeton: Princeton UP, 1970.

Eagleton, Terry. *William Shakespeare*. New York: Blackwell, 1986.

Else, Gerald F. *Aristotle's Poetics: The Argument*. Cambridge: Harvard UP, 1957.

———, trans. *Aristotle: Poetics*. By Aristotle. Ann Arbor: U of Michigan P, 1967.

Erickson, Jon. "The Objectification of the Subject in Performance Art." Unpublished essay, 1986.

Etherege, George. *The Man of Mode or Sir Fopling Flutter*. *The Plays of Sir George Etherege*. Ed. Michael Cordner. Plays by Renaissance and Restoration Dramatists. Cambridge: Cambridge UP, 1982.

Euripides. *Medea*. *Euripides I*. Trans. Rex Warner. Ed. David Grene and Richmond Lattimore. Chicago: U of Chicago P, 1955.

Fineman, Joel. *Shakespeare's Perjured Eye*. Berkeley: U of California P, 1986.

Foreman, Richard. *Pandering to the Masses: A Misrepresentation*. *The Theatre of Images*. Ed. Bonnie Marranca. New York: Performing Arts Journal Publications, 1977.

Fornes, Maria Irene. *Fefu and Her Friends*. *Word Plays: New American Drama*. New York: Performing Arts Journal Publications, 1980.

Foucault, Michel, *Discipline and Punish: The Birth of the Prison*. Trans. Alan Sheridan. New York: Random, 1979.

———. *The History of Sexuality Volume I: An Introduction*. Trans. Robert Hurley. New York: Random, 1980.

———. *Madness and Civilization*. Trans. Richard Howard. New York: Random, 1965.

———. *The Order of Things: An Archaelogy of the Human Sciences*. New York: Random, 1970.

———. *The Use of Pleasure*. Trans. Robert Hurley. New York: Random, 1986.

Freud, Sigmund. *The Interpretation of Dreams*. Trans. James Strachey. New York: Avon, 1965.

———. *Jokes and Their Relation to the Unconscious*. *The Standard Edition of the Complete Psychological Works of Sigmund Freud*. Ed. and trans. James Strachey, New York: Norton, 1960.

Frisch, Hartvig. *Might and Right in Antiquity*. Trans. C. C. Martindale. New York: Arno, 1976.

Genet, Jean. *The Balcony*. Trans. Bernard Frechtman. New York: Grove, 1966.

———. *The Maids and Deathwatch: Two Plays*. Trans. Bernard Frechtman. New York: Grove, 1961.

Girard, René. *Violence and the Sacred*. Trans. Patrick Gregory. Baltimore: Johns Hopkins UP, 1977.

Gordon, George. Lord Byron's *Manfred*. *Nineteenth-Century English Verse Drama*. Ed. Gerald B. Kauver and Gerald C. Sorenson. Madison: Fairleigh Dickinson UP, 1973.

Gordon, Mel, ed. *The Grand Guignol: Theatre of Fear and Terror*. New York: Amok, 1988.

Gould, Evlyn. *Virtual Theater: From Diderot to Mallarme*. Baltimore: Johns Hopkins UP, 1989.

Gramsci, Antonio. *An Antonio Gramsci Reader: Selected Writings*. Ed. David Forgacs. New York: Schocken, 1988.

Greenblatt, Stephen. *Renaissance Self-Fashioning: From More to Shakespeare*. Chicago: U of Chicago P, 1980.

Grotowski, Jerzy. *Towards a Poor Theatre*. New York: Clarion, 1968.

Grube, G. M. A. Introduction. *On Poetry and Style*. By Aristotle. Trans. and ed. G. M. A. Grube. New York: Liberal Arts, 1958.

Handke, Peter. *Kaspar and Other Plays*. Trans. Michael Roloff. New York: Farrar, 1969.

Herman, Edward S. "The Semantics of Terrorism." *ConvertAction Information Bulletin* 26 (1986): 9–13.

Herman, Edward, and Gerry O'Sullivan. *The "Terrorism" Industry: The Experts and Institutions That Shape Our Views of Terror*. New York: Pantheon, 1989.

Hesiod. *The Works and Days, Theogony, The Shield of Herakles*. Trans. Richmond Lattimore. Ann Arbor: U of Michigan P, 1959.

Holman, C. Hugh. *A Handbook to Literature*. Indianapolis: Bobbs, 1972.

Homer. *The Iliad*. Trans. Richmond Lattimore. Chicago: U of Chicago P, 1951.

——. *The Odyssey*. Trans. Richmond Lattimore. Chicago: U of Chicago P, 1967.

Huizinga, Johan. *The Waning of the Middle Ages*. New York: Doubleday, 1954.

Hume, Robert D. *The Development of English Drama in the Late Seventeenth Century*. Oxford: Clarendon, 1976.

Hutchinson, Ron. *Rat in the Skull*. London: Methuen, 1984.

Ibsen, Henrik. *An Enemy of the People. Ghosts and Three Other Plays*. Trans. Michael Meyer. New York: Anchor, 1966.

——. *The Master Builder, and Other Plays*. Trans. Una Ellis-Fermor. Baltimore: Penguin, 1958.

——. *Peer Gynt*. Trans. Rolf Fjelde. New York: New American Library, 1964.

Inchbald, Elizabeth. *Selected Comedies*. New York: Lanham UP, 1987.

Jameson, Fredric. "Imaginary and Symbolic in Lacan: Marxism, Psychoanalytic Criticism, and the Problem of the Subject." *Literature and Psychoanalysis*. Ed. Shoshana Felman. Baltimore: Johns Hopkins UP, 1982.

——. *The Political Unconscious: Narrative as a Socially Symbolic Act*. Ithaca: Cornell UP, 1981.

Jardin, Lisa. *Still Harping on Daughters*. Totowa: Barnes, 1983.

Jay, Martin. *The Dialectical Imagination: A History of the Frankfurt School and the Institute for Social Research, 1923–1950*. Boston: Little, 1973.

——. "The Politics of Terror." *Partisan Review* 38 (1971): 95–103.

Kant, Immanuel. *The Critique of Pure Reason, The Critique of Practical Reason and Other Ethical Treatises, The Critique of Judgment*. Ed. Robert Maynard Hutchins. Trans. Thomas Kingsmill Abbott, W. Hastie, and James Creed Meredith. Chicago: Encyclopedia Britannica, 1952.

Kellen, Konrad. "The Terrorist Individual." *Journal* Spring (1987): 31–33.

Kennedy, Adrienne. *In One Act*. Minneapolis: U of Minnesota P, 1988.

Kirby, E. T., ed. *Total Theatre*. New York: Dutton, 1969.

Kojeve, Alexander. *Introduction to the Reading of Hegel*. Trans. James H. Nichols Jr. Ithaca: Cornell UP, 1969.

Kott, Jan. *The Theater of Essence*. Evanston: Northwestern UP, 1984.

Kristeva, Julia. *Powers of Horror: An Essay on Abjection*. Trans. Leon S. Roudiez. New York: Columbia UP, 1982.

Kubiak, Anthony. "Disappearance as History: The Stages of Terror." *Theatre Journal* 39 (1987): 78–88.

Kyd, Thomas. *The Spanish Tragedy*. Ed. Andrew S. Cairncross. Regents' Renaissance Drama Series. Lincoln: U of Nebraska P, 1967.

Lacan, Jacques. *Ecrits: A Selection*. Trans. Alan Sheridan. New York: Norton, 1977.

———. *Speech and Language in Psychoanalysis*. Trans. Anthony Wilden. Baltimore: Johns Hopkins UP, 1968.

Laing, R. D., and D. G. Cooper. *Reason & Violence: A Decade of Sartre's Philosophy 1950–1960*. New York: Pantheon, 1971.

Laplanche, Jean. *Life and Death in Psychoanalysis*. Trans. Jeffrey Mehlman. Baltimore: Johns Hopkins UP, 1976.

Laplanche, Jean, and J.-B. Pontalis. *The Language of Psychoanalysis*. Trans. Donald Nicholson-Smith. New York: Norton, 1973.

Laquer, Walter. *The Age of Terrorism*. Boston: Little, 1987.

Laquer, Walter, and Yonah Alexander. *The Terrorism Reader*. New York: Penguin, 1987.

Liddell and Scott. *Greek-English Lexicon*. Oxford: Oxford UP, 1871.

Lukacs, Georg. *The Historical Novel*. Trans. Hannah and Stanley Mitchell. Lincoln: U of Nebraska P, 1962.

———. *History and Class Consciousness: Studies in Marxist Dialectics*. Trans. Rodney Livingstone. Cambridge: MIT P, 1971.

Lyotard, Jean-Francois. *The Postmodern Condition: A Report on Knowledge*. Trans. Geoff Bennington and Brian Massumi. Minneapolis: U of Minnesota P, 1984.

Markley, Robert. *Two Edg'd Weapons: Style and Ideology in the Comedies of Etherege, Wycherley and Congreve*. Oxford: Clarendon, 1988.

Marlowe, Christopher. *Edward II*. Ed. H. B. Charlton and R. D. Waller. New York: Gordian, 1966.

Marx, Karl. *Essential Writings of Karl Marx*. Ed. David Cante. New York: Collier, 1970.

———. *Selected Writings*. Ed. David McLellan. Oxford: Oxford UP, 1977.

McEvilley, Thomas. "Art in the Dark." *Artforum* 21.1 (1983): 62–71.

McGann, Jerome J. *The Romantic Ideology*. Chicago: U of Chicago P, 1983.

Meyerhold, Vsevolod. *Meyerhold on Theatre*. Trans. Alan Sheridan. New York: Norton, 1977.

Mickolus, Edward F. *Transnational Terrorism: A Chronology of Events, 1968–1979*. Westport: Greenwood, 1980.

Milhous, Judith, and Robert D. Hume. *Producible Interpretation: Eight English Plays 1675–1707*. Carbondale: Southern Illinois UP, 1985.

Müller, Heiner. *Hamletmachine and Other Texts for the Stage*. Ed. Carl Weber. New York: Performing Arts Journal Publications, 1984.

Mulvey, Laura. "Visual Pleasure and Narrative Cinema." *Narrative Apparatus, Ideology*. Ed. Philip Rosen. New York: Columbia UP, 1986.

Nietzsche, Friedrich. *The Birth of Tragedy*. Trans. Walter Kaufmann. New York: Random, 1967.

———. *On the Genealogy of Morals*. Trans. Walter Kaufmann. New York: Random, 1967.

Osinski, Zbigniew. *Grotowski and His Laboratory*. Trans. Lillian Vallee and Robert Findlay. New York: Performing Arts Journal Publications, 1986.

Otto, Rudolf. *The Idea of the Holy*. Trans. John W. Harvey. New York: Oxford UP, 1923.

Otway, Thomas. *Venice Preserved or a Plot Discovered*. *British Dramatists from Dryden to Sheridan*. Ed. George H. Nettleton and Arthur E. Case. Carbondale: Southern Illinois UP, 1969.

Paull, Philip. "Who Is a Terrorist?" *CovertAction Information Bulletin* 26 (1986): 14–15.

Pinter, Harold. *The Birthday Party and Other Plays*. London: Methuen, 1960.

Piscator, Erwin. *The Political Theatre*. Trans. Hugh Rorrison. New York: Avon, 1963.

Plato. *The Republic*. Trans. Francis MacDonald Cornford. New York: Oxford UP, 1945.

Preston, Thomas. *Cambyses, King of Persia*. *Drama of the English Renaissance I: The Tudor Period*. Ed. Russell A. Fraser and Norman C. Rabkin. New York: Macmillan, 1976.

Richardson, Alan. *A Mental Theater: Poetic Drama and Consciousness in the Romantic Age*. University Park: Pennsylvania State UP, 1988.

Roach, Joseph. R. *The Player's Passion: Studies in the Science of Acting*. Newark: U of Delaware P, 1985.

Sabatini, Arthur. "Terrorism and Performance." *High Performance* 9.2 (1986): 29–33.

Sartre, Jean-Paul. *Being and Nothingness: An Essay on Phenomenological Ontology*. Trans. Hazel E. Barnes. New York: Washington, 1953.

————. *The Wall*. Trans. Lloyd Alexander. New York: New Directions, 1975.

Scarry, Elaine. *The Body in Pain: The Making and Unmaking of the World*. New York: Oxford UP, 1985.

Schank, Theodore. "Mitchell's Death." *The Drama Review* 23.1 (1979): 43–48.

Schechner, Richard, and Mady Schuman, eds. *Ritual, Play and Performance: Readings in the Social Sciences/Theatre*. New York: Seabury, 1976.

Seneca. *Medea*. Trans. Frederick Ahl. Ithaca: Cornell UP, 1986.

————. *Oedipus*. Trans. E. F. Watling. Baltimore: Penguin, 1966.

Shakespeare, William. *Othello*. Ed. M. R. Ridley. London: Methuen, 1965.

Shelley, Percy Bysshe. *The Cenci*. *Nineteenth-Century English Verse Drama*. Ed. Gerald B. Kauver and Gerald C. Sorenson. Madison: Fairleigh Dickinson UP, 1973.

————. *A Defense of Poetry*. *English Romantic Writers*. Ed. David Perkins. New York: Harcourt, 1967.

————. *Prometheus Unbound*. *English Romantic Writers*. Ed. David Perkins. New York: Harcourt, 1967.

Shepard, Sam. *Seven Plays*. New York: Bantam, 1981.

Sloan, Stephen. *Simulating Terrorism*. Norman: U of Oklahoma P, 1981.

Stanislavsky, Constantin. *An Actor Prepares*. Trans. Elizabeth Reynolds Hapgood. New York: Theatre Arts, 1936.

States, Bert O. *Great Reckonings in Little Rooms: On the Phenomenology of Theater*. Berkeley: U of California P, 1985.

Strindberg, August. *The Dance of Death, Part I*. *The Strindberg Reader*. Trans. Arvid Paulson. New York: Phaedra, 1968.

————. *A Dream Play*. *Eight Expressionist Plays*. Trans. Arvid Paulson. New York: New York UP, 1972.

————. *The Father*. *Seven Plays by August Strindberg*. Trans. Arvid Paulson. New York: Bantam, 1960.

————. *The Pelican*. *Selected Plays*. Trans. Evert Sprinchorn. Minneapolis: U of Minnesota P, 1986.

Templeton, Joan. "The *Doll House* Backlash: Criticism, Feminism, and Ibsen." *PMLA* 104.1 (1989): 28–40.

"Terrorism and the Media: A Discussion." *Harper's* October 1984: 47–58.

Theweleit, Klaus. *Male Fantasies*. 2 volumes. Trans. Stephan Conway. Minneapolis: U of Minnesota P, 1987.

Turner, Victor. "Frame, Flow and Reflection: Ritual and Drama as Public Liminality." *Performance in Postmodern Culture*. Ed. Michel Benamou and Charles Caramello. Madison: Coda, 1977.

Wagner-Pacifici, Robin. *The Moro Morality Play: Terrorism as Social Drama*. Chicago: U of Chicago P, 1986.

————. "The Text of Transgression: The City of Philadelphia Versus Move." *Journal* Spring (1987): 20–29.

Webster, John. *The Duchess of Malfi*. *The Selected Plays of John Webster*. Ed. Jonathan Dollimore and Alan Sinfield. Plays by Renaissance and Restoration Dramatists. Cambridge: Cambridge UP, 1983.

Wilden, Anthony. "Lacan and the Discourse of the Other." *Speech and Language in Psychoanalysis* by Jacques Lacan. Trans. Anthony Wilden. Baltimore: Johns Hopkins UP, 1968.

————. *System and Structure: Essays in Communication and Exchange*. 2nd ed. London; New York: Tavistock, 1980.

Wilson, Robert. *A Letter to Queen Victoria*. *The Theatre of Images*. Ed. Bonnie Marranca. New York: Performing Arts Journal Publications, 1977.

Wordsworth, William. *The Borderers*. *Nineteenth-Century English Verse Drama*. Ed. Gerald B. Kauver and Gerald C. Sorenson. Madison: Fairleigh Dickinson UP, 1973.

INDEX

ANTHONY KUBIAK, Assistant Professor at Harvard University, teaches classes in poetry, performance, and theatre history and theory. He has published articles in *Theatre Journal, Comparative Drama,* and *Journal of Dramatic Theory and Criticism,* and is a contributor to the series *Psychiatry and the Humanities.*